# Nursing Malpractice

# Nursing Malpractice

Implications
for Clinical Practice
and Nursing Education

Janet Pitts Beckmann, Ph.D., R.N.

University of Washington Press

*Seattle and London*

Library of Congress Cataloging in Publication Data

Beckmann, Janet Pitts, 1946–
    Nursing malpractice : implications for clinical practice and nursing
    education / Janet Pitts Beckmann.
        p. cm.
    Includes bibliographical references and index.
    ISBN 0–295–97373–0 (alk. paper)
    1. Nurses—Malpractice—United States. 2. Nursing—United States.
    3. Nursing—Study and teaching—United States. I. Title.
        [DNLM: 1. Malpractice—United States—nurses' instruction.
    2. Nursing—United States—legislation,  WY 44  1994]
    KF2915.N83B36  1994
    346.7303'32—dc20
    [347.306332]
    DNLM/DLC
    for Library of Congress                                      94–10802
                                                                      CIP

The paper used in this publication is acid-free and recycled from 10 percent post-
consumer and at least 50 percent pre-consumer waste. It meets the minimum
requirements of American National Standard for Information Sciences—Perma-
nence of Paper for Printed Library Materials, ANSI Z39.48–1984.

## Dedication

Respectfully to

my loving parents Dorothy De Simone Pitts and Jack C. Pitts,
who taught me values and instilled in me a respect for education

my husband,
without whose loving support
this book would never have been written

the memory of my grandparents
Mrs. Elsie Cupo De Simone and The Reverend Francis De Simone

# Acknowledgments

I would like to thank Professor M. Minnette Massey of the University of Miami School of Law, a friend and teacher who first led me to consider that nursing malpractice is a reality. I am also indebted to J. B. Spence, Esquire, who made me aware that nursing malpractice is in fact a serious problem and who guided me in those early cases in which I served as an expert witness.

Stuart Z. Grossman, Esquire, also deserves special thanks. Over the years, he and other lawyers have deepened my understanding of the legal process that relates to nursing malpractice.

I am deeply grateful to Professor Rheba de Tornyay, Department of Community Health Care Systems and dean emeritus of the School of Nursing at the University of Washington, and to Leonard W. Schroeter, Esquire, who reviewed the entire manuscript and made most helpful suggestions for improvement. For review of the legal content in chapter 2, I would like to thank Andrew B. Yatta, Esquire, and Professor Richard S. L. Roddis, dean emeritus of the University of Washington School of Law.

Above all, I would like to thank my husband, George M. Beckmann, professor emeritus of East Asian Studies and provost emeritus of the University of Washington, for ideas and guidance that made this work possible.

# Contents

## Chapter 10. Problems Associated with Medication Administration 216

## Chapter 11. Problems Associated with Environmental Safety 243

## Chapter 12. Documentation 261

## Chapter 13. Summary and Recommendations 268

## Appendix A. The Nursing Process 279

## Appendix B. Common Departures from the Standard of Nursing Care 280

## Appendix C. Initial Nursing Assessment and Nursing History 281

# Nursing Malpractice

# Chapter 1

# Introduction

This book came about by chance. Through a very close friend and colleague, I was approached fifteen years ago by a prominent attorney to review a nursing malpractice case. I said I was not interested because I associated such cases with attorneys who were "out there" making trouble. To make a long story short, my friend twisted my arm and I looked at the case. What I learned shocked me. Never in my worst imaginings had I thought that nurses could or would provide such poor care.

Not only did I review that case but I also testified at the trial as a nurse expert witness. I was glad for an opportunity to set the record straight by testifying to the patient (plaintiff), the jury, the attorneys, the physicians, and the judge that the patient had indeed received care that was both irresponsible and negligent, and to explain that competent nurses deliver care quite differently. The jury awarded $660,000 to the patient (plaintiff). This happened in 1979, and the award was unprecedented for nursing malpractice at that time. I believe that this substantial award was justified.

The most disturbing aspect of the case was that basic principles of nursing care had been neglected. The patient had injured his knee while working at a construction job. Medial compartment arthritis developed which required surgery for its treatment. The patient had the elective surgical procedure, and a long leg cast was applied. Postoperatively, the nurse's notations in the medical record regarding the involved extremity indicated that the patient was suffering increasing pain, abnormal sensations progressing to loss of sensation in the foot, a change in the color of the toes and the foot progressing to cyanosis, and a change in extremity temperature where the toes ultimately became cold to touch. Nurses have the responsibility to inform the physician of changes in the patient's condition. In this case, the nurses failed to apprise the physician of the situation, and by the time the physician discovered it the next morning, it was too late. The patient sustained a permanent partial disability to the lower extremity.

I assumed that this case was an anomaly and that I would never again see anything like it. I was asked to review other cases, however, which opened my eyes to the serious problem of substandard nursing care when it occurs in today's hospitals. Today's hospitalized patients usually are in need of intense nursing care. Though "nursing malpractice" in the hospital setting is subsumed under the concept of hospital liability, nurses must face directly the issue of malpractice. In each case that I reviewed where nursing malpractice was evident, the common element was failure to provide basic nursing care of an acceptable professional standard. This in turn resulted in major injury to the patient or, in some instances, death.

According to the American Nurses' Association, the number of nursing malpractice suits is increasing. This increase is a cause for concern and is not adequately discussed in the nursing literature. Nursing malpractice obviously has implications both for nursing education and for clinical practice, but when I searched the nursing literature I found no systematic analysis of nursing malpractice cases or the problem of deviation from prevailing professional standards of nursing care. The nursing literature extensively addresses what should be done to provide safe and effective nursing care where the nursing interventions and actions are based on sound scientific principles. It does not describe, however, the pitfalls and problems associated with the delivery of substandard nursing care. In relation to the malpractice issue, the nursing literature discusses only isolated malpractice cases – that is, personal accounts of being sued; legal aspects of malpractice (e.g., elements of negligence, various laws, etc.); and general information on malpractice prevention (e.g., charting advice, malpractice insurance advice, etc.).

I have also searched the legal literature. It generally addresses the changing role of the nurse, which has resulted in increased responsibility and accountability. It also presents historical reviews of nursing, isolated case analyses, and the application of laws to nursing. The legal literature has no mechanism for reporting nursing malpractice cases systematically. Cases are published only if someone chooses to write about a particular case. Many cases, moreover, are settled out of court and are known only to those involved. Much nursing malpractice information is therefore lost. Little authoritative data exist (or are revealed) as to the magnitude of nursing malpractice, its problems and costs. Furthermore, useful and relevant statistical data are not available.

Given the significance of nursing malpractice as a health-care problem and the lack of available data regarding it, I have decided to address the issue based on my own experience as a consultant and expert witness.

My purpose is to improve nursing care and practice. This book of sixty case studies responds to a need in the nursing and legal literature for a concise and systematic analysis of nursing malpractice as it relates to nursing education and clinical practice.

I have served as an expert witness on nursing care for fifteen years and have reviewed many cases. Not all of these cases involved departures from prevailing professional standards of nursing care. For example, Patient G was admitted to a hospital with cholecystitis. Shortly after admission, she complained of a headache in addition to the abdominal pain. According to the medical record, the nurse caring for Patient G performed another pain status assessment fifteen minutes after the first complaint of a headache. This assessment revealed that the headache had become more intense and that Patient G was also complaining of weakness of the right arm. The physician was informed of the change in the patient's condition and came to the hospital immediately. But despite appropriate and necessary intervention by the nurse and the physician, Patient G suffered a massive cerebrovascular accident secondary to a ruptured berry aneurysm of the circle of Willis. The berry aneurysm was a congenital condition. Patient G was left with a residual neurological deficit. I did not find any departures from prevailing professional standards of nursing care and reported that conclusion to the patient's lawyer, who decided not to take any legal action.

I am not in the business of being a "professional expert." I have limited my consulting practice to a few highly reputable attorneys. By convenience, my clients are located in the state of Florida, primarily in one metropolitan area. Eighty percent of the cases used in this book are from this primary area, and twenty percent are in other metropolitan areas of the state of Florida. I am surprised that nursing malpractice is so pervasive in this one metropolitan area, but I believe this area is representative of other areas in the United States in terms of incidence of nursing malpractice. This, however, needs to be researched.

All of the nursing malpractice cases discussed in this book occurred at excellent hospitals – that is, the facilities were well funded and staffed, well respected in the community, and accredited by the Joint Commission on Accreditation of Healthcare Organizations (JCAHO).

All of the nurses involved in these cases were graduates of National League for Nursing (NLN) accredited programs, were licensed to practice nursing, and had good credentials. Some were technical nurses with an associate degree in nursing or a diploma from a hospital-based program.

Others were professional nurses with a bachelor of science in nursing. Nursing education produces both the technical nurse (ADN/diploma) and the professional nurse (BSN). The technical nurse, according to nursing educators, functions under the supervision of the professional nurse and is prepared to provide technical patient care. The professional nurse, on the other hand, is prepared for leadership, planning of patient care, and more advanced nursing practice. In the hospital setting, however, the distinction between the professional and technical nurse is generally not recognized and, in practice, professional nurses and technical nurses perform many of the same duties.

I would have expected to find a predominance of ADN/diploma nurses involved in nursing malpractice, simply because their education is of a limited technical nature with less theory to build on. By contrast, the BSN nurses have more extensive preparation in theory and in beginning clinical specialization. To my surprise, the nurses involved in the malpractice cases discussed in this book were equally divided between ADN/diploma nurses and BSN nurses.

I am alarmed by what I have learned about nursing malpractice, and I have come to realize that a major problem exists. Year after year I keep seeing the same failures in the delivery of nursing care. There has been little or no improvement. The shocking thing is that these failures generally involve fundamental principles of nursing care rather than sophisticated or complex nursing situations. In the cases presented in this book, with one exception, injury to or the death of the vulnerable and unsuspecting patient could and should have been prevented by delivery of nursing care in accordance with acceptable standards.

Each of the sixty cases discussed in this book was reviewed and evaluated by me on behalf of the plaintiff. Each involved nursing malpractice except for Case 3–2 (Endotracheal Tube Malposition), chapter 3, which illustrates techniques of case analysis in the absence of nursing malpractice. With few exceptions, the cases in this book are limited to the medical-surgical specialty and generally involve care of the adult in an acute-care setting. When direct quotations from medical records are utilized in this book, medical abbreviations are written out in full.

Nursing malpractice is costly, not only in terms of patient well-being but also in economic terms. Of the cases described in this book, three went to trial, and fifty-six more were settled out of court. These fifty-nine cases all resulted in payment to the plaintiff. For ten of these cases, the amount of settlement to the plaintiff is unknown. Settlements out of court are frequently confidential, whereas most trial awards are public knowledge. To protect confidentiality, the data regarding monetary awards can be summarized as follows:

| Award (in 1979–93 dollars) | | Number of Cases | Percentage of Cases |
|---|---|---|---|
| 10–49 | thousand | 4 | 6.78 |
| 50–89 | thousand | 8 | 13.56 |
| 90–149 | thousand | 5 | 8.47 |
| 150–499 | thousand | 6 | 10.17 |
| 500–999 | thousand | 11 | 18.65 |
| 1–4½ | million | 15 | 25.42 |
| [ ? ] [case settled] | | 10 | 16.95 |

The known awards in forty-nine of the cases totaled over $39 million. The median award was $500,000. When this $39 million is converted, year by year, into 1993 dollars, it amounts to over $53 million. Hospital malpractice insurance companies were responsible for the majority of these payments to the plaintiffs. Only in rare circumstances where an individual was named along with the hospital did the individual being sued have to make a portion of the payment because of lack of malpractice insurance.

Nursing malpractice contributes to the rising costs of health care because, ultimately, it is the consumer who pays. Malpractice litigation per se is expensive; the costs for both plaintiff and defense are substantial. For example, if a case goes to trial, average plaintiff costs may total $45,000, with 1,000 hours invested in the case by the plaintiff attorney, and average defense costs may total six or seven times more. These numbers do not include the monetary award, if one is made to the plaintiff. Even though payment of costs is covered by malpractice insurance, all of this adds to the cost of health care. In each case in this book involving monetary award to the plaintiff, malpractice could have been prevented in the first place through nursing care that conformed to the standard of practice.

When a nurse commits malpractice in the hospital setting as a key member of the health-care team, he/she often creates liability for other members of that team. This is because of the way hospitals are structured in terms of clinical services (e.g., medical-surgical staff, pathology, nursing, pharmacy, respiratory therapy) and management services (e.g., plant operations, administration, business office).

For example, in Case 10-9 (Wrong Medication Time), chapter 10, the nurse clearly committed malpractice but she also created liability for both the hospital and the physicians. The physician's order for a medication was incomplete. The nurse administered the medication, using the incomplete order, and the patient suffered anoxic brain damage. In this situation, the nurse had the obligation and responsibility to call the physician for clarification of the order and to obtain a complete order before administering the medication. The hospital's insurance company settled for $3 million, to which the physicians, while denying liability, contributed an additional $300,000 for a total of $3.3 million.

In another instance, nursing malpractice created liability for the hospital and the pharmacist (see Case 10–10, chap. 10). The pharmacy sent the wrong intravenous infusion solution to the neonatal intensive care unit, but it was labeled with the patient's name. The nurse failed to read the entire label on the bottle which identified the medication contained therein. The wrong fluid was administered, and the infant died. The hospital and pharmacist were sued, with payment awarded to the infant's parents.

Nursing malpractice thus may implicate hospital liability from the administrative and corporate perspective and also may lead to liability of the attending physician and others.

The case studies in this book, when analyzed in terms of errors leading to nursing malpractice, reveal the following repeated departures from prevailing professional standards of nursing care: (1) failure to observe or monitor a patient adequately; (2) failure to document and/or communicate a significant change in a patient's condition; (3) failure to execute a complete nursing history; (4) failure to formulate and/or follow the nursing care plan; (5) failure to perform a nursing treatment or procedure properly; (6) failure to provide a safe environment and to protect the patient from avoidable injury; (7) failure to execute a physician's medication order correctly and/or promptly; (8) failure to administer medications correctly; (9) failure to observe a medication's action; (10) failure to prevent infection; (11) failure to obtain help for a patient not receiving proper care from a physician; (12) failure to report that a patient is not receiving proper care from a physician; (13) failure to use equipment properly; (14) use of known defective equipment; (15) failure to make prompt, accurate entries in a patient's medical record; (16) altering a medical record; and (17) failure to follow hospital policy and/or procedure.

This book addresses these recurring departures from acceptable standards of nursing care and also formulates principles for the improvement of patient care. In analyzing these departures from prevailing professional standards, I have grouped them into problem areas associated with the following: (1) nursing assessment; (2) communication between nurse and physician; (3) physicians' departures from the standard of care; (4) nosocomial infection; (5) equipment and products; (6) nursing interventions and treatments; (7) administration of medications; (8) environmental safety; and (9) documentation. I have organized the book around these problem areas, utilizing case studies.

(1) Initial as well as continuous systematic assessment of the biopsychosocial status of the patient is a crucial part of the nursing process and is fundamental to the delivery of safe and effective nursing care. All of the members of the health-care team in the hospital setting depend upon these observations because only the nurse remains with the patient 24 hours a day. Chapter 4 addresses problems related to nursing assessment.

(2) Communication among members of the health-care team is vital to patient care. Nursing assessment information must be communicated promptly to the physician, especially when a change occurs in the patient's condition. Communication is the foundation for appropriate medical decision-making and action because the physician is usually with the hospitalized patient only briefly. Historically, the relationship between nurse and physician was based upon loyalty and obedience to the physician, with the nurse's role clearly subservient. Rarely did the nurse make judgments, act independently, or communicate patient information to the physician. Today, poor communication between members of the health-care team – especially between nurses and physicians – may lead to serious if not fatal consequences to the patient. Chapter 5 discusses problems of communication between the nurse and physician.

(3) Through the application of knowledge, the members of the health-care team are obligated to recognize inadequate patient care provided by any member of the team. One is expected to communicate patient-care problems, using hospital guidelines, so that help may be obtained for the patient's benefit. It is especially disturbing to note that nurses are frequently hesitant to do anything about inadequate care rendered by physicians.

Chapter 6 is concerned with problems related to a physician's departure from the standard of care.

(4) A safe biological environment for patient care is essential because nosocomial (hospital-acquired) infection is a serious threat to the hospitalized patient. This is especially true when the patient is subjected to treatments and procedures that are invasive. The entire health-care team must utilize principles and practices of medical and surgical aseptic technique. Chapter 7 deals with nosocomial infection as a consequence of the nurse's failure to provide a safe biological environment.

(5) The hospitalized patient is subjected to a number of nursing interventions as a part of the nursing care plan. In providing care, various pieces of equipment and products are used. Nurses must not only be knowledgeable about the proper use of equipment and products but must also keep up to date regarding new and unfamiliar equipment and products. In addition, for safe patient care, equipment must be maintained properly by the appropriate department. Chapter 8 addresses problems associated with use of equipment and products by the nurse.

(6) and (7) Nursing interventions include various treatments and procedures. Some are independent nursing actions initiated by the nurse (e.g., skin care), while others are dependent actions (e.g., administration of medication). To illustrate – accurate and safe administering of medication involves not only the nurse but the pharmacy department and the physician. Chapters 9 and 10, respectively, deal with problems associated with nursing treatments and procedures and with medication administration by the nurse.

(8) Nursing care must be provided in a safe environment where the patient is protected from injury. Unfortunately, falls are not uncommon among hospitalized patients. Chapter 11 discusses such problems.

(9) Nursing care and documentation go hand in hand. According to the American Nurses' Association *Standards of Nursing Practice,* documentation regarding the patient's health status must comprise a systematic and continuous collection of data that is recorded, accessible, and communicated. These standards have become increasingly important because the expanded role of the nurse demands greater accountability and responsibility. From a legal standpoint, good documentation can prevent the initiating of malpractice claims. Chapter 12 discusses this critical element in a nurse's duty to a patient, and preceding chapters incorporate discussions of nursing care standards applicable to specific

cases which include, among other things, nursing assessments that serve to illustrate appropriate documentation.

For ease of cross-reference, the Appendixes present in combination selected materials extracted from various parts of the text, including information regarding: the nursing process, common departures from the standard of nursing care, the initial nursing assessment and nursing history, systematic nursing assessment and independent nursing assessments, and nursing documentation.

In summary, I believe that the representative cases in this book have important implications for nursing education and nursing service administration. Nursing education programs are carefully planned, executed, and accredited. Nursing curriculum is well conceptualized and is revised frequently to reflect changes in nursing practice. Nursing service administrators are concerned with the delivery of excellent nursing care and, to this end, they have developed solid philosophies, policies, and procedures. Nonetheless, nursing malpractice does occur, and it occurs because of instances of failure to provide basic nursing care.

In the chapters that follow, specific problems of nursing malpractice will be identified so that they may be solved. The solution to these problems rests with individual nurses, nursing educators, and nursing service administrators. Principles on which good nursing care is based need to be emphasized throughout the entire nursing curriculum as well as reiterated continually in clinical practice.

We can all learn the larger lessons to be drawn from these unfortunate cases, and nursing care can be improved.

Chapter 2

# Nursing Malpractice and the Legal Process

Before proceeding to an analysis of nursing malpractice based on actual cases, it is important to understand this issue in the context of the legal process. Section One of this chapter presents a brief overview of the legal aspects of nursing malpractice, including a discussion of standards of care (definition, origins, forms, and use), negligence and malpractice, errors in judgment, and elements of negligence. This discussion is written for nonlawyers and is not confined to the laws applicable in any one state. While state laws may vary on particular issues, the ensuing general summary of the legal aspects of malpractice is valid for most states.

The role of the nurse expert witness is vital to the legal process. Section Two describes the nature, functions, and qualifications of the nurse expert witness and enumerates specific pretrial and trial responsibilities. In concluding this section, I offer some direct advice for effective deposition and trial testimony.

## Section One
## Legal Aspects of Nursing Malpractice

### *Standards of Care*

Concern for quality of care constitutes the nursing profession's major responsibility to the public. The nursing profession is thus accountable to the consumer for the quality of its services. One of the characteristics of a profession is the ability to set its own standards. *Nursing standards*, broad in scope, are established to create guidelines within the profession for assuring an acceptable quality of patient care. The standards of care are also used as the criteria to judge or determine whether appropriate care has been achieved. In practice, it represents the minimum acceptable level of care. These standards evolve or change as nursing practice changes with the onset of new information and technology.

Standards of nursing care are formulated by the nursing profession itself, including various professional organizations, nurses engaged in clinical practice, nursing educators, and nursing service administrators, all of whom contribute to the development of nursing standards. For example, the American Nurses' Association Congress for Nursing Practice has established basic standards for nursing practice that are applicable to all nurses in all settings. Within this framework, each of the divisions of practice of the American Nurses' Association sets standards for its specialty. In addition, agencies concerned with health care (such as the Joint Commission on Accreditation of Healthcare Organizations [JCAHO], which establishes guidelines for the operation of health care facilities, including hospitals) have contributed to the establishment of nursing standards.

Statements of ethical principles by the profession, in turn, influence the development of nursing standards. For example, the American Nurses' Association *Code for Nurses with Interpretive Statements* provides guidelines for the delivery of nursing care consistent with standards and ethical principles.

Standards of a profession may take many forms. Some standards of nursing care are in written form and may be included in recommendations by professional organizations; job descriptions; agency policies, procedures, and bylaws; textbooks; periodicals; federal regulations; and in some states, statutes and administrative codes (e.g., nurse-practice acts and regulations). Other standards, such as those intrinsic to the custom of nursing practice, are not found in writing.

The standards of nursing care should not differ from state to state nor between a large urban and a small rural community hospital. For example, if an acutely ill patient needing complex diagnostic and therapeutic measures is admitted to a small rural hospital, the health-care team is obligated to stabilize the patient and arrange for transfer of the patient to a tertiary hospital.

Locality and similar-locality rules for nursing care should effectively be replaced by a national standard of care. The nurse should be held to this national standard of care rather than to a local one. It is the nurse's responsibility to know and understand the standards of nursing care. Failure to comply with the standard of care can result in liability, because the nurse has a professional duty to provide patient care consistent with the standard.

In suits alleging nursing malpractice, prevailing professional standards of nursing practice are utilized to evaluate the actual nursing care provided a patient. That is, a nurse is judged according to what any reasonably prudent nurse would have done in the same situation at that particular point in time.

Until recently, nurses were not regarded by the courts as qualified to serve as experts on nursing care standards. Physicians were called instead to testify and to establish the prevailing standards of nursing care for a patient. Over time, the courts recognized that nurses were in fact more knowledgeable than physicians in determining the quality of nursing care. Nurse expert witnesses now perform this function. Some of the cases in this book contributed to establishing the precedent that nurses are more proficient and reliable than physicians in determining whether the nursing care meets the prevailing professional standards of nursing practice. In an early nursing malpractice trial, the judge called me into his chambers after my testimony to thank me for educating the court about the nature and scope of nursing practice and to engage me in a lively discussion about the nursing profession.

## *Negligence and Malpractice*

*Negligence* occurs when a person is harmed because of another person's failure to exercise a standard of care that a reasonable person of ordinary prudence would use under the same circumstances. *Malpractice* is negligence by professionals in conducting a professional activity. Malpractice, then, is liability for professional negligence. Malpractice occurs when a reasonable or prudent professional person departs from the prevailing professional standard of care with harmful consequences to the party under care. Thus, any person can be negligent, but only a professional may be charged with malpractice.

Certain factors must be proven in court before a person can be declared liable for negligence. To show liability, the plaintiff (the injured party filing the complaint) in most cases bears the burden of proof. That is, the plaintiff must prove by a preponderance of evidence that the defendant (the party against whom suit is brought) was negligent. By preponderance of evidence, it is meant that the weight of the evidence is more likely than not in the plaintiff's favor. To establish negligence, four elements must be present: (1) duty owed; (2) breach of duty owed; (3) injury or damage; (4) causation. In other words, for negligence to occur, a person must owe another person a duty. When that duty is breached and when injury or damage results from the breach of duty, liability is present.

Ordinarily, the plaintiff bears the burden of proving all four elements of the right to recover for negligence. When the plaintiff does in fact prove all four prerequisites, he/she is said to have put on or presented a *prima facie* case. Sometimes, however, the courts will permit the jury to conclude that the plaintiff's injury resulted from negligent conduct by the defendant without direct evidence. This happens when the instrumentality that caused the injury was within the control of the defendant, or of defendants acting together, and when the nature of the accident was such that it ordinarily does not occur in the absence of negligence. In this situation, the *trier of fact* (the jury, or sometimes the judge) is permitted to infer the negligence of the defendant because "the thing speaks for itself," or in the Latin phrase used by lawyers, it is *res ipsa loquitur.* A simple example of this concept would be the finding of a surgical instrument inside a patient's abdomen at a later date. By common knowledge, in the absence of error, surgical instruments are not normally present in the abdominal cavity, and thus "the thing speaks for itself."

## Errors in Judgment

One quick word about judgment is in order here. If a nurse provides nursing care to a patient but makes an error in judgment, the nurse is not liable for negligence. The law evaluates a nurse's actions by the action a "reasonable or prudent" nurse would take under "the same or similar circumstances" (i.e., the prevailing professional standard of nursing care). For an action to be considered an error in judgment, two conditions must be met. First, the nurse must possess knowledge and skills comparable to those of an average member of the nursing profession; and second, the care provided must conform to prevailing professional standards of nursing care.

## Elements of Negligence

The element of *duty* in a nursing malpractice suit is synonymous with the prevailing professional standard of nursing care. *Breach of duty* by the nurse is the actual departure from the standard of care that is owed to a patient. The nursing care is evaluated and judged on the facts as they are determined to be at the time of the occurrence. Only the standard of care at the time of the incident (the prevailing standard) is applied. Furthermore, foreseeability (reasonableness of conduct) in relation to breach of duty is a legal requirement. This means that the perceived chance that *harm* may result is great enough, when coupled with the probable severity of the harm, that a reasonable person will take precautions. For example, when safety measures such as bedside rails or restraints are not employed, and a restless, disoriented patient falls out of bed, the event is foreseeable.

Causation of injury to a patient by the nurse's departure from prevailing professional standards of nursing care (breach of duty) is the fourth prerequisite element in a nursing malpractice case. Causation can be divided into *cause in fact* and *proximate cause*. Cause in fact establishes that the injury was actually caused by the breach of duty. That is, there is a factual connection between the event and the harm. In law suits, the term "proximate cause" is used by the courts to mean that there is a legal causal relationship. A legal causal relationship establishes that within reasonable probability (more likely than not, or greater than 50 percent of a chance) the injury (harm) was caused by the breach of duty (departure from accepted standards of nursing care, i.e., negligence).

In a nursing malpractice suit, then, the actions of the allegedly negligent nurse are examined in relation to these four elements – duty owed, breach of duty owed, injury or damage, and causation. That is, the nurse's actions are measured against the prevailing professional standard of nursing care. Expert nursing evaluation and testimony are essential to this process and may address the following: (1) What was the prevailing professional standard of nursing care (duty owed)? (2) Did the nurse depart from the prevailing professional standard of nursing care (breach of duty)? (3) If there was breach of duty owed, did an injury occur? (4) If there was an injury, was the cause of the injury within reasonable nursing probability a result of the breach of duty?

Information is presented to the trier of fact (judge or jury), which has the responsibility to determine whether the elements of negligence have been proven by the plaintiff. The malpractice process, from inception through trial, is summarized in figures 1 and 2. While this process may vary from state to state, these figures present a general overview.

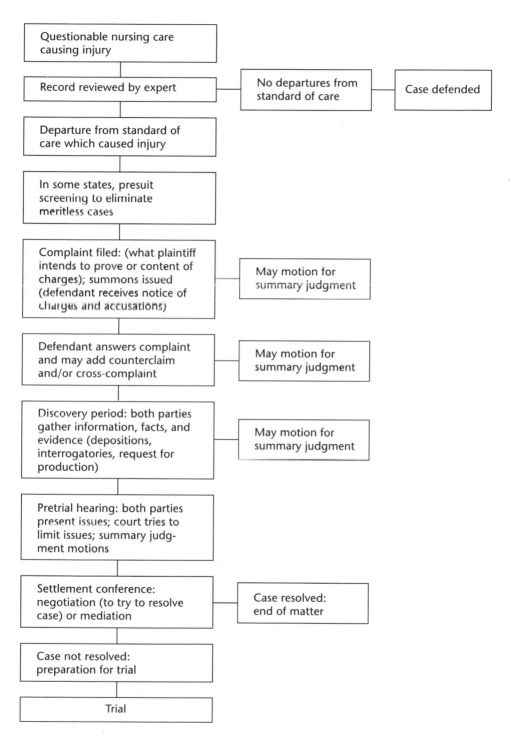

**Figure 1** Systems Diagram of the Malpractice Action Process

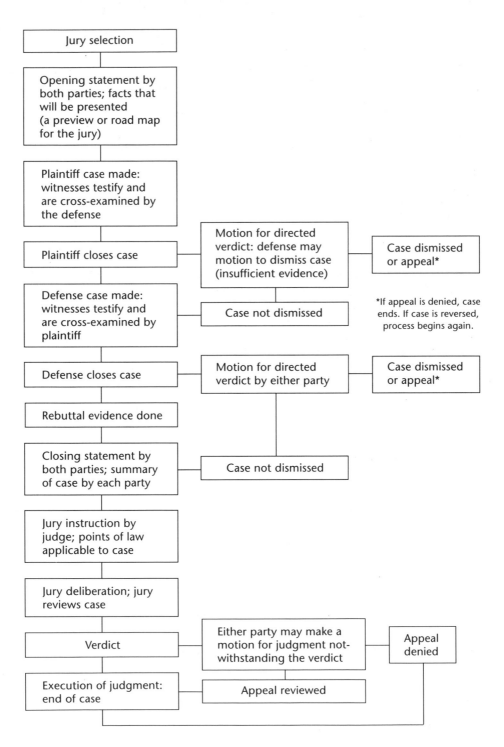

**Figure 2** Systems Diagram of the Trial Process

Section Two

# The Nurse Expert Witness

## *The Expert's Role*

An expert has specialized knowledge through education and/or experience beyond that of the ordinary layman. An expert witness, therefore, is qualified by virtue of specialized knowledge to express an opinion on a technical subject related to the field of expertise. The nurse expert witness is a valuable member of the legal team. Every time an expert witness testifies, his/her reputation is put on the line in a public forum. The expert is not an advocate, for that role is best left to the attorney. The attorney builds the case for the jury by witnesses who provide facts, and the nurse expert witness synthesizes the facts and puts them in terms that the jury will understand. Throughout the development of the case and in the courtroom, the expert functions as an educator. In general, the functions of a nurse expert may include the following: (1) analysis of facts; (2) establishment of facts; (3) interpretation of facts (showing cause and effect); (4) testimony as to prevailing professional standards of nursing care; (5) testimony as to the standards of nursing care applied to a particular case; and (6) testimony to establish causation.

Carl Sandburg defined an expert as "a damned fool a long way from home." Experts are often treated with mistrust or hostility, yet courts need expert opinions. Unfortunately, the negative image is sometimes deserved. It stems from the perception that one can always get an expert to espouse one's cause for a fee, and that many poorly qualified, unethical, and unscrupulous people call themselves experts. There are people willing to accept money (sometimes outrageous fees) to express a particular opinion in a case where that opinion is unfounded and does not conform to expected standards. This behavior is detrimental to the whole legal process and tarnishes the credibility of valid expert witnesses.

## *Qualifications of an Expert Witness*

An expert witness is qualified to render an opinion by virtue of knowledge, skill, education, and demonstrated mastery of a subject. An expert's credentials must match or exceed those of the opposing party. A solid *curriculum vitae* or résumé, emphasizing relevant advanced-educational preparation and showing substantial clinical experience, favorably influences all parties involved in a case – especially the judge and jury, if the case goes to trial. In addition to solid credentials, the expert must have earned a sound professional reputation for expertise and must exhibit honesty, integrity, and stability.

The nurse expert witness must truly *be* an expert in fact regarding the area the case represents, because nursing practice has become increasingly complex and specialized. Thus it is impossible for one nurse to possess knowledge and clinical experience in all specialty areas. An expert's credibility is determined by his/her area of expertise. Credibility is questioned when an expert is represented as one type of specialist (e.g., neonatal intensivist) in one case and another type of specialist (e.g., geriatric practitioner) in another situation. There are, however, certain basic nursing interventions that cut across all specialties, and an expert may testify to those principles. For example, it is perfectly acceptable for an expert who is a specialist in physiological nursing (care of the adult patient whose major problem is a physiological alteration) to be involved in a pediatric case where the issue is safe medication administration. Similarly, the physiological nursing specialist may testify in a psychiatric case addressing special safety requirements if the patient is placed on a medical and/or surgical unit. One must be a good generalist in nursing before becoming a specialist, and an expert may effectively address the basic nursing principles that cut across specialties.

To credentials and credibility, add communication skills. Excellent knowledge and clinical practice skills alone will not suffice. For one to be an effective expert witness, the ability to communicate information accurately, concisely, and persuasively is vital. Specific communication skills are discussed in this chapter in the section on Trial Responsibilities.

To summarize, a case may be enhanced and facilitated by an expert witness with an outstanding reputation. Cases have been settled out of court based solely on an expert's reputation for honesty, knowledge, and skill. If an expert is highly respected, the opposition is at a real disadvantage!

## *Pretrial Responsibilities*

Initially, the nurse expert is retained by the attorney to evaluate nursing care administered to a patient in a particular case. This is done by review and analysis of the medical record and any other documents deemed appropriate. The process may be complex and may demand exceptional analytical and organizational skills. Chapter 3 is devoted to a discussion of this process.

After review of the medical record and related documents, the expert then compares the patient's actual nursing care with the prevailing professional standard of nursing care and formulates an opinion. This opinion as to whether a nurse departed from the standard is based on the facts of the case contained in the medical record and other documents, and on the expert's professional education, knowledge, and clinical experience. The opinion is communicated only to one's client (the attorney). It is communicated orally or in writing, depending upon the client's preference and the discovery laws of the state.

If a written report is requested, it must be carefully conceptualized. The expert must be able to stand behind every statement, and the expert's reputation is at stake. Frequently, a well-written report (when requested) serves as the basis for settlement of the case. One must not be tempted to stray from one's area of expertise and write about an obvious deficiency in the care provided by another professional, say a physician. For example, in Case 3–2 (Endotracheal Tube Malposition) it was obvious that the patient's ultimate demise resulted from the anesthesiologist intubating the esophagus rather than the trachea. My written report in this case addressed only nursing care and stated that there were no departures from prevailing professional standards of nursing care. Based upon general nursing knowledge, however, I recommended in conversation with my client that the case be reviewed by an anesthesiologist.

The nurse expert may be called upon to educate the attorney/client regarding the nature of nursing as well as the scope of the nurse's responsibility and accountability. An understanding by the attorney of standards of nursing practice, the nursing process, technical aspects of nursing, and related sciences such as anatomy and physiology may be essential for case preparation. Other educational responsibilities of the expert may include the organization of evidence, preparation of summaries and/or charts, analysis of and comment on opposing experts' facts and opinions, interpretation of facts and issues, and procurement of technical information. The development of visual aids by the expert may enhance communication of facts and evidence to the court.

The *discovery period* occurs early in the malpractice action and the expert may be involved in this process. At this time, both plaintiff and defense attorneys gather facts and evidence, and they attempt to uncover every pertinent detail about the case. *Discovery devices* are legal procedures for obtaining information and may include interrogatories, requests for production of documents and related items, and depositions.

An *interrogatory* is a set of questions to discover facts. It is formulated by one party and directed to the other party. Written answers to the questions are required and they must be made under oath.

Both parties during discovery may file a *request for production* to obtain all pertinent records and relevant documents. The nurse expert may assist in this process by educating the attorney regarding the various types of documents available. Not subject to production, though, are communications between attorney and client (protected by attorney-client privilege), attorney work-product (working papers), and proprietary processes and patents.

A *deposition* is an oral examination under oath in order to (1) discover facts; (2) record a witness's recall of an event (fact witness); (3) impeach a witness's testimony (see pp. 38–41 below on cross-examination and impeachment); and (4) present testimony in the event a witness is unable to appear at trial. The deposition is taken outside of court and the oral testimony is recorded.

The nurse expert may be asked by the attorney/client to frame questions for the interrogatories and the deposition of adverse (opposing) witnesses. By the same token, the expert will probably also be required to respond to an interrogatory and/or be deposed by the opposing side. Each opposing side is entitled to discover what the other side's expert witness knows. Because the witnesses need only respond to direct questions, the attorneys need to know what questions to ask.

Specific requirements and recommendations for effective testimony are presented in the section below on Trial Responsibilities. These recommendations are applicable to the deposition as well and should be reviewed.

A few words are in order about some aspects of the deposition which differ from the trial testimony. The deposition takes place outside court and may appear informal, with attorneys chatting back and forth. Nonetheless, the proceeding is absolutely serious; the nurse expert must respect the process and must not be caught off guard. A *discovery deposition* usually takes place at the office of the opposing attorney(s). Prior to the start of the deposition, the expert is usually introduced to the opposing attorney(s) and there may be small talk. Beware of an overly friendly opposing attorney, because this is a technique sometimes used to put the expert witness off guard. The attorney softens the witness and then goes for the jugular. Always remember, the opposing attorney represents the interests of the opposing client.

At the discovery deposition, the nurse expert witness must respond to questions truthfully but should provide as little information as possible. The opposing attorney may try to use this deposition for his/her own education regarding technical matters and strategy.

A number of techniques used by the opposing side during a deposition are designed to "fluster" the expert witness, cast testimony in a more favorable light for the opposition, and/or discredit the witness. Some of these techniques are illustrated below, with excerpts from actual deposition testimony. OA is the opposing attorney, EW is the expert witness, and PA is the plaintiff attorney. The opposing attorney sometimes stands very close to the expert witness in an attempt to create an uncomfortable environment, as noted in the following testimony:

OA: Let me ask you to look at the physician's progress record for 7 July, and just to save time, if it doesn't bother you, I'd like to look over your shoulder a moment. This note shows a physician who's seen a patient, and he's very pleased with his condition at that time?

EW: I don't know if the physician is pleased with the patient's condition. The physician just outlines his observations.

OA: Having a good blood pressure is good?

EW: Yes.

OA: Having a pacemaker functioning well after it had been just put in is good?

PA: Object to the form.

EW: I would hope so.

OA: Then we have another note here by [Dr. D]. . . . He certainly doesn't write anything about cardiac instability or respiratory problems or heart rate problems or any such thing?

EW: He doesn't address any of those observations in that note.

PA: Hold on one second. Let's stop here a minute [to OA]. I don't really think it's appropriate that you're hovering over the witness. Why don't you sit down.

The opposing attorney may also try to intimidate by implying that the expert witness is too critical:

OA: Do you sit back at night and try to just make a list of everything you can find that's wrong?

PA: Object to the form.

OA: Is that essentially your perspective as an expert?

EW: As an expert, I evaluate nursing care.

OA:   But I mean you sit there and try to just find every problem you can possibly find . . .

PA:   Object to the form.

OA:   . . . with what was done? Is that how you view what you do as an expert?

PA:   Object to the form – multiple questions.

OA:   You do that by trying to find everything wrong you can find?

PA:   Object to the form.

EW:   I review the record and compare the nursing care in it to what the nursing standard is.

OA:   But do you also, as part of that, try to find everything you can that was subject to criticism?

EW:   I evaluate the record according to the standard. Some medical records are beautiful and they reflect the standard.

OA:   Can you send it to me, please? I mean for Christmas. Tell me it's in this case. Tell me it's in this case.

Another attempt at intimidation reads as follows:

OA:   You make mistakes? You make mistakes?

EW:   Plenty.

OA:   You put the wrong date on a check?

EW:   Yes.

OA:   Have you ever failed to put the date on a check all together?

EW:   No. I manage to get a date on checks.

OA:   I do that all the time.

PA:   He actually runs out of checks, from what he told us yesterday.

OA:   We are human beings, right?

EW:   That is correct.

OA:   I mean let's be fair with each other, we are human.

PA:   Object to form.

OA:   And we can fail in a given moment, even you, in terms of documentation. I'm talking about human weakness, human frailties, human – the human condition. We can do things where we fail in some way or another to document.

EW:   It is possible that some minor point might be left out but we are talking about a situation where documentation was not done over a period of hours and hours. Nurses are taught to document all care.

A flow sheet (see chap. 3) is useful for organizing one's presentation. The opposing side is entitled to know each and every criticism of nursing care that the expert witness makes. If the witness is not well organized, the opposing side may use this to fluster the witness. It is not enough to make general statements such as "the patient was not systematically assessed." The expert witness must be prepared to state each and every assessment that was not made, and this is where the flow sheet comes in handy, as in the following:

OA: Tell me if you would, in order, what the heart rates were, insofar as what you have documented between 4:30 and 10:45.
EW: There was a heart rate of 72 at 8:00 P.M. on 7 July.
OA: The next, please.
EW: There was no assessment of heart rate again until –
OA: Just tell me what *is* there. I know you want to tell me everything that *isn't* there. My question is, please tell me what is there. It will be a lot shorter that way, believe me. You got a lot of empty boxes there. We'll be here all day.
PA: That is, if you would let her answer the question, you would have gotten your answer.
OA: What is the next heart rate you have?
EW: Midnight, a heart rate of 72. Next, at 8:00 A.M. on 8 July, of 76 – and that's all.

The opposing attorney may frequently try to skew testimony by reinterpreting facts so they appear more favorable to the opposing side. This has happened to me a number of times when discussing documentation. In the four situations presented, the line of questioning is typical of this technique. The first situation involves a nurse charting observations that she did not make:

OA: You're saying [Nurse C] wrote down things she didn't see herself?
EW: Yes, sir.
OA: And you're talking about which notes, please?
EW: Let me refer to her deposition where she testifies about helping [Nurse J] care for her patient.
OA: That's good for nurses to help each other, isn't it?
EW: Yes, it certainly is.
OA: I would think you'd say that's just wonderful, if one nurse is tied up in the crisis, that the other nurse smoothly and confidently takes over and assumes her responsibilities?
PA: Object to the form.
EW: I have no problem with that.
OA: It's just that it's good – it's good, isn't it?
EW: That's good, but the problem is . . . that this nurse charted observations that she did not make.
OA: Teamwork is good?
EW: Yes.
OA: So you're not critical of [Nurse C] and [Nurse J] for helping each other, are you?
EW: Absolutely not.

OA:   But what then is your criticism?

EW:   My criticism is that [Nurse C] recorded nursing observations in the patient
      record which she did not actually make herself.

   Lack of patient assessment is another situation where the opposing
side tries to reinterpret facts. The testimony that follows illustrates this
technique, as well as techniques of intimidation:

OA:   In the deposition didn't she say that she came to assess the patient after
      [Nurse C] gave the Tylenol?

EW:   Yes, but there is nothing in the record indicative of this.

OA:   Well, you're not saying she is a liar, are you?

EW:   Absolutely not.

OA:   You're not saying she didn't come in as she said she did, are you?

PA:   Object to the form.

EW:   I don't know when she came in, because if in fact she did assess the patient's
      condition, it would have appeared in the record.

OA:   Okay. You have read [Nurse J's] testimony, have you not?

EW:   That is correct.

OA:   She said she came back in to see the patient after he had been medicated for
      pain. Is that correct?

EW:   That is what she says.

OA:   She said she did so because she wanted to see if he had any – had any relief
      from pain, and how he was doing, if it was better or if it was worse?

EW:   That is what she says.

OA:   It's good nursing practice to check on a patient after he's been medicated for
      pain and to see how he's doing?

PA:   Object to the form.

EW:   Definitely.

OA:   That's good practice, whether it's documented or not?

PA:   Object to the form.

EW:   No. The nursing act of assessment goes hand in hand with the documenta-
      tion.

OA:   You're just going to say that, no matter what question I ask – that whatever
      they did, it was not documented. The treatment wasn't good because it should
      have been documented, is that right?

PA:   Object to the form.

EW:   Nursing acts go hand in hand with documentation.

OA:   That's what you're going to say no matter how many times I ask you the
      question, you're going to say the treatment wasn't right, even if given, because
      if it wasn't documented, it should have been?

PA:   Object to the form. Argumentative. Let's move on.

OA:   Right?

EW:   Nursing care and documentation go hand in hand.

OA:   And one without the other is meaningless?

EW:  Yes.

OA:  Ma'am, I'm sorry. I just get frustrated when I sit here for four hours and listen to stuff like that. So, I apologize.

PA:  Object to form. Move to strike. Let's go on.

Another common situation involves the attorney implying that nursing care was in fact given but was "merely" not documented, as in the following:

OA:  When you used the terminology "it wasn't done," what you're saying wasn't done was documentation in the nurse's note.

PA:  Object to form.

OA:  Is that correct?

EW:  What I said was that the heart rate was not assessed because it did not appear in the record. The act of nursing care and documentation go hand in hand.

OA:  I understand. You have convinced me of that completely. But the monitor is showing second by second, apart from whatever documentation you're referring to at 8:00 P.M. or midnight, or whatever time?

EW:  I don't know whether there was anybody out there looking at the monitor, or even if the patient was on the monitor at that time. We don't have anything regarding heart rate during that time documented in the record.

OA:  Let's not get too metaphysical. You don't think there's somebody out at the monitor station that day between these times that we have just discussed?

EW:  I don't know.

OA:  Well, I mean, why would you think there wouldn't be?

EW:  I'm not thinking that there wouldn't be. All I'm saying is that the heart rate was not assessed.

OA:  And yet you don't feel that you are too picky?

PA:  Object to the form.

EW:  No. We are talking only about the prevailing professional standard of nursing care – care that the patient was entitled to and should have received.

In another instance from deposition testimony, the opposing attorney attempts to make an incomplete order appear complete:

OA:  [Dr. R] wrote an order at around 8:45 A.M. to 9:00 A.M. Is that correct?

EW:  Yes, sir.

OA:  The order states that the patient should receive 7,000 units of Heparin, I.V. push. Is that correct?

EW:  That is all the order states.

OA:  Let me just do one step at a time, if I can. There is an order for Heparin written by [Dr. R] that morning at about 9:00 A.M.

EW:  Yes.

OA:  The order reflects that the patient should receive 7,000 units of Heparin.

EW:  Yes, sir.

OA:  It also directs that it should be given I.V. push?

EW:  That is correct.

OA:  It also directs that the Heparin should be given after the wires are removed?

EW:  It does not specify the time.

OA:  It says "after the wires are removed." Is that correct?

EW:  That's what it says.

OA:  Okay. Just bear with me. I know you're going to be critical, and I know you don't like the order, and I know I'm not going to change your mind, but just bear with me. . . . [Nurse C] gives Heparin to this patient?

EW:  Yes.

OA:  She gave 7,000 units of Heparin?

EW:  Correct.

OA:  She gave an I.V. push?

EW:  Correct.

OA:  She gave it after the pacemaker wires were removed?

EW:  The order states "after the pacemaker wires are removed," and that is too non-specific for a nurse to administer a medication.

OA:  I know you don't like the order, but she gave it after the pacemaker wires were removed?

EW:  Yes, she did.

OA:  So if we take the order we have here, and we take [Nurse C's] actions over here – we have got Heparin being given?

EW:  Correct.

OA:  Now, if the person giving the order meant for it to be given 7,000 units I.V. push after the wires were removed, and the person who is obligated to follow that order gives the Heparin 7,000 units I.V. push after the wires are removed, there is a perfect communication there between the person giving the order and the person carrying out the order?

PA:  Object to form.

OA:  Is that correct?

EW:  No. The person is not obligated to give Heparin according to this order, because the order is incomplete.

OA:  What is incomplete about it?

EW:  The time is not specified.

OA:  What is wrong with that?

EW:  It doesn't specify a time.

OA:  Is that confusing to you?

EW:  Very.

OA:  Is that ambiguous to you?

EW:  Yes. Confusing, ambiguous, and incomplete.

OA:  You don't understand?

EW:  Absolutely not.

OA:  But [Nurse C] did, didn't she?

EW:  She gave Heparin.

OA:  Did [Nurse C] understand the order or not?

EW:  I don't know.

OA:  Did she herself feel that she understood the order?

EW:  I can't answer for her.

OA:  I mean, the person ordering it knows what they mean by it, and the person giving it knows what they meant by it, and the two are the same. Would you agree that there's no ambiguity, at least between [Dr. R] and [Nurse C]?

PA:  Object to the form.

OA:  That just logically follows?

EW:  I can't speak for [Dr. R] or [Nurse C], but I can say a competent nurse would not administer Heparin by the way this order was written.

OA:  We got the medication, we got the dose, we got the route, and we got the time?

EW:  The time is absolutely inadequate. The time is not specific.

OA:  Now if the nurse, for whatever reason, even though she had no doubt about what [Dr. R] meant, and [Dr. R] didn't have any doubt about what he meant, but let's assume that you showed up that day and said, "Well, even though the two of you understood each other perfectly, [Nurse C], I would feel better if you'd call [Dr. R] and ask him about the order"– that's what you're saying she should have done, right?

EW:  Definitely, because the order was incomplete.

In some situations the opposing side appears to become desperate and attempts to "make something out of nothing." Several times, I have been confronted with an actual count of entries into a medical record. It was implied that the care was good simply because of the quantity of entries, as this excerpt from testimony illustrates:

OA:  From 4:30 P.M. on 7 July until 11:15 A.M. on 8 July we have twenty-two notes?

EW:  Oh, I see where you are. You counted them.

OA:  That comes out to a note about every forty-five minutes?

EW:  I'm terrible at mathematics.

OA:  Well, we have more than one note per hour during that whole time, and that doesn't include the other notes that may be on the medication sheets, or notes written on the physician order sheets, or physician visits. Is that correct?

EW:  If that's what you counted.

OA:  We then have a visit by [Dr. R] also on the 7th?

EW:  Yes.

OA:  A visit in the morning by [Dr. R] and [Dr. J]?

EW:  Correct.

OA:  A visit a couple hours later by [Dr. L]?

EW:  Yes.

OA:  And then three doctors entering the room at about 11:15 A.M.?

EW:  Yes.

OA: So, if we added up all the different doctors' notes and nurses' notes, we would have probably in the range of thirty entries covering this 18-hour period?
PA: Object to the form.
EW: Okay. If that's what you say.
OA: Does that suggest anything to you?
EW: No, sir.
OA: That doesn't? That doesn't mean anything to you that we have got thirty different entries about this patient in an 18-hour period?
PA: Object to the form.
EW: It means absolutely nothing.
OA: I think that – that probably that one question and one answer, probably, I think, says it all for the deposition; wouldn't you agree?
PA: Object to the form; move to strike.
OA: You don't know what I mean?
EW: I don't understand the question.

Finally, the opposing attorney may attempt to get an expert witness to state an opinion outside his/her expertise, as illustrated by the following:

OA: Are you saying that [Dr. R] was negligent for writing the Heparin order that he did?
PA: Pardon me. Hold on. Object to the form.
EW: The order was incomplete from a nursing standpoint. I can't evaluate [Dr. R's] care because I am not a physician.
OA: You just said it was written improperly?
EW: It was incomplete from a nursing perspective.
OA: So, [Dr. R] improperly wrote an order?
EW: It was incomplete from a nursing standpoint.
OA: The person who wrote it was [Dr. R]?
EW: Correct.
OA: Therefore, you think what he did was wrong?
EW: I am not here to evaluate the care provided by [Dr. R].
OA: Were the doctors happy with the nursing care that afternoon? I mean, we had two doctors in to see the patient. They both wrote progress notes; they both were there to assess the patient. Were they dissatisfied with the nursing care?
EW: I have no idea.
OA: Do you have an opinion as to the cause of the patient's arrest?
EW: No, sir. I defer to a physician expert.
OA: Do you have an opinion as to whether a cardiac tamponade occurred in this case?
EW: No, sir.
OA: Do you have any opinions about the patient's life expectancy?
EW: No, sir.

OA: Do you have any opinions about his future medical needs?
EW: No, sir.
OA: Do you have any opinions about his present condition?
EW: No, sir.

Another technique used by the opposing side to fluster an expert witness during the deposition is to provide an uncomfortable physical environment. On more than one occasion, when testifying by deposition at the opposing attorney's office, I encountered a room with sealed windows or no windows, with no air conditioning or ventilation, with an outside temperature in the low 90s. A witness is entitled to a comfortable environment and must speak up, because such a situation can negatively affect performance.

Bladder contests sometimes occur when the deposition goes on and on for many hours! Again, an expert witness must be comfortable, and it is appropriate to ask for a short break if no one else has suggested such. Personally, I prefer to restrict fluids to avoid this physiological need and the distracting interruption!

Distractions must be handled. Problems such as needing a drink of water or being seated in a place with the sun shining directly into one's eyes must be addressed. A deposition is a serious matter and concentration is essential.

One final comment about the deposition regards eye contact. To be an effective witness, it is necessary to look the attorney in the eye whenever you are asked questions or whenever you are answering questions. One exception to this is when the deposition is being videotaped. In this situation, the expert witness must look at the camera, so eye contact is made with the viewer. This takes some getting used to because it is such a habit to look at the people to whom one is talking.

Settlement of a case may be instigated by an effective discovery deposition.

## Trial Responsibilities

Testimony by expert witnesses is an essential ingredient of a malpractice trial for both plaintiff and defense. The nurse expert witness testifies at a malpractice trial and acts as an educator to assist the court (trier of fact, the judge or jury) in understanding technical facts, issues, and evidence that are not matters of common knowledge. The ambience of the courtroom may be intimidating to some, but I like to think of it as a classroom with students eager to learn. Often, malpractice trials are battles of experts.

The expert witness provides information about prevailing professional standards of nursing care and assists the court in understanding the criterion against which a nurse's action is measured. Proof of appropriate duty or breach of duty is established by expert testimony. To do this, the expert witness states an opinion (based upon analysis of facts) as to whether a nurse has departed from prevailing professional standards of nursing care. The court expects the opinion to be based on a reasonable degree of nursing probability, with more evidence (51 percent or greater) for the opinion than against it. The opinion is sometimes expressed in the form of an answer to a hypothetical question. The expert witness is asked to assume certain facts and then to express an opinion based upon those facts. The following is an example of a hypothetical question posed by the attorney during trial in Case 5–2 (Neurovascular Embarrassment):

Please assume what is in the chart for the G. S. Hospital for the subject admission. By that I am referring to the preoperative diagnosis, the operative record, the nursing notes, etc.

Assume that on 26 January, [Dr. G] performed a tibial osteotomy upon [Patient B] as indicated. Assume that up until 5:10 P.M. [Dr. G] had been in attendance with his patient, and that after 5:10 P.M. [Dr. G] left the hospital and returned either to his home or his office. Assume that at approximately 7:00 P.M. [Dr. G] received a telephone call from a nurse at G. S. Hospital who indicated that [Patient B] was having pain and was tense, and that [Dr. G] responded by ordering Valium for the patient at 7:10 P.M. in the dosage indicated in the chart.

Assume that from that point in time, that is 7:00 P.M. on 26 January up until the next morning when [Dr. G] returned to G. S. Hospital at approximately 7:00 A.M., he was not called and was not notified about any changes in the condition or any complaints that [Patient B] made to any of the nursing staff, as is reflected in the nurse's notes. Assume that [Dr. G] had, of course, left postoperative orders as contained in the chart. Now, in this context, I want to read to you a portion of a sworn deposition that was taken from [Nurse K], who was on duty from 3:00 P.M. until 11:00 P.M. on 26 January. I want you to assume that [Nurse K] is a registered nurse who graduated in 1958 from S. Hospital in Troy, New York, and has been licensed as a registered nurse in Florida since 1966. I want you to assume that she has worked on the surgical and orthopedic floor at S. M. Hospital and L. Hospital, that she was working on the surgical and orthopedic floor at G. S. Hospital on the night of 26 January, and that she was in attendance with [Patient B].

I am about to read to you the portions of [Nurse K's] deposition and I want you to assume that she was under oath at this time and was telling the truth when she gave her answers to these questions. Please take these questions and answers in conjunction with the nurse's notes that you see on page 125 of the record at 9:00 and 9:30 P.M.

Q: "Do you know whether or not [Dr. G] was told at the time about complaints of burning?" (This refers back to the 7:10 P.M. call.)

A: "He did not have any complaints of burning until, I would say – well, I can't. I don't have them exactly when he, when he exactly started it, but he started it after 8:00."

Q: "After 8:00 he had burning and numbness?"

A: "And numbness, you know, alternate. As I said, every time I went in there was a different . . ."

Q: "You would walk in and sometimes he'd say it was burning and sometimes he would say it was not. Correct?"

A: "Right."

Q: "Now, how many times – just give us an approximate figure, if you can – how many times would you say you went in to see him that evening?"

A: "I'd say I had at least seen him between eight and ten times that evening."

Q: "During these times then he would make the alternate complaints as you have described?"

A: "Earlier it was just a lot of pain."

Q: "Before 8:00, approximately?"

A: "Uh-huh."

Q: "He complained of pain?"

A: "Uh-huh."

Q: "Then at 8:00?"

A. "Around then."

Q: "Around 8:00?"

A: "I'd say around then."

Q: "During the eight or ten times you went in, he'd sometimes say it's burning, he'd sometimes say it's numb: is that correct?"

A: "Uh-huh."

Q: "You have to answer audibly."

A: "Yes."

I want you to assume that no member of [Dr. G's] professional association was notified of these complaints by [Nurse K] or any other member of G. S. Hospital's nursing staff, and that [Nurse K] did not suggest to her head nurse or any other nurse that these doctors be called, nor was any other physician called by any nurse at G. S. Hospital to see this patient.

The question is, based upon your experience as a nurse and [as a teacher of] nurses who work in hospitals like G. S. Hospital, do you have an opinion within a reasonable degree of nursing probability . . . as to whether the failure of [Nurse K], in view of these complaints that she testified were given to her, departed from accepted standards of nursing care? Do you have an opinion as to whether she did, assuming that there was no communication of these complaints [by Nurse K to the doctor]?

Please answer these questions within reasonable nursing certainty.

Testimony by deposition or at a trial is a serious matter. The witness is sworn to tell the truth and nothing but the truth. Witnesses should never agree to testify unless they can fully tell the truth and unless they absolutely believe in the opinion they will express. Anything that is said in a deposition or open court is public record and such statements will remain with the expert witness for the rest of his/her career.

Preparation for testifying may extend over time, so one's records pertaining to a case should be kept on file. Frequently, many months or even a year or two may elapse between the time an expert witness analyzes a case and is finally called to testify. Prior to testifying, therefore, it is important to review carefully the medical records and all relevant documents, including a transcription of the expert's deposition, if one was given.

A planning session with the client/attorney takes place before the expert testifies, to review the expert's opinion and discuss the scope of the testimony. The attorney, along with the expert, may simplify complex testimony and may agree to limit testimony to only two or three main points.

The nurse expert will be expected to bring to the deposition or trial all the documents that have been reviewed. The opposing party is entitled to know exactly what materials were provided for review and what facts were used by the expert in formulating an opinion.

The expert witness must be thoroughly familiar with all the reviewed documents but does not have to memorize medical records or related materials. It is permissible to refer to these documents during testimony. The witness should organize these records beforehand so that relevant sections can be accessed rapidly during testimony. Facts in the documents that contribute to the expert's opinion can be underlined and markers can be placed on pages. The witness should not make notes or produce any written materials unless requested to do so.

The case is confidential and should never be discussed with anyone except at the direction of the client/attorney. During examination, the expert witness will probably be asked with whom the case has been discussed. The witness's credibility will be destroyed if the case was discussed, for example, with a neighbor or a friend, and credibility is central to effective communication with the jury.

This brings us to the issue of courtroom behavior as it bears upon the witness's credibility – that is, the witness's ability to deliver information in ways that inspire the jury's trust in his/her expertise. It is well known in advertising and politics that people's attitudes are changed as much by a persuasive communicator as by the actual message. Courtroom dynamics are the same. The impression made by the expert witness, together with the information imparted, are critical to the effectiveness of the expert and the outcome of the trial. The purpose of the expert witness, remember, is to assist the trier of fact, and the expert witness must convince members of the jury. If opposing expert witnesses differ in opinion, which is frequently the case, the jury usually believes the expert who is the more effective communicator.

Effective courtroom behavior can best be illustrated by example, so it will be useful from this point on to offer some practical guidelines to the nurse expert witness, based on a typical day in court as I have experienced it and interspersing direct advice with a number of general observations.

The appearance and manner of the nurse expert witness while on the witness stand significantly influence the jury's impression of the expert's credibility. Conservative, businesslike attire along with neat and tidy grooming are mandatory. You should walk with poise toward the witness stand and should avoid looking nervous. When taking the oath, you should stand up straight, saying "I do" clearly and firmly. Credibility is influenced not only by demeanor but by tone of voice.

Upon instruction to be seated, sit in an attentive position with both feet on the floor and with hands folded in your lap. Smile cordially at the jurors. Project a positive and confident attitude.

The first few minutes of testimony are critical in establishing a rapport with the jury. Look attentively at the examiner (the attorney asking questions), but be sure to look at the jury when providing the answer. Responding to the individual examiner with eye contact is easy and natural, but one must concentrate on looking at the jurors while replying. Eye contact with each juror in turn during testimony is vital.

Speak only in response to a question, and listen carefully to all questions. Be animated and do not bore the jury, but at the same time do not be rushed into replying without collecting your thoughts. Answer questions as briefly as possible because jurors do not want to spend the rest of their lives in the courtroom! Make the main points of testimony with conviction, and never talk down to the jury. Make direct statements of fact, avoiding such qualifiers as "I think," "Many say," "It seems like," or "It appears." Express emotion calmly, with appropriate vocal inflection and facial expression, but never with an outburst.

Some jurors tend to think abstractly while others are concrete in thinking. Throughout testimony, express opinions in different ways tailored to the different thinking styles. Everyday analogies and visual aids are helpful in expressing technical concepts. If you are presenting a demonstration or writing/drawing on a blackboard, be careful not to block the view of the jury.

I will never forget the first time that I testified at a trial in front of a jury. Before being called to the witness stand, I convinced myself to look upon the jurors as a class of beginning nursing students. This technique worked well and it was a very interesting experience. One juror looked tired and bored at the beginning of my testimony. It was rewarding later to observe him shift position, sit up straight (almost at attention), lean forward, and appear to show interest. Another juror who was listening attentively seemed to have a blank look on her face. All of a sudden, her expression appeared insightful, as if a light bulb had gone on in her head.

From my experience in testifying at trials, I have observed that jurors respond to teaching. I have the utmost respect for jurors in a complex malpractice trial, because they are concerned citizens who listen and learn well.

Answers to questions must be articulate, factual, and to the point, with a yes or no when possible. Answer only what is asked and do not volunteer information, elaborate, lecture, or editorialize. Answer slowly and thoughtfully to be in control of the questioning process, but be aware that hesitating too long before replying may give the jury the impression that you are not knowledgeable or are being evasive. Speak clearly, confidently, and at the appropriate volume (not loud) so that you are heard easily.

You should let the examiner know if you have not heard or understood the question. Furthermore, it is all right to say "I do not know" or to defer to another expert if the question is not within your area of expertise. As an expert witness, you should not try to figure out whether a particular answer will "help or hurt" the case. You are obligated simply to answer a question truthfully.

If requested, you may have to answer with a yes or no. If this is impossible, say so and ask that the question be rephrased. If the question can be answered with a yes or no, but the yes or no needs explanation or qualification, say so. An expert witness has the right to explain the yes or no. Some attorneys will try to cut you off, but it is important to go ahead and provide the explanation. Questioning can get nasty. To intimidate the expert witness, an attorney may ask the judge to instruct the expert witness to answer with a yes or no. The judge will usually do this, but the instruction does not prohibit the witness from providing an explanation as in "yes, but. . . . "

Speak simply, using lay terms and avoiding medical vocabulary. When necessary, obtain permission prior to testimony to use visual aids in the courtroom and arrange to have them on hand. Testimony about a medication error, for example, is facilitated by using a blackboard to demonstrate to the jury the proper calculation of a drug dosage or the proper site to give an injection. It is also useful to show the equipment under discussion (e.g., syringes, restraints).

Just as in the deposition, the opposing attorney may ask questions in an abrasive manner or may imply that you are an idiot. This is a technique used to make you "lose your cool," to distract you, to shake your confidence, and to destroy your presence. Never take this personally. Recognize it as part of the process and remain calm, polite, and professional in manner. Furthermore, the opposing attorney may purposefully rephrase your answer to a previous question, stating it inaccurately with the meaning twisted about. Again, you must not become angry or argumentative. Calmly set the record straight.

Occasionally during testimony, opposing counsel will object to a question. You must stop speaking immediately and answer only when instructed. Do not be alarmed by an objection. Sometimes this is a technique simply to distract a witness. If the objection concerns relevance of testimony, however, the expert may need to present information in another way to show that it applies to the case.

The first part of the witness's testimony is the *direct examination*. The expert witness is examined by the attorney representing the party on whose behalf the expert has been called. The first questions usually asked of the expert witness concern professional qualifications. Here, a current *curriculum vitae* or résumé is useful. When testifying about qualifications, do not be modest.

You will then be asked by the attorney if you have formed an opinion about the standard of nursing care in the case. This question is usually answered with a yes or no. If yes, you will be asked to state the opinion, and then the basis of (your reason for) the opinion.

In addition to testimony about standard of care or breach of duty in the case, you may be asked to testify about causation. The expert witness is concerned with convincing the jury that the breach of duty did or did not in fact cause the patient's injury or death.

*Cross-examination* is then conducted by the opposing attorney to diminish the effect of evidence presented by the expert witness during direct examination. The opposing attorney's questioning regarding your professional qualifications may be lengthy and detailed. Be prepared to provide specific information regarding all your professional positions, especially those showing relevant clinical practice experience. Do not be disturbed by implications that you are not qualified for the case. The expert witness would not be testifying if he/she were not qualified!

At some point in this questioning, the opposing attorney usually asks about the expert witness's fees. Questions are sometimes framed in a negative manner, implying to the jury that the expert is an overpaid and avaricious person, hired to state a certain opinion. It is important that questions about fees be answered calmly, matter-of-factly, and objectively. One should not be embarrassed about discussing fees because, as a professional like the lawyer, the expert witness is entitled to compensation for services rendered. Ethics dictate that an expert witness be compensated on a fee-for-service basis rather than on a contingency arrangement. A contingency fee could create bias because compensation is based on the case outcome.

The nurse expert witness may also be questioned about advertising his/her services. In my opinion, advertising by nurse expert witnesses (in legal journals, etc.) destroys credibility. This practice suggests one is in the business of being a "professional expert witness" rather than a nurse. If one is a competent expert, advertising is not necessary because one's skills become known by word of mouth. By the same token, if one serves as an expert witness too often, one's credibility as a nurse also suffers. Or if an expert is used too many times by the same attorney, the opposing attorney may bring this out and may convince the jury that the expert "appears to be in the attorney's pocket."

During cross-examination, the nurse expert will usually be expected to testify in detail as to how his/her opinion was formulated. General statements of principle are not sufficient. For example, if the expert states that there was failure to observe a patient systematically, the expert is usually requested to state what specific observations were omitted. Furthermore, the expert witness must be prepared to state each and every instance that the observation was not made. That is when a well-organized medical record is useful. If the medical record is lengthy, and if nursing observations are scattered all over the record, a flow sheet may facilitate testimony. The preparation and use of a flow sheet is addressed in chapter 3.

If the nurse expert has addressed causation, questions will be asked. In many cases, numerous breaches of duty cause injury or death. The expert witness may be asked to address which specific breach of duty caused the injury. For example, in Case 3–1 (Infection of Intravenous Infusion Site), the patient developed an overwhelming infection and died as a result of the nursing staff's failure over a number of days to provide proper intravenous infusion care. I was asked to state which specific departure from prevailing professional standards of nursing care caused the infection. It was impossible to pinpoint the one event that caused the infection, because the intravenous infusion site had not been properly maintained over a number of days. For each departure I had described (e.g., failure to observe the intravenous infusion site for infection on 2 October, failure to change the intravenous infusion catheter within the maximum of 72 hours, etc.), I was asked if that one particular departure caused the infection. Furthermore, I was instructed to answer only yes or no. Obviously, one would have to answer "no" or "I do not know" to each and every departure. In effect, by the end of testimony, I would have said that not one of the departures caused the infection, when in fact the continuing improper care of the intravenous infusion site *did* cause the infection. This is when it is important to know that the expert witness can qualify a yes or no answer. Thus, I replied regarding each questioned departure: "No, in and of itself the departure did not cause the infection. The infection was caused by the poor nursing care manifested by the numerous departures from the standard of care over a period of days."

Cross-examination is also used to impeach or discredit testimony and destroy credibility. The truthfulness and competence of the expert witness is tested in several ways during cross-examination. For example, when testimony by the witness relies for authority on specific sources in professional literature (textbooks, monographs, and/or periodicals) the witness may be cross-examined on that material. If during cross-examination, the testimony of the witness is found to be inconsistent with the stated authoritative source(s), the witness may be impeached. In addition, the opposing attorney examines the witness's prior statements for consistency. That is, previous speeches, writings, affidavits, deposition testimony, and trial testimony are reviewed, and inconsistencies with current testimony are brought to light.

During cross-examination the expert witness may be subjected to challenging questions about anything that was discussed during direct examination. The duty of the cross-examiner is to make the expert witness re-examine the facts so they can be interpreted more favorably for the opposing side. (This may also occur in deposition.) When answering questions, the expert witness should not guess. He/she should clarify multiple meanings, straighten out confusions immediately, and admit if an answer given was a mistake. Beware of questions that assume a fact. Watch out for alternative questions (it may not be A or B that is proposed), and be alert to paraphrases.

The strategy during cross-examination is to make the expert feel like a fool, thereby causing him/her to become negative and defensive in attitude. Methods vary from impugning the witness's qualifications to intimidating and confusing him/her on the issues. The purpose is to confuse the expert witness so that he/she appears and feels unprepared, unprofessional, and incompetent. The ultimate goal of this attack is to make an expert witness go on the offensive so that he/she no longer appears neutral.

The examiner during cross-examination attempts to distract the witness so that he/she ignores the jury. Inflammatory words may be used (e.g., "Do you mean to tell me that you actually disagree with the other distinguished experts?") along with histrionic behavior. The expert witness must maintain a professional demeanor by remaining calm and objective in the presence of the opposing attorney. The goal of the cross-examiner is to engage the expert witness in an emotional debate and provoke sarcastic or flippant behavior.

During cross-examination the expert witness may expect to encounter the following techniques: (1) an attack on qualifications and credentials in hopes the expert witness will be sensitive to criticism and will appear nonobjective; (2) the "hired gun" routine, which implies that payment for professional services causes bias and is unethical; (3) an initial review of obvious facts on which both sides agree (requiring a simple yes answer by the witness), and then a sudden, skillful shift to gray areas with an attempt to push the expert witness into agreement with areas favorable to the opposing side; (4) the "hedge," which attempts to confuse issues so that the expert witness contradicts, changes, or qualifies an answer given previously on direct examination or at a deposition; (5) confrontation with errors or contradictions in the expert witness's work; (6) confrontation (based upon research of the expert witness's professional life) with inconsistencies in previous testimony, reports, and writings; (7) a hypothetical question, which can represent a dangerous situation for the expert witness but also an opportunity if the expert listens and answers carefully.

Impeachment of a witness is an important goal of the opposition. Impeachment calls into question the veracity of a witness. This may be done by demonstrating bias, prior inconsistent statements, contradiction of fact, or poor character. Some ways to avoid impeachment include the following:

1.  Testify only within your area of expertise. An effort may be made to tempt the expert witness to answer obvious and simple questions specific to another aspect of medical care. Defer to the appropriate expert.
2.  Base opinions on the case facts, your knowledge, and your experience. Do not testify in a case if you must review the literature to clarify the standard of care.
3.  Know the relevant professional literature. If you state that any particular literature source is authoritative, be familiar with it, because if it is the least bit inconsistent with your testimony, it may be used to impeach you.
4.  Review and organize all documents. Refer to the actual document during testimony. Do not rely on memory.
5.  Do not use or rely on any summaries prepared by someone else.
6.  Do not be afraid to say "I do not know." This assertion can in fact reassure a jury of the witness's honesty and expertise.
7.  Stay calm and professional in manner. Do not become angry, hostile, argumentative, or sarcastic.
8.  Maintain the conviction of your opinion. Do not under any circumstances be pressured into altering an opinion.
9.  Do not volunteer information, because this will give the examiner more to explore.
10. Listen to objections during testimony. They may provide a clue to a difficult question or a question with a slightly different but significant slant.

Finally, telling the truth at all times will prevent impeachment by prior inconsistent statements.

After the cross-examination, the nurse expert witness may be examined again by the party who first called the witness. This is the redirect examination, and it provides an opportunity for the witness to clarify aspects of his/her testimony. This may be followed by the recross-examination and, finally, with questions asked by the judge. Think of the judge as part of the jury. The expert is present to educate the judge also, because it is the judge who must prepare the important jury instructions.

Expert testimony on many occasions is like being on trial. The attorney cross-examining an expert witness has had substantial education and experience directed toward discrediting a witness. The nurse expert must be prepared. The battle of wits can be mentally exhausting, but it is at the same time a challenging and exciting experience. The expert witness must skillfully and calmly defend credentials, opinions, theories, and prior statements without becoming defensive. There is nothing to fear in this process when the nurse expert has evaluated the case with integrity and has arrived at an opinion through thoughtful and careful deliberation.

Chapter 3

# Analysis of Medical Records and Related Documents: Two Case Studies

W hen nursing malpractice is at issue, a nurse expert is the person asked to evaluate nursing care. Prevailing professional standards of nursing practice provide the criteria for the evaluation of nursing care. The nurse consultant knows the standard of care through both clinical experience and education. Medical records and related documents are analyzed to determine the actual nursing care provided to a patient. The actual care provided to the patient is then compared with the prevailing professional standard of nursing practice. The nursing care either conforms to or departs from the prevailing professional standard. This chapter provides an overview of this process.

## Section One
## Nursing Care Evaluation: Nursing Malpractice

Accepting or rejecting the case is the first decision to be made after a nurse consultant is asked to evaluate a potential nursing malpractice case. Two important criteria when considering a case are (1) whether the case falls within one's area of expertise, and (2) the professional reputation of the referring law firm. It is impossible to evaluate a case accurately and efficiently unless one possesses expertise in the prevailing professional standard of nursing care relevant to the case. The reputation of the law firm that refers the case is also an important criterion. Some attorneys accept cases of dubious merit – that is, cases with insignificant departures from the standard of care where it is highly questionable whether the patient was even harmed by the departure. The goal of these attorneys appears to be immediate monetary gain. Since it is costly and time-consuming to take a case to trial, the insurance company pays a small amount of money ("nuisance settlement") to settle the case. This is most unfortunate, but it happens. Obviously, a competent nurse consultant does not want to be associated with such attorneys or law firms.

Whether one is asked to evaluate a case for plaintiff or for defense counsel makes no difference in terms of the process, because the nurse consultant objectively reviews and evaluates nursing care. The following case illustrates the process of analyzing the medical record and related documents in a nursing malpractice suit.

## Case 3–1
### *Infection of Intravenous Infusion Site*

#### Problem and Outcome

A 46-year-old man fell and sustained a fractured skull and a fracture of the left iliac bone. He recovered from these injuries but died later from an infection related to the intravenous infusion catheter.

#### The Patient

On 1 October, Patient B fell from a ladder while repairing the roof of his home and was injured. His wife took him to the hospital. The patient, a laborer, was the father of three children and provided the only source of income for his family.

#### Treatment

Examination in the emergency department after the fall on 1 October revealed that Patient B had sustained a basilar skull fracture, a cerebral concussion, and a fracture of the left iliac bone. He was admitted to the intensive care unit in a restless and confused state with periods of lethargy. Patient B responded to medical treatment, and his neurological condition gradually improved.

On 6 October, Patient B was transferred to a medical-surgical unit. His neurological and orthopedic conditions continued to improve. During this time, however, Patient B developed symptoms of an intravenous infusion catheter-related complication. It was treated with ice pack and K-pad applications by the nursing staff. The physician noted that Patient B was "fully recovered" at the time of discharge on 13 October.

Patient B was readmitted to the hospital 17 October with the chief complaint of headache and elevated temperature. Upon admission, Patient B was alert, although somnolent, toxic, and tachycardiac. His complete blood count revealed leukocytosis with a shift to the left. Liver-function studies were abnormal. A *Candida albicans* infection was present in the oral cavity, and it was thought to be a function of the steroid therapy prescribed for the head injury.

A diagnosis of septic suppurative thrombophlebitis (left arm) and *Staphylococcus aureus* bacteremia was made. Intravenous antibiotics were administered, and an evaluation for infectious metastatic foci was made.

Patient B was taken to the operating room 19 October for exploration of the left forearm along with segmental resection of the left forearm vein, and debridement and drainage of an abscess of the left forearm. The patient "tolerated the procedure well," and he was taken to the intensive care unit in serious condition. Later in the day, however, Patient B developed disseminated intravascular clotting which was secondary to the sepsis from the *S. aureus* bacteremia.

An aortic insufficiency murmur also developed, but it was without hemodynamic compromise. Echocardiograms revealed vegetation on the aortic valve confirming the suspicion of aortic valve endocarditis. The endocarditis resulted from the original infection at the intravenous infusion catheter site in the left forearm from the previous hospitalization. Antibiotics were continued and the patient was followed clinically. By 25 October, Patient B developed severe aortic regurgitation secondary to the bacterial endocarditis. He was treated conservatively, and the developing congestive heart failure was controlled with the cardiac glycoside Lanoxin (digoxin) and the diuretic Lasix (furosemide). The disseminated intravascular clotting problem was resolving at this time.

A gallium scan of the chest on 31 October revealed increased isotopic uptake in the mediastinum which suggested myocardial abscesses. This data, along with the presence of a pericardial effusion and increasing congestive heart failure, led to the conclusion that Patient B needed thoracic exploration and an aortic valve replacement.

On 1 November, the aortic valve was replaced with a Bjork-Shiley valve. Patient B tolerated the procedure well and he was returned to the intensive care unit at 12:25 P.M. According to the nurse's notes at 1:10 P.M. an "irregularity in the arterial-line pattern, although patient in sinus rhythm" was called to the attention of the physicians. By 1:25 P.M., the nurse's notes state that "while in sinus rhythm, arterial-line indicated that patient was not profusing, . . . closed chest massage done by [Dr. B] and patient moved back to operating room." A re-exploration of the aortic valve using cardiopulmonary bypass was done, because it had been observed that not all of the cardiac beats opened the Bjork-

Shiley valve. The valve was rotated and a plasty of the aortic wall was accomplished.

Patient B was then taken back to the intensive care unit in "good condition." Two hours later at 5:25 P.M., it was recorded in the nurse's notes that "patient started missing pulse rate in arterial-line, very irregular and more frequently – [Dr. B] notified immediately." Orders were received and executed. At 6:00 P.M., the nurse's note read, "patient very unstable . . . patient has rare missing beat now." By 8:00 P.M., it was noted "patient more stable, normal sinus rhythm without ectopies, arterial-line regular," and at 9:00 P.M., "patient stable, regular rhythm, no more missing beats in arterial-line." At 2:45 A.M., 2 November, however, the nurses wrote, "patient missing beats rare but longer than before." The physician was called and a volume challenge was started. By 3:15 A.M. Patient B completely failed to open the aortic valve. Cardiopulmonary resuscitation was instituted but it was ineffective in restoring circulation. Patient B was pronounced dead at 3:52 A.M.

## Departures from the Standard of Care

Significant departures from prevailing professional standards of nursing care are evident in this case. They are all related to the care and maintenance of the original intravenous infusion site. Deviations from acceptable standards of nursing practice for the 1–13 October hospital admission include the following:

1. Failure to record the size and type of intravenous infusion catheter inserted into the patient
2. Failure to observe systematically the intravenous infusion site
3. Failure to change systematically the intravenous infusion administration tubing
4. Failure to clean systematically the intravenous infusion site and change dressings
5. Failure to change the intravenous infusion catheter and site after a maximum of 72 hours
6. Failure to provide appropriate nursing care with corticosteroid usage
7. Failure to inform the physician (by 7 October) of intravenous infusion catheter–related problems
8. Failure to chart when the intravenous infusion catheter was removed
9. Failure to follow hospital policy and procedures regarding intravenous infusions

## Discussion

During the first hospitalization an intravenous infusion was started in the emergency department. There was, however, no notation in the medical record regarding the size and type of intravenous infusion catheter used.

Further review of the medical record revealed that systematic nursing assessment and care of the intravenous infusion site during this hospitalization did not occur. Specifically, inspection of the intravenous infusion site for catheter-related complications at least every eight hours was not carried out; the intravenous infusion administration tubing was not changed every 24 hours; site dressings were not done; and the intravenous infusion catheter and site were not changed within the maximum of 72 hours. Finally, there was no notation by the nursing staff as to when the intravenous infusion catheter was, in fact, removed.

During this time Patient B was receiving Decadron (dexamethasone), a synthetic adrenocortical steroid as treatment for the head injury. It is common nursing knowledge that corticosteroids may mask the signs of infection. Important nursing responsibilities are to protect the patient from infection and make careful observations for early and subtle signs of infection. There was no evidence of this in the medical record.

On 7 October, according to the nursing notes, Patient B was "complaining of pain at intravenous site of left arm." It was noted that ice packs were applied. Other references in the nurse's notes regarding intravenous infusion site problems include: 8 October "Both hands are jaundiced"; 9 October "Old intravenous site on left forearm has puffiness and reddened area size of a dime . . . both hands continue to be jaundiced"; 10 October "Small swelling in over arm (old intravenous site) . . . small area of swelling noted on left arm . . . redness and warmth also seen"; 11 October "Dressing applied to left arm from infiltrated intravenous site."

There were no nursing notations that the physician was informed of these problems. Patient B was discharged from the hospital 13 October with an active infection at the intravenous infusion site.

The death of the patient resulted, ultimately, from the absence of nursing care to prevent infection and to control contamination at the intravenous infusion site. The severe infection could have been prevented in all probability by nursing care that conformed to the prevailing professional standard.

## Review of the Medical Record

The medical record is the first document I analyze. Sometimes a *summary* of the medical record is supplied by the law firm, but I do not use this because I prefer to evaluate the case from the *entire* medical record. Also, I have seen a number of inaccurate summaries written by people who are not health-care professionals. An initial review of the entire record provides a general overview of the case and supplies basic information about the patient and the presenting problem.

During this review, the first step is to check the *chronological order* of the record. Frequently, various sections of the medical record (particularly the nurses' notes) are not in chronological order. This must be corrected, and doing so can consume a good amount of time, especially if the case involves a long hospitalization. Medical records can constitute a jigsaw puzzle when the date or time are omitted from many pages. When this occurs, the content has to be carefully analyzed and integrated accordingly.

The medical record must also be complete for accurate review and evaluation. Thus, the next priority is to ascertain the *completeness* of the medical record. It is not uncommon to have several pages of the medical record missing (or pages from another patient's record included), especially if the record is lengthy. Another thing that must be checked is the quality of the photocopy. Frequently parts of pages are not legible, and at times sections of pages are cut off by Xeroxing.

In Case 3–1 (Infection of Intravenous Infusion Site), the first copy of the medical record that I received was incomplete, and various pages were difficult to read because of poor Xeroxing. I requested a complete and readable copy of the record. Several weeks later, I received a microfiche copy of the entire record, rather than just the missing and illegible pages. In this situation, my first task was to compare both copies of the medical record, page by page.

When I compared the first set of medical records for Patient B with the microfiche copy, several differences were noted. The discharge summary by Dr. D, dictated 14 October and transcribed 14 October, was not present in the microfiche copy. In its place was a discharge summary for this first hospital admission that was dictated 20 November (after Patient B had died) and transcribed 22 November. The content of this discharge summary was substantially different from the first one, in that it included a detailed discussion of the intravenous infusion–related problem. The first discharge summary did not mention such a problem. The face sheet of the microfiche copy of the medical record for the 17 October admission also differed from the first copy in terms of the final diagnosis section. The microfiche copy contained six diagnoses, whereas the first copy contained four diagnoses.

In addition, the microfiche copy contained eight pages of a form (labeled "Nursing Progress Notes") not present in the first set of records. This form included items specifically to document intravenous infusion–site care. Under the category of "skin condition" was a space to record "dressing/wound care." Under the category of "tubes" was a space to record "I.V. tubing change" and "I.V. site changed." Nothing, however, was recorded on the eight pages under these categories regarding intravenous infusion–site care.

I did not formulate an opinion about the reason for the differences between the two copies of the medical record because to do so was not within the scope of my expertise. I did communicate the information to my client, however, with the suggestion that a physician address the discharge summaries and a medical records custodian address the extra pages of nursing notes.

The third step of the review process, reading the now-complete medical record, provides *base line data* for a comprehensive picture of the patient. All of the nursing care that a patient received, including patient assessment, is documented in the various nursing sections of the medical record. The nursing documentation regarding the condition of the patient is compared with the notes of other members of the health-care team. Discrepancies, if any, are noted. The physician's history and physical examination along with the admission note provide additional baseline data. Laboratory studies, operative report(s), and the physician's progress notes provide information regarding daily patient status. Treatment information is gathered from review of the physician's orders along with consultation reports and progress notes. Social service, nutritional, and other information may be gathered from reports and/or progress notes made by other members of the health-care team. The discharge summary by the physician addresses patient outcome. All of this information provides basic data for analysis of nursing care and for formulating an opinion about the kind of nursing care a patient required. "The Patient" and "Treatment" sections of Case 3–1 (Infection of Intravenous Infusion Site) derived from this process.

At this point in the review process, if I do not feel absolutely competent to evaluate the type of nursing care that is involved, I return the records and recommend someone else. To evaluate a medical record properly, the nurse consultant must be thoroughly familiar with the applicable prevailing professional standard of nursing care. One must be knowledgeable about both the theoretical and clinical-practice aspects of the case. This knowledge base is internal; that is, one draws upon one's own educational and clinical-practice experience. A quick trip to the library to "study up" on an unfamiliar aspect of the nursing care is not appropriate in this situation.

After the initial review of the medical record is completed, a very detailed *analysis* follows. Every page and every word of the medical record is carefully scrutinized, including such things as addressograph stamps, stamped-on time/dates, and dates when documents were dictated and transcribed. Unusual neatness or unusual completeness of sections of the medical record, particularly *after* an incident, warrant close examination. In some situations, it may be necessary to compare the Xerox copy of the medical record with the original record, because alteration of the record may not be evident in the Xerox copy.

The nurse's notes, graphic sheets, medication record, intake-output record, and all other pages of the medical record that are a nursing responsibility are then analyzed in greater depth. This may be difficult if the case is complex, or involves a long hospitalization, or if nursing assessments and interventions are recorded inconsistently throughout the medical record. In some medical records, for example, it can be difficult merely to determine the frequency with which vital signs were taken, if they have been recorded inconsistently within the record. That is, some vital signs may be found in the narrative portion of the nurse's notes, while others may be found on the graphic sheet, on a nursing treatment record, on a flow sheet, or on a medication record. In order to determine the frequency of the vital signs, all of these pages must be synthesized. This becomes more complicated with numerous nursing assessments and interventions. Therefore, to simplify analysis, I devise a *flow sheet* for the case.

### The Flow Sheet

The left-hand column on the flow sheet contains a list of the necessary nursing assessments and interventions along with the appropriate frequency (that is, the standard of care). The date and time is designated across the top. The nursing data in the medical record are then entered on the flow sheet. The flow sheet works well not only to organize data for evaluation of nursing care but also as a graphic tool to illustrate important aspects of nursing care.

The flow sheet has a space for all appropriate nursing assessments and/or interventions. If the assessment/intervention was not done, the space is empty. In cases where nursing assessment/intervention was inadequate, the empty spaces on the flow sheet dramatically illustrate the departures from the standard of care. In addition, the flow sheet facilitates discussion of the case with the client. During testimony, it is useful because all pertinent nursing data being evaluated is available and clear. Frequently, during testimony, the expert witness is asked to specify each and every nursing assessment/intervention that was not done for a patient. In complex cases this may involve numerous references. This is when the flow sheet is invaluable. The flow sheet not only saves time, because the expert witness does not have to leaf through the medical record page by page, but it enhances accuracy. It is sometimes difficult to track nursing assessments/interventions page by page, because one nurse may chart vital signs, for example, on the graphic sheet while another nurse may chart them only in the narrative portion of the nursing note.

| Date and Nursing intervention/ assessment | October | | | | | | | | |
|---|---|---|---|---|---|---|---|---|---|
| | 1 | 2 | 3 | 4 | 5 | 6 | 7 | 8 | 9 |
| Insertion of catheter Date/time/type (every 48-72 hours) | I.V. started | | | | | | | | I.V. D/C |
| Intravenous tubing change (every 24 hours) | | | | | | X | | | |
| Intravenous site cleaned/dressed (every 24 hours) | | | | | X | | | | |
| Intravenous site assessment (every 8 hours) | | | | | | | | X | X |

X = assessment/intervention executed

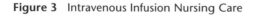

**Figure 3**  Intravenous Infusion Nursing Care

All of the nursing care Patient B, Case 3–1 (Infection of Intravenous Infusion Site), should have received in relation to the intravenous infusion, as well as all of the actual nursing care he received, is summarized on the flow sheet in figure 3. Thus, from the flow sheet, one can easily identify departures from the prevailing professional standard of nursing care for intravenous infusions. Other cases discussed in this book where flow sheets were helpful include Case 4–3 (Respiratory Fatigue), Case 5–1 (Brain Herniation), Case 6–1 (Excessive Chest-Tube Bleeding), Case 6–3 (Postoperative Abdominal Sepsis), Case 6–4 (Increased Intracranial Pressure), Case 9–3 (Paraplegia), and Case 10–9 (Wrong Medication Time).

To summarize, review and analysis of the complete medical record permits one to determine the actual nursing care a patient received. This actual care (as reflected in the medical record) is then compared with the standard of care (the type of nursing care a patient *should* receive), and an opinion regarding quality of nursing care is formulated. The section titled "Departures from the Standard of Care" in Case 3–1 (Infection of Intravenous Infusion Site) reflects this process.

## Reports

When communicating opinions and observations to a client, it is important to establish whether the report is to be in oral or written form. In some states, written reports may be discoverable (used as evidence) by opposing counsel. If I am asked for a written report, I include only professional opinions and observations based upon the facts. I have reviewed a number of expert reports that were potentially damaging because (1) the expert rendered opinions about care issues that were not within the area of expertise, or (2) the expert made derogatory remarks about the patient or the involved health-care professionals. I do not editorialize nor do I express personal opinions or judgments. I write each report in such a way that, if it were made public, it would not be embarrassing or unprofessional. Many law firms prefer an oral report.

A consultant's written notes, if any, may also be discoverable, so it is wise to be cautious as to what one writes in notes. Personally, I underline or highlight relevant sections of the medical record, depositions, and other materials that speak to the care the patient received. I do not make case notes, but I do make a list of departures from prevailing professional standards of nursing care when they are present. In addition, for a complex case, I make a flow sheet(s) synthesizing data in the medical record.

## The Discovery Process

Approximately one year after the medical record was reviewed in Case 3–1 (Infection of Intravenous Infusion Site) the *discovery process* began. During the discovery process, both plaintiff and defense attorneys gather facts and evidence, and they attempt to uncover every pertinent detail about the case. Discovery devices are legal procedures for obtaining information and may include interrogatories, depositions, and requests for production of related documents and items. I was asked to help formulate questions to be used in discovery devices. Also additional materials were provided for review. These consisted of depositions of the involved nurses and physicians, and the hospital policy-and-procedure manual.

The section on intravenous infusion care, in particular, was reviewed in the hospital policy-and-procedure manual. Its recommendations for the nursing care of intravenous infusions were consistent with the accepted standards of nursing practice. Thus, it was determined that the nurses caring for Patient B had also deviated from hospital policies and procedures.

The depositions in this case were reviewed and analyzed. Conflicting and/or inconsistent testimony was noted. Testimony was also reviewed to see if it shed additional light on the case or provided new information. Sometimes deposition testimony is quite helpful in clarifying information in the medical record. To illustrate this process, selected comments follow from some of the nurse's depositions for Case 3–1 (Infection of Intravenous Infusion Site).

According to the testimony of Nurse P, she did not document any observations regarding the intravenous infusion site while she cared for Patient B. She further testified that, "had there been something wrong with the site, it would have been charted." This testimony was in conflict with the hospital policy-and-procedure manual as well as acceptable standards of nursing care. The hospital's *Intravenous Fluid Policy,* statement four, reads: "The condition of the area surrounding insertion site dressing is to be documented in the Nursing Progress Notes every shift." This policy statement does not specify that only abnormal site findings are to be documented. It specifies that the "condition" (which could be normal or abnormal) of the area be documented.

Nurse C, when asked if the intravenous infusion site had been inspected on 8 October stated, "I can't remember, because I haven't charted it." The intravenous infusion site should have been inspected, because the medical record indicates that on 7 October, the patient experienced pain at the site and ice packs were applied. Nurse C further testified that on 12 October she did not know why there was a K-pad on the patient's left arm. When asked on several occasions if she observed the patient's left arm, she stated that she did not or could not remember. This testimony was not consistent with acceptable standards of nursing care.

One further comment about Nurse C's testimony: she states, "Anything that's irregular as regards to a patient's condition or unsatisfactory, I do make a note of it." According to the medical record, problems with the patient's left arm were noted commencing 7 October. Nurse C did not make note of these problems in the medical record. Incomplete charting represents a deviation from acceptable standards, and this testimony is in conflict with the medical record.

The testimony of Nurse N is consistent with the medical record of Patient B in that Nurse N states that he did not document the condition surrounding the intravenous infusion insertion site. Nurse N further testified that he documents only "problems" rather than "nursing actions." This is in conflict with hospital policy and procedure as well as acceptable standards of nursing care.

Nurse B testified that she cared for Patient B on 4 through 6 October. She agreed that intravenous infusion site care and intravenous infusion catheter information should appear in the nurse's progress notes. Nurse B testified that she could not determine how long the intravenous infusion catheter was left in the left forearm prior to 4 October by looking at the nurse's notes. She further stated that she changed the intravenous infusion site on 5 October, but that she "forgot" to chart it. This statement was difficult for me to understand, because at the beginning of the deposition Nurse B testified that she remembered very little about the patient. How, then, could she remember one year later that she changed Patient B's intravenous infusion site on 5 October? Also, it was difficult to comprehend her "forgetting" to chart an intravenous infusion site change.

Since the testimony of Nurse B did not seem consistent with the medical record, I requested an itemized printout of all Patient B's hospital charges. The printout was produced, and all charges related to the intravenous infusion were compared with documentation in the record. The charges for each bag of solution matched the medical record. There was only one charge for an intravenous infusion catheter, and that was on 1 October. There was no charge for an intravenous infusion catheter on 5 October. This further decreased the credibility of the testimony of Nurse B.

Nurse S in testimony could not answer specific questions about the condition of Patient B's left arm on 10 through 12 October, because she had no recollection of the patient and the information was not present in her charted notes. Furthermore, this nurse testified that the patient's left arm must have been normal, and that she could not remember why she applied the K-pad to the left arm. Standard nursing practice dictates that one does not apply a K-pad to an extremity except for reason. Nurse S also testified that it was hospital procedure not to chart findings that were within normal limits. That statement was neither consistent with acceptable standards of nursing care nor hospital policy. Furthermore, this nurse contradicted herself because she did in fact chart findings that were within normal limits (e.g., 10 October, 8:00 A.M., "awake and alert, oriented times three").

Nurse N, who cared for Patient B on 10 October, noted redness, warmth, and swelling of the left arm. She testified that she did not notify the physician of these findings because "if I were to find something like this and it hadn't been reported to me, or there was no entry in the chart previously, I would call the doctor and report it to him." Based upon this testimony, Nurse N had assumed that the physician had been notified of this problem, but she did not verify her assumption with the medical record. Good nursing practice dictates that the physician be informed of problems.

The testimony in all of the depositions reviewed for Case 3–1 (Infection of Intravenous Infusion Site) did not alter my initial opinion based upon the facts in the medical record (see Case 3–1, *Departures from the Standard of Care*). This is frequently the situation. The majority of depositions reviewed concerning a case are consistent with the medical record, and the medical record speaks for itself.

Case 3–1 (Infection of Intravenous Infusion Site) did go to a jury trial. Prior to the trial, I was deposed twice and my expressed opinions about nursing care are included in Case 3–1 under *Departures from the Standard of Care* and *Discussion*. The first deposition was on behalf of the defense during discovery, and the second deposition was videotaped for use at the trial were I was unable to appear in person.

I testified in person on behalf of the plaintiff at the trial regarding issues of nursing care. During the trial, I explained in lay terms that the percutaneous insertion of a needle or catheter in a vein breaches the integrity of the skin. Because of this, the patient is at risk for iatrogenically induced problems such as nosocomial infection, infiltration, and inflammation.

I pointed out that, for prolonged intravenous infusions, the use of a plastic, indwelling venous catheter brings with it enhanced risk of infection and phlebitis. I stated that it is common nursing knowledge that the risk of infection with the catheter increases with the duration of the catheterization, and that the risk of bacteremia secondary to an infected catheter may be as high as 2 percent. I explained that *Staphylococcus aureus* is the most common pathogen isolated from catheter tips and from bacteremias related to catheterization. *S. aureus* can disseminate from local lesions by invasion of the bloodstream with spread to any tissue or organ of the body and can produce abscesses. In addition, factors such as steroid therapy, diabetes, treatment with immunosuppressive drugs, or the presence of diseases that compromise host defenses may enhance susceptibility to *S. aureus* infections.

I told the jury that the nurse is responsible for the safety of parenteral infusions via intravenous catheters as well as for the comfort of the patient. I explained that the safety of an intravenous infusion depends upon surgical asepsis in the placement and maintenance of the catheter, accuracy of administration, early detection of inflammation, infection or infiltration and preservation of the patient's usable veins.

I emphasized to the court that scrupulous nursing care of the intravenous infusion site must be rendered to control contamination and prevent the introduction of microorganisms in the blood stream. Acceptable nursing care includes the following procedures, with documentation:

1. The use of sterile technique for insertion of the intravenous infusion catheter, and documentation of date and time of insertion and type of catheter inserted
2. Observation of the intravenous infusion site at least every eight hours for catheter-related problems
   a. Palpation of the site for tenderness and/or pain
   b. Observation of the site and areas along the course of the vein for redness, swelling, and increased skin temperature
3. Securing the intravenous infusion catheter as needed to decrease

motion that might injure the vein or allow microorganisms to enter the wound

4. Changing the intravenous infusion administration tubing every 24 hours
5. Observing the amount of fluid infused, the kind of fluid infused, and the rate of fluid flow
6. Cleansing the intravenous infusion catheter site every 24 hours or sooner and applying dressings as needed
7. Changing the intravenous infusion catheter and site at least every 48 to 72 hours, provided there are no catheter-related complications
   a. At the earliest sign of malfunction or catheter-related complication, the catheter and site are changed
   b. Removal of the catheter is mandatory after 72 hours
8. Notifying the physician of any signs of infection or inflammation at the intravenous infusion catheter site

Two other experts testified for the plaintiff, a board-certified specialist in infectious diseases who was the author of guidelines on nosocomial infections for the Centers for Disease Control and Prevention, and a board-certified cardiovascular pathologist with the National Institute of Health in Bethesda, Maryland.

At the end of the trial and after three and one-half hours of deliberation, the jury awarded $485,000 to the estate of the plaintiff. It was determined that departures from the prevailing professional standards of nursing care contributed to the development of the left forearm abscess and septic thrombophlebitis. This infection, in turn, caused the bacteremia, which then resulted in the bacterial endocarditis. The aortic valve insufficiency with cusps perforation developed secondary to the bacterial endocarditis. Thus, the verdict was that deviations from acceptable standards of nursing care contributed to the demise of Patient B.

While the monetary award was not as much as was hoped for in such a tragic case, it definitely represented a victory for the victim's rights in a malpractice case.

The local media had adversely influenced the jury award. Physicians, through statements on television and in newspapers, had strongly objected to increases in their malpractice insurance rates. In some instances, they took dramatic public actions (such as refusing to provide

```
┌──────────────────────────────────────────────┐
│                                                │
│  Case accepted for review                      │
│                                                │
│  Purpose: to evaluate nursing care             │
│                                                │
│  Criteria for evaluation:  the prevailing      │
│      professional standard of nursing care     │
│                                                │
└──────────────────────────────────────────────┘
                        │
┌──────────────────────────────────────────────┐
│                                                │
│  Initial review of the medical record          │
│                                                │
│  Ascertain completeness                        │
│  Order chronologically                         │
│  Obtain overview                               │
│  Define care required                          │
│  Reassess expertise                            │
│                                                │
└──────────────────────────────────────────────┘
                        │
┌──────────────────────────────────────────────┐
│                                                │
│  Detailed review of the medical record         │
│                                                │
│  Analyze each page                             │
│  Do flow chart as necessary                    │
│  Determine actual nursing care                 │
│     given to patient                           │
│                                                │
└──────────────────────────────────────────────┘
                        │
┌──────────────────────────────────────────────┐
│                                                │
│  Review of related materials                   │
│                                                │
└──────────────────────────────────────────────┘
                        │
┌──────────────────────────────────────────────┐
│                                                │
│  Actual nursing care given,                    │
│     compared with standard of care             │
│                                                │
└──────────────────────────────────────────────┘
                        │
┌──────────────────────────────────────────────┐
│                                                │
│  Opinion of care formulated                    │
│                                                │
│   Basis: facts & expertise as consultant       │
│                                                │
│  Communication of opinion                      │
│                                                │
└──────────────────────────────────────────────┘
```

**Figure 4**   Nursing Malpractice Review and Evaluation Process

medical care in emergency departments, with the result that some emergency departments had to close for a time). This had created an almost-insurmountable burden for the plaintiff's attorneys.

A claim against the physician, Dr. D, was pursued at a later date. A large out-of-court settlement resulted.

The outcome of this case not only provided monetary compensation for the surviving spouse and children but it also created positive changes in the provision of health care to the public, especially at the hospital where the incident occurred.

Figure 4 summarizes the process of review and evaluation used to analyze nursing care in a potential nursing malpractice case.

## Section Two

# Nursing Care Evaluation: Malpractice by Non-Nurse Members of the Health-Care Team

A number of plaintiff cases that I reviewed presented no nursing malpractice – that is, there were no departures from prevailing professional standards of nursing care. I communicated this opinion to the law firm, and my involvement with the case ended. In a few such cases, however, I continued to provide advice regarding physiological events throughout the development of the case, and I made suggestions regarding appropriate experts. This section illustrates in Case 3–2 (Endotracheal Tube Malposition) the analysis of a case in which nursing care conforms to prevailing professional standards, but care by other members of the health-care team is questionable.

## Case 3–2

### *Endotracheal Tube Malposition*

#### Problem and Outcome

A 40-year-old woman had elective gynecological surgery. During the surgery, she suffered a prolonged period of hypoxia because the endotracheal tube was placed in the esophagus rather than the trachea. The result was severe, irreversible brain damage.

#### The Patient

Patient S, the wife of a physician, was admitted to a hospital 23 August with the diagnosis of a right ovarian cyst (confirmed by pelvic ultrasound). She presented with a gynecological history of irregular vaginal bleeding of two-month's duration and an atypical Papanicolaou's test (Pap smear). She was allergic to catgut sutures and had a history of bronchial asthma (most recent attack, six to seven years prior).

### Treatment

Patient S was scheduled for a dilatation and curettage, cone biopsy, laparotomy, and possible hysterectomy on the day following admission. She was seen by a physician from the anesthesia department who wrote a preoperative note, and who also classified her as ASA II (American Society of Anesthesiologists Classification of Physical Status). Preoperative medication consisting of Demerol (meperidine) 50 milligrams, Phenergan (promethazine hydrochloride) 25 milligrams, and atropine 0.4 milligram was ordered and given on call. The surgery was performed by Dr. C and the anesthetic was administered by Dr. G.

According to the medical record, anesthesia was induced at 6:50 P.M. (24 August) utilizing Ketalar (ketamine) 125 milligrams intravenously, and oxygen at 6 liters per minute with 3 percent Fluothane (halothane) by mask. Anectine (succinylcholine chloride) 80 milligrams was administered intravenously, and the patient was intubated. Anesthesia was maintained with Nitrogen monoxide (nitrous oxide), oxygen, Fluothane (halothane), and an Anectine (succinylcholine chloride) drip. At 7:10 P.M., it was noted that the Nitrogen monoxide (nitrous oxide) was turned off and 100 percent oxygen was administered because the "ventilator [was] not functioning well." Manual ventilation was attempted but it was "almost impossible due to poor compliance." It was stated that the endotracheal tube was checked and found to be in the appropriate position. The cone biopsy was almost completed at this time, and with the second incision into the cervix, the surgeon noted that the blood was dark and called this to Dr. G's attention. He informed the surgeon that he was having difficulty in providing adequate ventilation to Patient S. He was attempting to do this with 100 percent oxygen and Fluothane (halothane). At 7:10 P.M. an Isuprel (isoproterenol) spray and drip, followed by Adrenalin (epinephrine) and steroids were tried, without any improvement in the ability to ventilate.

The anesthesia record states that at 7:15 P.M. Dr. G extubated the patient and found that it was impossible to ventilate the patient by mask. He reintubated the patient without any benefit. At 7:20 P.M., a cardiac arrest occurred. The graphic portion of the anesthesia record shows, basically, unchanged blood pressures from the induction of anesthesia up to 7:25 P.M., five minutes after the arrest was diagnosed.

With the diagnosis of cardiac arrest, cardiac massage was started. Sodium bicarbonate solution, Adrenalin (epinephrine) and calcium chloride solution were given. It is not clear according to the medical record how long it took to reestablish the heart beat. The anesthesia record shows a blood pressure resuming at 7:40 P.M. An emergency department physician assisted with resuscitative efforts. He states that when he arrived in the operating room, the patient was intubated and being ventilated with difficulty. No pulse was present and various drugs were given over a twenty-minute period. Dr. G, in his note, states that after several minutes the "bronchospasm" eased, and circulatory stability was achieved.

Patient S remained in the operating room until 8:20 P.M. She was then transferred to the intensive care unit. An endotracheal tube was in place and she was being mechanically ventilated. She was deeply comatose. A blood gas recorded on the anesthesia page of the medical record shows a pH of 7.30, $pCO_2$ (mmHg) of 52 and a $pO_2$ (mmHg) of 15. This presumably was taken at 7:15 P.M. and shows gross hypoxia with moderate metabolic acidosis. The 7:45 P.M. blood gas demonstrated remarkable improvement with a pH of 7.58, $pO_2$ (mmHg) of 336 and a $pCO_2$ (mmHg) of 25. A chest X-ray taken on admission to the intensive care unit was normal. On 25 August, a left pneumothorax was noted, and a chest tube was inserted. The tube was removed on 26 August.

Patient S remained deeply comatose and in a vegetative state. An electroencephalogram (EEG) on 25 August demonstrated features of severe hypoxic encephalopathy, and a repeat study on 28 August showed no cerebral activity whatsoever. She continued neurologically unchanged until 15 May of the next year, when it was decided to discontinue mechanical life support.

### Departures from the Standard of Care

There were no departures from prevailing professional standards of nursing care. Review of this case, though, did suggest that care provided by the attending surgeon and the anesthesiologist needed to be evaluated by physician experts.

### Discussion

The first cause for concern in this case was the absence of a preoperative history and physical examination in the medical record. A notation by the charge nurse indicated that it was "done by her husband [Dr. S]." From a nursing standpoint, this is very poor practice on behalf of the hospital and the admitting physician. In addition, it is customary that physicians do not treat their family members for obvious reasons. A complete history and physical examination preoperatively provides valuable information to the members of the health-care team. This should have been accomplished by the admitting physician.

Unusual events occurred in the operating room. Anesthesia was induced at 6:50 P.M., and at 7:10 P.M. difficulty in ventilating the patient was noted. This was attributed to a bronchospasm, and the condition persisted until a cardiac arrest occurred at 7:21 P.M.

Adequate anesthesia should be provided to a patient where there is suspicion of an irritable airway, before ever attempting to "instrument" the larynx, let alone intubate the trachea. Furthermore, while the choice of inhalation agent Fluothane (halothane) was appropriate, no time was allowed here for its intended beneficial bronchodilator effect, since induction at 6:50 P.M. was immediately followed by intubation and surgery. In other words, a "two syringe" technique was used here, where the inducing agent is quickly followed by Anectine (succinylcholine chloride) and intubation. In this case, if the endotracheal tube was indeed inserted in the trachea, an inadequate plane of anesthesia existed when this was done. In a person with irritable airways, this will trigger immediate and serious bronchospasticity; what is more, it will trigger a certain tracheobronchial reaction in any patient. Still accepting that bronchospasm did occur, why was it not diagnosed at its outset? How can it be that the anesthesia record shows smooth induction, stable blood pressure and pulse rate for fifteen minutes intra-anesthetic, and then suddenly at 7:10 P.M. , the ventilator requires 50 cmHOH pressure to deliver the tidal volume?

The term "bronchospasm" is to some extent a misnomer, because it suggests that the spasm occurs in the bronchi. In actual fact, the spasm occurs in the smooth muscle of the bronchioles, which are smaller divisions of the tracheobronchial tree. Bronchospasm is seen during anesthesia in patients who have "irritable" bronchial trees, that is, in patients with chronic bronchitis, emphysema, or asthma. It may then be triggered by such events as surgical stimulation under too light a level of anesthesia, mechanical or chemical irritation of the tracheobronchial tree, or the passage of the endotracheal tube. It produces a form of respiratory obstruction, which is more severe on expiration than on inspiration. It is characterized and accompanied by loud noises and wheezes, which are heard all over the chest on auscultation. When features of bronchospasm appear (increased resistance to respiration, noisy breathing), it is mandatory to eliminate those conditions that simulate a true bronchospasm. These include (1) surgical stimulation under an inadequate level of anesthesia, (2) coughing and bucking the endotracheal tube, and (3) most commonly, respiratory obstruction due to a kinked, blocked, or misplaced endotracheal tube or some defect in the anesthesia apparatus. Only when these conditions have been excluded should the physician make the diagnosis of a true bronchospasm and proceed to treat it with such drugs as aminophylline and steroids. In practically all instances, deepening the anesthesia, administering Anectine (succinylcholine chloride), or removing the mechanical obstruction eliminates the problem of bronchospasm immediately.

In the analysis of further events, I considered the matter of blood gasses. Patient S's arterial blood gas at 7:15 P.M. revealed a partial pressure of oxygen of 15 mmHg. In general, the arterial blood gasses reflect ventilatory efficiency, the ability of hemoglobin to carry oxygen and carbon dioxide, the rate of metabolism, and the state of the buffer systems. The partial pressure of oxygen reflects the amount of oxygen that has diffused through the alveoli into arterial blood. The normal amount of oxygen carried in this form is small, but it provides the essential driving force for oxygen to combine with hemoglobin (the majority of oxygen is carried in this form). A partial pressure of oxygen of 15 mmHg is outstandingly low and indicates profound hypoxia. The partial pressure of carbon dioxide is inversely proportional to alveolar ventilation, and the 7:15 P.M. value of 52 mmHg also indicated poor alveolar ventilation.

This situation was consistent with the endotracheal tube being positioned in the esophagus; hence, ventilation was nonexistent for the length of time between intubation and extubation, when an attempt was made to mask and bag-ventilate the patient. This would account for the extraordinarily low $pO_2$ of 15 mmHg. The mechanism was obviously that of continued perfusion (heart action sustained) while alveoli remained nonventilated. Thus, no alveolar-arterial gradient for oxygen existed, though the patient was "receiving 100 percent oxygen." In fact, if the most severe degree of bronchospasm had really been present, some of the oxygen flow would have reached some of the alveoli. The partial pressure of oxygen might have been relatively low, but not to the magnitude reported in this case. The arterial blood gasses at 7:45 P.M. (after Patient S was reintubated) presented a markedly improved picture regarding partial pressure of oxygen and carbon dioxide. Even with the dramatic improvement of the arterial blood gas values, however, the severe, irreversible brain damage had already been caused by the prolonged period of hypoxia.

The anesthesia record was unusual from a physiological standpoint. The pulse rate and blood pressure recordings on the graphic portion of the anesthesia record were remarkably stable right up to 7:25 P.M. (24 August). The cardiac arrest was noted on this sheet to have occurred at 7:21 P.M., and the vital signs were thus inconsistent with this. It is unusual to have such a stable blood pressure and heart rate under conditions of such extreme hypoxia (arterial blood partial pressure of oxygen of 15 mmHg at 7:15 P.M.), because physiological compensatory mechanisms come into play and vital signs change.

When a person engaging in nonviolent exercise stops breathing for one through three minutes, the heart rate increases. At about three minutes, the heart rate will slow rather remarkably. This appears to be part of the so-called diving reflex. Bradycardia continues over the next seven minutes, at least. The average is somewhere around eighteen minutes.

Also, at about the three-minute mark, the oxygen level of the blood, measured as $pO_2$, drops below 40 mmHg (muscular activity shortens this time). The blood turns dark, and the lips and nail beds become cyanotic if the patient is not anemic. At this point, the brain starts to be markedly affected by the lack of oxygen. The brain has a differential level of sensitivity to the lack of oxygen; the higher centers, such as those which control voluntary muscle activity are affected first. The brain stem, with the primitive centers, is affected last. This is why one cannot commit suicide by holding one's breath. The higher centers, which are involved in voluntary holding of the breath, quit functioning; the brain stem, which controls automatic breathing, takes over. The medical record does not reflect this tachycardia, nor the bradycardia associated with lack of ventilation.

Sympathetic stimulation in response to acute hypoxemia (mediated by chemoreceptors at vasomotor centers) causes an increase in cardiac output, primarily as a function of increased heart rate and an increased total peripheral resistance (secondary to vasoconstriction). These increase the blood pressure. If one adds all these factors to the Ketalar (ketamine) anesthetic used, known to increase heart rate and blood pressure, one cannot accept the stability of the vital signs reflected in the medical record from induction to arrest.

Another unusual event happened when the surgeon (Dr. C) actually left the operating room at the time Patient S had the cardiac arrest and a Code Blue was called. According to a narrative statement of facts by Dr. S (the patient's husband):

> While I waited in the surgeons' lounge for a happy outcome of the operation, and while talking to [Dr. M], all of a sudden the surgeons' lounge door connected with the operating room opened, and [Dr. C] in complete panic told me to rush to the operating room because my wife had stopped breathing. I rushed into the operating room with [Dr. M] and [Dr. R], and found my wife with no vital signs and no breathing sounds on her lungs. I found complete absence of heart or lung activity. I automatically started ordering cardiotonic medications and medications used in this kind of cardiorespiratory arrest as part of the code. You could see a very big, protuberant, distended stomach – which she never had before the moment of the operation.

Dr. C, the surgeon, left her patient rather than assisting in the resuscitation efforts. This was totally inappropriate.

Physician consultants were retained after physiological analysis, and it was concluded by physicians that, in this case, the esophagus rather than the trachea was intubated, and that this went unrecognized. The statement by Dr. S regarding the distended abdomen, the absence of wheezes and noises in the chest, and the improvement in oxygenation with reintubation certainly confirmed the conclusion.

As a nurse expert, I helped the legal team understand the physiological basis of the case as outlined. The case went to trial, physician expert witnesses testified as to the standard of medical care, and the jury found for the plaintiff.

## Chapter 4

# Problems Associated with Nursing Assessment

Systematic nursing assessment is a vital nursing responsibility. It is a crucial part of the nursing process and is fundamental to the delivery of systematic, scientifically based, effective nursing care. Nursing assessment establishes the data base, which is the foundation of the initial and evolving nursing care plan. Florence Nightingale asserted that without the habit of ready and correct observation, nurses are useless, no matter how devoted.

Nurses must continually monitor the biopsychosocial status of the patient. Monitoring may not always eliminate a problem, but it does ensure early recognition of problems, thereby facilitating appropriate intervention. Most nursing malpractice cases I have reviewed involve in varying degrees the failure to assess the condition of the patient systematically. This serious departure from prevailing professional standards of nursing practice is apparent in the majority of the cases in this book. The cases in this chapter, illustrating this problem, involve patient injury or death because of inadequate nursing assessment.

The American Nurses' Association *Standards of Nursing Practice* emphasizes that the systematic and continuous collection of data regarding the patient's health status is a nursing responsibility. Systematic nursing assessment of the patient includes basic observations with which every licensed registered nurse should be familiar. Yet these observations are frequently not present in the medical record.

It is amazing how often the initial nursing assessment and nursing history are incomplete or inadequate in the medical record. Even when the hospital provides a specific form for the initial nursing assessment and nursing history, the data is often not complete. In fact, I have reviewed patient medical records in which these forms are devoid of any entries except the patient's name. In such instances, it is impossible to substantiate whether the patient's condition was assessed upon admission or, more important, whether a baseline patient problem existed. Valuable patient information is thus lost to the health-care team.

An initial nursing assessment with a nursing history must be part of each patient's medical record. This thorough and accurate data base is essential to proper formulation of the nursing care plan and should include such data as the following:

1. Patient's chief complaint (onset of illness, complete description of symptoms and condition)
2. Past medical history
3. Social and family history
4. Behavioral status
5. Respiratory status
6. Circulatory status
7. Neurological status
8. Body temperature status
9. Integumentary status
10. Renal function and fluid status
11. Gastrointestinal status
12. Weight and height
13. Musculoskeletal status
14. Endocrine and metabolic status
15. Sensory and perceptual status
16. Immune status

I have reviewed many medical records, and I have found that where the initial nursing assessment was incomplete or absent, the nursing care plan was also incomplete and inadequate.

Ongoing systematic nursing assessments were also incomplete and inadequate in many medical records. Ongoing systematic nursing assessment consists of nursing observations made and recorded over a 24-hour period. This includes, among other things, the following:

1. Respiratory status assessment
2. Circulatory status assessment
3. Body temperature status assessment
4. Neurological status assessment
5. Integumentary status assessment
6. Renal status assessment
7. Fluid status assessment
8. Pain status assessment (when applicable)
9. Gastrointestinal status assessment

10. Musculoskeletal status assessment (when applicable)
11. Endocrine and metabolic status assessment (when applicable)
12. Sensory and perceptual status assessment (when applicable)
13. Immune status assessment (when applicable)

In a hospital setting, nurses monitor the patient 24 hours a day in order to observe for pertinent biopsychosocial alterations. All members of the health-care team are dependent upon these observations. The nurse determines the frequency with which these observations are made as well as their specificity according to the patient's condition. Specifically, the nurse has the knowledge base to observe, record, and report, without a physician's order, the following major assessments:

1. Respiratory status assessment
   a. Patency of airway
   b. Respiratory rate
   c. Respiratory rhythm
   d. Respiratory character
   e. Breath sounds
   f. Ease of respiration
   g. Duration of inspiration vs. expiration
   h. General chest expansion
   i. Presence/absence of intercostal retractions
   j. Posture of the patient and facial expression
   k. Presence/absence of fatigue with breathing
   l. Effectiveness and frequency of cough
   m. Sputum amount and character
   n. Percussion of chest – noting intensity, pitch, quality, duration, and equality of sound
   o. Arterial blood gas interpretation
   p. Tidal volume
   q. Minute volume
   r. Vital capacity
2. Circulatory status assessment
   a. Pulse rate
   b. Pulse rhythm
   c. Pulse quality
   d. Blood pressure
   e. Skin color

   f. Skin temperature
   g. Central venous pressure and other hemodynamic line measurements
   h. Circulation in extremities (peripheral pulses, temperature and color of extremity, blanching sign, motor and sensory function)
3. Body temperature status assessment
4. Neurological status assessment
   a. Response to stimuli
   b. Orientation
   c. Level of consciousness
   d. Response to commands
   e. Pupillary response (size, equality, and reaction to light)
   f. Ocular movements (noting if eyes move, if movement is conjugate [together] or disconjugate [separate] and direction of eye movement when head rotated [doll's head maneuver])
   g. Motor and sensory function (movement and strength in extremities, abnormal sensations)
   h. Reflexes
   i. Behavioral changes
   j. Headache or seizure activity
5. Integumentary and wound status assessment
   a. Description of trauma
   b. Character of drainage
   c. Amount of drainage
   d. Condition of dressings and/or suture lines
   e. Condition of skin
6. Renal status assessment
   a. Urinary output
   b. Character of urine
7. Fluid status assessment
   a. Intake (amount, kind, route, rate)
   b. Intake vs. output
   c. Estimated or actual fluid loss
8. Pain status assessment
   a. Qualitative aspects
   b. Quantitative aspects
   c. Topographic aspects
   d. Temporal aspects

  e. General level of comfort
9. Gastrointestinal status assessment
  a. Appearance of abdomen
  b. Bowel sounds
  c. Presence/absence of nausea, emesis
10. Musculoskeletal status assessment
  a. Sensory and motor function
  b. Mobility
11. Endocrine and metabolic status assessment
12. Sensory and perceptual status assessment
13. Immune status assessment
14. Psychosocial status assessment

These observations must be systematic, and all applicable categories of the patient status assessments outlined above must be present in the medical record throughout each day. The systematic nursing observations provide the data base for early detection of problems and, if necessary, facilitation of appropriate intervention.

The frequency of assessment and the details included in the assessment are of course determined by the individual patient's primary problem and condition. The above outlines are not intended to convey that there is only one way to present this information in a patient's medical record. The nurse is at liberty to determine how this information is documented within the guidelines of hospital policy. I have seen medical records where the information is presented effectively in narrative form, or where a flow sheet is used with check marks, or where a check list and narrative are combined. The important thing is that all observations (both normal and abnormal) must appear in the medical record. This is the responsibility of the nurse in caring for the patient.

I have heard and refuted testimony that "negative" and "normal" observations need not be recorded. The meaning of "negative observations," as defined by defense attorneys, is that there is no problem or alteration. Such failures to record or chart assessments/observations deviate from prevailing professional standards of nursing care. Explanations of these failures, by referring to "negative observations," do not, moreover, hold up in Court. In these circumstances, a jury will not be convinced that a patient actually was systematically assessed by the nurse. The old adage "If the nursing action or observation is not charted, it was not done" still applies today. In fact, in all of the cases discussed in this chapter, it was determined that vital nursing assessments were not made because they did not appear in the medical record.

Testimony by defendant nurses that they always gave "good nursing care" by "observing" their patients, but that they did not chart "normal" or "negative" observations was not convincing. By the time these defendant nurses testified by deposition or at trial, a significant period of time (sometimes one to two years) had usually elapsed since they had cared for a particular patient. They could not remember the patient, let alone what specific assessments or observations they had made.

In summary, nurses are held accountable for determining the type and frequency of patient assessment that is required. A physician should not have to order or even address the type and frequency of nursing assessment for a patient, because this is solely a nursing responsibility.

The cases in this chapter illustrate problems associated with nursing assessment specifically in the areas of respiratory, circulatory, neurological, wound, fluid, and pain status assessment.

In all of the cases presented in this chapter, a lawsuit was filed. The hospital was named as a defendant because it employed the nurses who departed from prevailing professional standards of nursing care. All of these cases settled with substantial payment made to the plaintiff or the estate of the plaintiff.

## Section One
# Assessment of Respiratory Status

The three cases in this section illustrate different types of respiratory alterations leading to progressive hypoxia and, ultimately, death. The first case involves upper airway obstruction secondary to postoperative sedation; the second involves failure to maintain a patent endotracheal tube; and the third involves failure to institute ventilatory support. In all three cases, had systematic nursing assessment been done, the hypoxic states would have been detected in a timely fashion, and three deaths could have been prevented.

Case 4–1

## Postoperative Airway Obstruction

### Problem and Outcome

Lack of systematic nursing assessment in the immediate postoperative period led to the failure to detect hypoxia. This resulted in the death of a 32-year-old woman.

### The Patient

Patient A was a happily married woman. She and her husband were of Iranian descent and had lived in the United States for eleven years. Her husband, who held a Ph.D. in economics, was successfully self-employed and Patient A assisted in his business.

Patient A was involved in a motor-vehicle accident and was taken to the emergency department of a general hospital 3 December with multiple injuries. She was alert and cooperative. X-rays revealed multiple facial fractures including the following: Le Fort I midface fracture, Le Fort II midface fracture, Le Fort III midface fracture, nasal complex fracture, fracture of the midline of the palate of the maxilla, fracture of the symphysis of the mandible (right), and an alveolar segment fracture of the anterior mandible involving teeth numbers 25 and 26.

### Treatment

Plastic closure of facial lacerations, closure of an intra-oral laceration, and manual reduction of a retruded maxilla were executed on the evening of the accident.

Patient A's condition improved, and five days after admission she was taken to surgery for bilateral exploration of the orbits, open reduction of the fracture of the floor of the orbits, and exploration of the frontozygomatic sutures with open reduction; open reduction of a mandibular fracture; dental extraction of tooth number 9; debridement of the alveolar ridge and diagnostic dental impressions of the mandible and maxilla. Patient A was taken to the recovery room in good condition, and after one and one-half hours she was transferred back to the surgical floor. Her condition continued to improve.

Seven days later, 15 December, the patient was returned to surgery on an elective basis for application of upper and lower precontoured Erich arch bars; closed reduction of the alveolar ridge fracture of the mandible with stabilization of the symphyseal fracture of the mandible; closed reduction of the midpalatal split fracture; removal of teeth numbers 4 and 5; repair of nasal complex fracture, and placement of a frontal screw with internal suspension wires from the frontal screw to the oral cavity. After this four-hour procedure, the patient was transferred to the recovery room "in excellent condition."

After a thirty-minute stay in the recovery room, Patient A was transferred back to the surgical floor. Approximately three hours later, Patient A suffered a cardiopulmonary arrest.

Resuscitation was instituted, but Patient A remained comatose with little improvement. The patient suffered a second cardiopulmonary arrest ten days later, 25 December. Repeated electroencephalograms were iso-electric, and Patient A was pronounced dead 27 December.

### Departures from the Standard of Care

Analysis of the case revealed the following departures from prevailing professional standards of nursing care:

1. Failure to observe the patient for a sufficient length of time in the recovery room after the 15 December surgery
2. Failure to observe and assess the patient systematically on the surgical floor after the 15 December surgery
3. Failure to consider seriously the patient's complaint of shortness of breath postoperatively 15 December
4. Failure to respond to the husband's pleas for help on 15 December
5. Failure to detect a change in the patient's condition and obtain help for the patient

### Discussion

Postoperatively, on 15 December, good nursing care would have prevented the demise of Patient A. First of all, a thirty-minute stay in the recovery room was insufficient in view of the type, extensiveness, and length of the surgery. Thirty minutes is far too short a time to determine whether the anesthetic drugs were adequately reversed and adequately metabolized. The immediate postoperative period is a critical one for the patient, and diligent nursing assessment and intervention are necessary.

The basic nursing-care objectives for Patient A should have included the following: maintenance of pulmonary ventilatory status, maintenance of circulatory status, maintenance of environmental safety, and promotion of comfort. Adequate pulmonary ventilatory status is necessary to prevent hypoxemia and hypercapnia. Nurses caring for Patient A should have realized that two of the most common causes of inadequate pulmonary exchange, in the immediate postanesthetic period, are airway obstruction and hypoventilation. Airway obstruction most frequently occurs as a result of the tongue (relaxed from anesthesia) falling back against the pharynx, or as a result of secretions (or other fluids) collecting in the pharynx, trachea, or bronchial tree. While caring for Patient A, it was essential for the nurse to recognize that all noisy breathing (e.g., snoring, gurgling, wheezing) is indicative of some type of airway obstruction. It is equally important, however, to realize that obstruction can occur without being accompanied by noise.

The nurses caring for Patient A on 15 December should also have recognized that hypotension and cardiac arrhythmias are the most commonly encountered cardiovascular complications of the immediate postanesthetic period. Early recognition and management of these complications before they become serious enough to diminish cardiac output is dependent upon frequent assessment of the patient, especially of vital signs. Hypoxemia and hypercapnia are common causes of postoperative cardiac arrhythmias.

Testimony by the recovery room nurse revealed that vital signs were taken only one time before the physician was contacted for an order to transfer Patient A to the surgical floor. In addition, the physician was told simply that "the patient is fine and ready to go." The Aldrete scoring system for postanesthesia recovery was used, and the patient was rated nine on admission at 12:10 P.M. and ten at 12:30 P.M. Of interest is that the patient was given a score of only one in consciousness. It is difficult to understand the scores of two in both activity and respiration in light of the score of one in consciousness. The score of ten at 12:30 P.M., twenty minutes after arrival, was viewed as highly suspicious by experts reviewing the case.

The recovery room nurse, Nurse G, had permission to leave the hospital as soon as the recovery room closed that day. After further questioning, the reason given for discharging the patient to the floor after only thirty minutes was that "she was ok . . . yes, the annual hospital Christmas party was that night . . . as soon as I closed the recovery room, I left . . . yes, I got my hair done on the way home."

The nursing care that Patient A received upon transfer to the surgical floor was also inadequate. The transporter/orderly told the nurse on the surgical floor that "We're going to need more help; this lady is very sleepy." This comment was in reference to transferring the patient from the stretcher to the bed. Upon admission to the floor, the nursing note reads: "Appears sleeping soundly. Complained of not being able to breathe." Vital signs at this time were pulse rate 92, respiratory rate 14, and blood pressure 150/90 mmHg. The patient was not seen again by any member of the health-care team, including a nurse, until forty minutes later at 1:20 P.M., when it was noted: "patient very sleepy – complains of not being able to breathe."

During the next one hour and forty minutes, the patient's husband became alarmed about his wife's condition and attempted to seek help from the nursing staff. Her husband described the situation as follows:

[Patient A] was breathing terribly hard, and she was alone in the room. It was curious how she was breathing. It seemed that she had too much trouble to breathe. She even wouldn't be breathing that way if she had been running one mile fast and without any break. I started to call [Patient A]. I shake her, I called her again and again, but there was no response at all. It seemed that she was in a deep sleep. . . . It must have been around 3:00 or 3:30 P.M. as I saw the things were turning worse and [Patient A] was breathing less and less. I ran out of the room, because I preferred to catch a nurse than to ring and wait. I saw [Nurse M] again. I asked her to come and see [Patient A's] condition. She replied her duty is over. [This nurse also had permission to leave early to buy decorations for the hospital Christmas party.] After hesitating, she came and said the same thing again – that everything is normal and I shouldn't worry. . . . I went to another nurse. . . . She just watched [Patient A's] pulse and went to the telephone. . . . Attempts were being made at last to get a doctor to [Patient A]. Nobody came. At this time I was getting excited and went out to see what was going on. On the floor I met [Dr. W]. [Dr. W] came to [Patient A's] room."

At this point in time, Patient A suffered a cardiopulmonary arrest. Between 1:20 P.M. and the time of the arrest, there were no notes by the nurse in the medical record. Resuscitation was instituted, and the patient was transferred to the intensive care unit.

Minimal nursing care that Patient A should have received on the surgical floor includes the following: (1) *respiratory status assessment* (patency of airway; depth, rate, character, and rhythm of respirations); (2) *circulatory status assessment* (blood pressure; pulse rate, rhythm, and quality; color and temperature of skin); (3) *neurological status assessment* (level of consciousness); (4) *wound status assessment* (amount and type of drainage); (5) *patient comfort status assessment*; (6) *patient safety assessment* (side rails; maintaining functional integrity of tubes; providing scissors and/or wire cutter at bedside).

These systematic assessments should have been made at an initial frequency of every fifteen minutes, with the expectation of improvement in level of consciousness and respiratory character. If Patient A's condition failed to improve after a reasonable time (that is, two assessments over thirty minutes), as it did, the nurse should have informed the physician of the situation. Patient A became progressively hypoxic because of upper airway obstruction secondary to heavy sedation, which in turn led to the respiratory arrest and a subsequent cardiac arrest.

The plaintiff's case was based on the determination that the departures from prevailing professional standards of nursing care caused the demise of Patient A. The case settled with payment to the estate of the plaintiff.

## Case 4–2
### Endotracheal Tube Obstruction

#### Problem and Outcome

Failure to prevent the patient from "biting on the endotracheal tube" and failure to detect hypoxia caused an unnecessary death.

#### The Patient

Patient A was a 37-year-old female with a known history of asthma. She was brought to a hospital emergency department by her husband on 24 December at 12:25 A.M. because of a severe asthma attack.

#### Treatment

While in the emergency department, Patient A experienced a seizure and respiratory arrest. She was bagged, various medications were administered, a central venous pressure line was established, and the patient was restrained because of "restlessness." At 1:15 A.M., she was intubated.

Patient A was transferred to the intensive care unit at 2:45 A.M. and was then connected to a ventilator. At 7:49 A.M. she developed ventricular tachycardia which progressed to ventricular fibrillation. Resuscitation efforts failed, and Patient A expired at 8:00 A.M., 24 December.

#### Departures from the Standard of Care

Serious deviations from prevailing professional standards of nursing care existed in this case, and they included the following:

1. Failure to make systematic nursing observations
2. Failure to detect respiratory problems leading to hypoxia
3. Failure to inform the physician of continued respiratory problems
4. Failure to maintain a patent airway
5. Failure to provide a safe environment for the patient

## Discussion

Between 2:45 A.M., 24 December, and the time that Patient A went into ventricular fibrillation at 7:49 A.M., the only vital signs recorded in the medical record included the following:

2:45 A.M.  Temperature 98.8; Sinus tachycardia 148; Respiration 40/10 and shallow, 140/80.
3:40 A.M.  Sinus tachycardia 143; Respiration 40/10, 110/70.
4:30 A.M.  Pulse 40–120; Respiration 40/10, 70/50.

It was noted that at 1:30 A.M., 24 December, Patient A was "awake and alert and pulled out the endotracheal tube." She was then reintubated. At 4:00 A.M., it was noted "patient restless, keeps on biting tube – extubated herself . . . reintubated." From 5:30 A.M. through 7:00 A.M., notations were made that the patient was "biting on the endotracheal tube all the time."

Maintenance of a patent airway is vital to life. Attentive nursing care could have prevented Patient A from biting on the endotracheal tube and consequently occluding her airway. In addition, permitting Patient A to extubate herself repeatedly and thus traumatize the airway was totally unacceptable.

Progressive hypoxia was not detected because systematic nursing assessment was absent. Nursing observations with particular emphasis on respiratory, circulatory, and neurological status should have appeared in the medical record at least hourly.

The only explanation offered for this dreadful nursing care was that "we were short-staffed because it was holiday time and people want to be home with their family. . . . You can't do everything."

The plaintiff's case was based on the determination that the departures from prevailing professional standards of nursing care contributed to the demise of Patient A. The case settled with payment to the estate of the plaintiff.

Case 4–3

## *Respiratory Fatigue*

### Problem and Outcome

Premature extubation and ultimate failure to provide mechanical ventilatory support led to the hastened death of a young woman.

### The Patient

Patient R, a bright and dynamic 31-year-old woman, had a full social and professional life. Graduating *summa cum laude* from Georgia College with a Bachelor of Arts degree and a major in psychology, Patient R greatly enjoyed working at a psychiatric hospital as a psychology technician.

She suffered from a progressive neuromuscular scoliosis secondary to amyotonia congenita. The condition, however, was in a state of arrest, and the situation was compatible with ten to twenty more years of productive life. Patient R was admitted to the hospital 5 September for elective correction and stabilization of the progressive spinal deformity.

Past medical history revealed no significant illnesses other than the primary muscle disorder. Patient R was confined to a wheelchair at approximately eight years of age and became essentially quadriplegic over the years. Due to the amyotonia congenita, her vital capacity was approximately 50 percent of normal, and she had trouble coughing effectively. In addition, structural deformities of her rib cage existed.

### Treatment

On 7 September, Patient R had the first stage of the operative procedure, an anterior spinal release of thoracic vertebra number ten through sacral vertebra number one (T10–S1), with anterior interbody fusion. The second-stage operative procedure, a posterior spinal fusion with spinal osteotomies and segmental instrumentation, was accomplished 19 September. Patient R tolerated both procedures well.

On 23 September, however, Patient R developed hematemesis and hypotension. Upper gastrointestinal endoscopy revealed a massively bleeding gastric ulcer. During the endoscopic procedure, Patient R was actively bleeding and in shock. The examination was discontinued when the patient went into respiratory arrest. Resuscitation was successful and the patient was taken to the operating room at 2:55 P.M. where an exploratory laparotomy with gastrotomy, oversewing of a bleeding gastric ulcer, pyeloroplasty, inadvertent splenectomy, and attempted vago-tomy were performed.

Immediate postoperative problems on 23 September included coagu-lopathy, hypercarbia, and marginal urinary output. The patient did aspi-rate blood preoperatively and continued to be intubated and mechanically ventilated. Patient R was extubated at 8:35 A.M. on 27 September but was reintubated at 10:00 P.M. because of respiratory distress. At 5:00 A.M., 28 September, she went into cardiopulmonary arrest. Resuscitation was suc-cessful, but she sustained anoxic encephalopathy.

Intra-abdominal sepsis developed, and Patient R was returned to the operating room 8 October for a tracheostomy, an exploratory laparotomy, gastrostomy, drainage of a subfacial abscess, and insertion of a feeding jejunostomy. Patient R continued to have problems with abdominal sep-sis and then pulmonary sepsis. Her vital signs became unstable, and she went into cardiac failure. On 3 November at 3:55 P.M., Patient R was pro-nounced dead.

### Departures from the Standard of Care

Based upon review of the medical record, serious deviations from pre-vailing professional standards of nursing care occurred 27 through 28 Sep-tember and included the following:

1. Failure to make systematic nursing assessments
2. Failure to establish an arterial line and obtain timely arterial blood gas analyses
3. Failure to have a physician evaluate the patient at 7:40 P.M., 27 Sep-tember
4. Failure to discontinue the continuous positive airway pressure every two hours for ten minutes
5. Failure to detect respiratory distress and profound hypoxia in a timely manner
6. Failure to institute ventilatory support in a timely manner
7. Failure to maintain a patent airway prior to the cardiopulmonary arrest
8. Failure to execute a program of pulmonary hygiene
9. Failure to suction the patient with appropriate frequency
10. Failure to properly visualize the patient from the nurses' station

| Date | 27 September | | | | | | 28 September | | |
|---|---|---|---|---|---|---|---|---|---|
| Time | am 8:00 | am 9:00 | am 11:30 | pm 3:30 | pm 8:00 | pm 11:00 | am 12:00 | am 2:00 | am 4:00 |
| Blood pressure | 170/90 | 148/0 | 130/0 | 134/74 | 126/0 | 134/90 | 134/90 | 150/100 | 194/0 |
| Pulse rate | 140 | 158 | 160 | 150 | 160 | 146 | 146 | 150 | 140 |
| Respiratory rate | 28 | | 30 | 29 | 30 | 36 | 36 | 26 | 28 |
| Effectiveness of cough | Poor | | | | Poor | | | | |
| Sputum characteristics and amount | Thick–small | | | Thin–large | | Thick–large | | | |
| Breath sounds | Equal | | | Rales–rhonchi | | | | Clear | |
| Mental acuity and orientation | | | | Alert x3 | Alert x3 | | | | |

**Figure 5**   Nursing Assessment Data

## Discussion

Comprehensive systematic nursing assessments were not documented during a critical period of this patient's hospitalization. Figure 5 presents all of the nursing assessment data charted from 5:00 A.M., 27 September, through 4:00 A.M., 28 September.

In this particular case, necessary nursing observations include the following:

A. Basic assessments
  1. Blood pressure
  2. Patency of airway
  3. Pulse rate, rhythm, and quality
  4. Ease of respiration
  5. Respiratory rate, rhythm, and character
  6. Duration of inspiration vs. expiration
  7. General chest expansion
  8. Presence or absence of intercostal retractions
  9. Posture of patient
  10. Skin color and temperature
  11. Breath sounds/adventitious sounds
  12. Presence/absence of fatigue with respiration

B. Expanded assessments
   1. Effectiveness and frequency of cough
   2. Sputum characteristics (amount, color, consistency)
   3. Determination of tactile fremitus
   4. Percussion of the chest, noting intensity, pitch, quality, duration, and equality of sound
   5. Arterial blood gasses
   6. Tidal volume
   7. Minute ventilation
   8. Vital capacity
   9. Mental acuity status

Prior to extubation (from 5:00 A.M. through 8:35 A.M., 27 September), the observations comprising the basic nursing assessments should have been documented every hour. Expanded nursing assessment observations with the exception of arterial blood gasses should have been documented every two hours during this period.

At 8:35 A.M., 27 September, when Patient R was extubated, the basic assessment observations should have been documented every fifteen minutes for the first hour of extubation and then, if stable, every hour thereafter. Expanded assessment observations should have been documented every two hours with the exception of arterial blood gasses.

Systematic nursing assessment was particularly important at this point because, after three days of mechanical ventilatory support, all of the breathing effort was now provided by the patient. This was no small feat for a frail young woman who had just undergone her third major operation in sixteen days, with a minimal amount of nutrition over that period of time. With weakened breathing muscles (from the muscular dystrophy) as well as the superimposed incision in the upper abdomen, she had to provide all her own energy for breathing.

Great difficulty with suctioning was noted to begin at 5:00 P.M. on 27 September. Repeated unsuccessful suctioning attempts were made. This is known to stress a patient, both psychologically and physiologically. An arterial line should have been established at this time and arterial blood gasses obtained immediately to determine the patient's oxygenation and acid-base status. Arterial blood gasses were not obtained until 7:40 P.M., and they indicated hypoventilation by the rising $pCO_2$ of 61 mmHg. Based upon this $pCO_2$, Patient R needed intervention by the physician. Also, basic and expanded nursing assessments thereafter needed to be made every fifteen minutes and every hour, respectively. Special attention should have been directed at observing for fatigue with her respiratory effort.

Problems continued, and Patient R was reintubated orally at 10:00 P.M. and was placed on a T-piece with continuous positive airway pressure (CPAP) of 5 cmHOH. Again, basic and expanded nursing assessment observations should have been continued every fifteen minutes and every hour, respectively. It is well known that an artificial airway adds resistance and promotes shallow breathing. In addition, the CPAP should have been discontinued for ten minutes every two hours to provide a period of rest from the increased ventilatory workload. When CPAP is utilized, it is essential that the patient be observed for fatigue and hypercapnia because of the increased work of breathing. At the first sign of fatigue and/or alteration of arterial blood gas values, the nurse must contact the physician and provide for mechanical ventilatory support.

It is the nurse who is with the patient continuously; it is the nurse's responsibility to recognize the onset of respiratory failure. Simple bedside monitoring, as outlined previously, alerts the nurse to subtle signs of impending problems. The flow sheet developed for analysis of nursing care in this case follows on pages 84–90. Nursing assessments that should have been made are listed in the left-hand column, while the appropriate frequency of the assessment appears across the top of the flow sheet. The assessment data on this flow sheet was taken from the medical record and includes all nursing entries made.

Astute observation of pulmonary function over time is vital. Cardinal signs of respiratory distress and profound hypoxia were not detected by the nursing staff until Patient R was found at 4:20 A.M., 28 September, "staring off into space. Hands clasped together moving up and down. Biting up and down on endotracheal tube." At this time, an extreme emergency existed. The establishment of an effective airway and ventilatory support should have been instituted immediately. The Ambu bag is the nurse's first line of defense for acute respiratory failure, but it was not until 4:45 A.M. that the nursing staff "began bagging 100 percent oxygen." Cardiopulmonary arrest occurred at 5:00 A.M.

The nursing staff failed to observe Patient R properly. In addition, there is no record that they instituted a vigorous program of pulmonary hygiene. It was documented by the physician upon admission that Patient R had a "severely reduced vital capacity and trouble coughing up secretions." It was also noted by the physician that "she does not move unless pushed to do so." The nursing staff should have used this information in planning her care. Rigorously managed pulmonary hygiene and frequent position changes along with encouragement to cough and deep-breathe might have prevented some of the respiratory problems.

Testimony by Nurse M revealed that there was limited visibility of the patient from the nurses' station on 27 through 28 September. This situation demands that a nurse not leave the patient unattended for over fifteen minutes. When Nurse M was asked about the frequency with which patients were observed, she stated that one was "supposed to make rounds, I understand it, every hour." This is totally inadequate.

When asked about her assessment of Patient R at 4:20 A.M., Nurse M stated that she suspected the patient was having a stroke or seizure. Nurse M did not address in her testimony the obvious problem of inadequate oxygenation. Nurse M also stated that she believed the patient did not need ventilatory support from 4:20 A.M. to 4:45 A.M. because "the patient was OK in that area." This nurse should have summoned a physician immediately when Patient R began biting down on the endotracheal tube.

The plaintiff's case was based on the determination that if systematic nursing assessments had been made, and that if mechanical ventilation had been instituted at the first sign of hypoxia, this tragic event in all probability could have been prevented. These departures from prevailing professional standards of nursing care contributed to the patient's suffering an anoxic episode between 2:00 A.M. and 4:25 A.M. on 28 September. This anoxic episode in turn caused brain injury, which contributed to the patient's death on 3 November. The case settled with payment to the estate of the plaintiff.

## Section Two

# Assessment of Circulatory Status

The series of cases in this section deal primarily with circulatory problems. These cases involve, among other things, failure to detect in a timely manner cardiopulmonary arrest, hypovolemic shock, a thromboembolitic episode, and permanent pacemaker malfunction.

## Case 4–3 Flow Sheet

**Assessment Standard for Patient**          **Minimum Frequency of Assessment**

| Assessment | Variable | 27 September 5:00 am | 6:00 | 7:00 | 8:00 | 8:35 | 8:45 |
|---|---|---|---|---|---|---|---|
| **Respiratory status** | Patency of airway | | | | small thick secretions | | |
| | Respiratory rate | | | | 28 | | |
| | Respiratory rhythm | | | | | | |
| | Respiratory character | | | | poor cough | | |
| | Breath sounds | | | | equal | | |
| | Ease of respiration | | | | | | |
| | Inspiration vs. expiration | | | | | | |
| | Chest expansion | | | | | | |
| | Intercostal retractions | | | | | | |
| | Posture of patient | | | | | | |
| | Fatigue with respiration | | | | | | |
| **Neurological status** | Mental acuity | | | | | | |
| **Circulatory status** | Blood pressure | | | | $\frac{170}{90}$ | | |
| | Heart rate | | | | 140 | | |
| | Heart rhythm | | | | | | |
| | Pulse quality | | | | | | |
| | Skin color | | | | | | |
| | Skin temperature | | | | | | |

**entries indicate assessments that were made)**

| 9:00 | 9:15 | 9:30 | 10:30 | 11:30 | 12:30 pm | 1:30 | 2:30 | 3:30 | 4:30 | 5:00 | 5:15 | 5:30 |
|---|---|---|---|---|---|---|---|---|---|---|---|---|
| | | | | | | | | large thin secretions | | | | |
| | | | | 30 | | | | 29 | | | | |
| | | | | | | | | | | | | |
| | | | | | | | | | | | | |
| | | | | | | | | rales rhonchi | | | | |
| | | | | | | | | | | | | |
| | | | | | | | | | | | | |
| | | | | | | | | | | | | |
| | | | | | | | | | | | | |
| | | | | | | | | | | | | |
| | | | | | | | | | | | | |
| | | | | | | | | alert oriented x3 | | | | |
| $\frac{148}{0}$ | | | | $\frac{130}{0}$ | | | | $\frac{134}{74}$ | | | | |
| 158 | | | | 160 | | | | 150 | | | | |
| | | | | | | | | | | | | |
| | | | | | | | | | | | | |
| | | | | | | | | | | | | |
| | | | | | | | | | | | | |

## Case 4–3 Flow Sheet (continued)

**Assessment Standard for Patient**                **Minimum Frequency of Assessment**

| Assessment | Variable | 27 September 5:45 pm | 6:00 | 6:15 | 6:30 | 6:45 | 7:00 |
|---|---|---|---|---|---|---|---|
| **Respiratory status** | Patency of airway | | | | | | |
| | Respiratory rate | | | | | | |
| | Respiratory rhythm | | | | | | |
| | Respiratory character | | | | | | |
| | Breath sounds | | | | | | |
| | Ease of respiration | | | | | | |
| | Inspiration vs. expiration | | | | | | |
| | Chest expansion | | | | | | |
| | Intercostal retractions | | | | | | |
| | Posture of patient | | | | | | |
| | Fatigue with respiration | | | | | | |
| **Neurological status** | Mental acuity | | | | | | |
| **Circulatory status** | Blood pressure | | | | | | |
| | Heart rate | | | | | | |
| | Heart rhythm | | | | | | |
| | Pulse quality | | | | | | |
| | Skin color | | | | | | |
| | Skin temperature | | | | | | |

entries indicate assessments that were made)

| 7:15 | 7:30 | 7:45 | 8:00 | 8:15 | 8:30 | 8:45 | 9:00 | 9:15 | 9:30 | 9:45 | 10:00 | 10:15 |
|---|---|---|---|---|---|---|---|---|---|---|---|---|
| | | | | | | | | | | | | |
| | | | 30 | | | | | | | | | |
| | | | poor cough | | | | | | | | | |
| | | | | | | | | | | | | |
| | | | | | | | | | | | | |
| | | | | | | | | | | | | |
| | | | | | | | | | | | | |
| | | | | | | | | | | | | |
| | | | | | | | | | | | | |
| | | | alert oriented x3 | | | | | | | | | |
| | | | $\frac{126}{0}$ | | | | | | | | | |
| | | | 160 | | | | | | | | | |
| | | | | | | | | | | | | |
| | | | | | | | | | | | | |
| | | | | | | | | | | | | |
| | | | | | | | | | | | | |

## Case 4–3 Flow Sheet (continued)

**Assessment Standard for Patient**                    **Minimum Frequency of Assessment**

| Assessment | Variable | 27 September 10:30 | 10:45 | 11:00 | 11:15 | 11:30 | 11:45 |
|---|---|---|---|---|---|---|---|
| **Respiratory status** | Patency of airway | | | large thick secretions | | | |
| | Respiratory rate | | | 36 | | | |
| | Respiratory rhythm | | | | | | |
| | Respiratory character | | | | | | |
| | Breath sounds | | | | | | |
| | Ease of respiration | | | | | | |
| | Inspiration vs. expiration | | | | | | |
| | Chest expansion | | | | | | |
| | Intercostal retractions | | | | | | |
| | Posture of patient | | | | | | |
| | Fatigue with respiration | | | | | | |
| **Neurological status** | Mental acuity | | | | | | |
| **Circulatory status** | Blood pressure | | | $\frac{134}{90}$ | | | |
| | Heart rate | | | 146 | | | |
| | Heart rhythm | | | | | | |
| | Pulse quality | | | | | | |
| | Skin color | | | | | | |
| | Skin temperature | | | | | | |

**(entries indicate assessments that were made)**

| 28 September 12:00 am | 12:15 | 12:30 | 12:45 | 1:00 | 1:15 | 1:30 | 1:45 | 2:00 | 2:15 | 2:30 | 2:45 | 3:00 |
|---|---|---|---|---|---|---|---|---|---|---|---|---|
|  |  |  |  |  |  |  |  |  |  |  |  |  |
| 36 |  |  |  |  |  |  |  | 26 |  |  |  |  |
|  |  |  |  |  |  |  |  |  |  |  |  |  |
| clear |  |  |  |  |  |  |  |  |  |  |  |  |
|  |  |  |  |  |  |  |  |  |  |  |  |  |
|  |  |  |  |  |  |  |  |  |  |  |  |  |
|  |  |  |  |  |  |  |  |  |  |  |  |  |
|  |  |  |  |  |  |  |  |  |  |  |  |  |
|  |  |  |  |  |  |  |  |  |  |  |  |  |
|  |  |  |  |  |  |  |  |  |  |  |  |  |
| $\frac{134}{90}$ |  |  |  |  |  |  |  | $\frac{150}{100}$ |  |  |  |  |
| 146 |  |  |  |  |  |  |  | 150 |  |  |  |  |
|  |  |  |  |  |  |  |  |  |  |  |  |  |
|  |  |  |  |  |  |  |  |  |  |  |  |  |
|  |  |  |  |  |  |  |  |  |  |  |  |  |
|  |  |  |  |  |  |  |  |  |  |  |  |  |

## Case 4–3 Flow Sheet (continued)

**Assessment Standard for Patient**            **Minimum Frequency of Assessment**

| Assessment | Variable | 28 September 3:15 am | 3:30 | 3:45 | 4:00 | 4:15 |
|---|---|---|---|---|---|---|
| **Respiratory status** | Patency of airway | | | | | |
| | Respiratory rate | | | | 28 | |
| | Respiratory rhythm | | | | | |
| | Respiratory character | | | | | |
| | Breath sounds | | | | | |
| | Ease of respiration | | | | | |
| | Inspiration vs. expiration | | | | | |
| | Chest expansion | | | | | |
| | Intercostal retractions | | | | | |
| | Posture of patient | | | | | |
| | Fatigue with respiration | | | | | |
| **Neurological status** | Mental acuity | | | | | |
| **Circulatory status** | Blood pressure | | | | $\frac{194}{0}$ | |
| | Heart rate | | | | 140 | |
| | Heart rhythm | | | | | |
| | Pulse quality | | | | | |
| | Skin color | | | | | |
| | Skin temperature | | | | | |

Case 4-4

## Postoperative Cardiopulmonary Arrest

### Problem and Outcome

Due to inadequate observation in the recovery room, a cardiopulmonary arrest was not detected in a timely fashion. A 30-year-old man suffered profound hypoxic encephalopathy and died one year later.

### The Patient

Patient H, a mailman with a wife and two children, was admitted to the hospital 13 March for elective surgery. The preoperative diagnosis included bony mass on the lateral aspect of the left patella and nonunion of the radial styloid with a ganglion of the right wrist. Past medical and social history was insignificant and the patient was in good general health.

### Treatment

An arthrotomy of the left knee and excision of a ganglion of the right radial styloid was performed. The surgery was uneventful, but a cardiopulmonary arrest occurred in the recovery room. Resuscitation was instituted, but hypoxic encephalopathy, manifested clinically by coma, occurred. The hospital course of Patient H was complicated and prolonged. Patient H never regained consciousness, and he expired one year after the incident.

### Departures from the Standard of Care

Failure to assess Patient H systematically in the recovery room was the major departure from prevailing professional standards of nursing care in this case.

### Discussion

Postanesthetic notes by the anesthesiologist stated: "Lifting head and blowing nose. Patient complaining of stuffy nose. To recovery room in good condition." The charted vital signs on admission to the recovery room at 2:30 P.M. were "blood pressure 125/65, pulse 75, and respiration 20." The nurse's note on admission reads "Patient alert, talking and sitting up on admission. Patient blowing his nose and asked for urinal." No other nursing entries were charted for the next thirty minutes. At 3:00 P.M., Dr. B, the surgeon, went to the recovery room to check the patient.

He found Patient H with dilated pupils and without blood pressure, pulse, or respiration.

The nurse caring for Patient H should have realized the critical nature of the immediate postoperative period. Many problems can arise. A patient can appear alert, oriented, and be breathing well one minute, and be apneic the next.

Patient H should have been diligently observed and systematically assessed at least every fifteen minutes. The assessment should have included the following: (1) *respiratory status* (patency of airway; depth, rate, character, and rhythm of respirations); (2) *circulatory status* (blood pressure; pulse rate, rhythm, and quality; color and temperature of skin); (3) *neurological status* (level of consciousness); (4) *wound status* (amount and type of drainage, circulatory status of extremities); (5) *patient comfort status*. Systematic observation enables the nurse to detect signs of impending problems.

Investigation of the incident revealed that there were six nurses on duty in the recovery room. Testimony indicated the following with respect to the activities of each:

1.  Nurse LV, the recovery room supervisor, was not actively engaging in patient care. She was physically present but was reviewing a proposed revision of the nursing care notes form.
2.  Nurse JW was leaving the recovery room to take another patient to the floor just as Patient H arrived. She did not return until at or about the time of Patient H 's arrest.
3.  Nurse CW had just come on duty and was doing the narcotics count in the medication area.
4.  Nurse CH was assigned to two other patients and was not responsible for Patient H.
5.  Nurse CA admitted Patient H and estimated that she spent two to three minutes with him. Thereafter, she paid no further attention to him because she was discussing the proposed revision of the nursing-care notes form with the supervisor.
6.  Nurse MH attended to Patient H when he arrived and assisted him with the urinal. She then went to care for another patient who had undergone a laparotomy and was not doing well. Her attention was not drawn back to Patient H until the surgeon found the patient unresponsive and asked, "What's going on here?"

Hypotheses as to why Patient H suffered a cardiopulmonary arrest include the following: (1) the patient had a full bladder, and when he tried to void, a vagal response was elicited (vagal stimulation may cause bradycardia, and if the bradycardia is profound, it may cause cardiac arrest); (2) during the act of blowing his nose (if forceful), a Valsalva maneuver (forcible exhalation against a closed glottis) was performed (holding the breath increases intrathoracic pressure and causes a reduction in cardiac venous return and ventricular filling – releasing the breath causes venous return to increase markedly along with a rise in the arterial pressure – this drastic change in the velocity of the venous blood flow activates a vagal response at the sino-atrial [SA] node, and bradycardia occurs); (3) there was inadequate reversal of the neuromuscular blocking agent; or (4) the patient had an idiosyncratic reaction to Prostigmine (neostigmine bromide), the agent used to reverse the neuromuscular blocking agent, which resulted in a profound bradycardia or cholinergic crisis (a state characterized by increasing muscle weakness which, through involvement of the muscles of respiration, may lead to respiratory arrest), even though atropine was administered with the Prostigmine (neostigmine bromide) to counteract adverse effects. These are some of the problems that can occur in the recovery room, and this is why patients must be intensely observed.

The plaintiff's case was based on the determination that, had the cardiopulmonary arrest been discovered in a timely fashion and treatment instituted promptly, in all probability Patient H would not have suffered hypoxic encephalopathy. The case settled with payment to the estate of the plaintiff.

## Case 4–5

### *Hypovolemic Shock*

#### Problem and Outcome

Unrecognized hypovolemic shock eliminated an 18-year-old's chance for survival after a motor-vehicle accident.

#### The Patient

A young man, Patient P, was struck by a motor vehicle while on a skateboard and was transported to a hospital by a fire-rescue unit. His injuries included subarachnoid hemorrhage, ruptured spleen, multiple rib fractures, compound fractures of the right tibia and fibula, numerous pulmonary contusions, and many contusions and abrasions of the skin.

### Treatment

Upon admission to the emergency department at 8:50 A.M. on 26 April, Patient P was evaluated by the emergency-department physician. The patient was reported to be combative and thrashing about. Pulse rate was 100, lungs were clear to percussion and auscultation, and the abdomen was noted to be firm with absent bowel sounds. The initial examination was "limited" because the patient was "thrashing about" and uncooperative. Various laboratory studies were ordered along with requests for consultation. Intravenous fluid therapy instituted at the scene of the accident was continued and whole blood replacement commenced. At 9:40 A.M., Nembutal (pentobarbital) 100 milligrams was administered intramuscularly.

Patient P was then transported to the radiology department for X-rays, with a nurse in attendance. At 9:55 A.M., a respiratory arrest was noted, but spontaneous respirations resumed at 9:58 A.M. Shortly thereafter, bradycardia developed. At 11:00 A.M., while still in X-ray, the patient suffered a cardiac arrest. Cardiopulmonary resuscitation commenced, and the patient was taken to the operating room at 12:00 P.M. with resuscitation efforts in progress. An exploratory laparotomy revealed a massive hemoperitoneum primarily related to a ruptured spleen. A left thoracotomy with open cardiac massage was performed, but the patient was in advanced shock and expired at 12:35 P.M.

### Departures from the Standard of Care

Significant departures from prevailing professional standards of nursing care were evident in this case and included the following:

1. Failure to do a comprehensive initial nursing assessment
2. Failure to observe the patient systematically at appropriate intervals
3. Failure to question a medication order

### Discussion

The nursing care Patient P received, as documented in the medical record, was most incomplete and inadequate. There is little in the record to indicate what occurred between admission and the cardiac arrest. The first and certainly the major departure from the standard of care was failure to recognize shock. Unfortunately, no blood pressures were taken on this patient. His pulse rate was initially 100 but increased rapidly to 150, which should have alerted the nurses to shock. His combativeness, although suggestive of intracranial pathology, was classical evidence of hypoxia and shock and, in the absence of lateralizing neurological signs, should have been assumed to have been related to shock.

A patient in shock, or threatening to go into shock, is seriously ill. The nurse must act rapidly and precisely to detect early signs of impending problems to protect the patient from complications. Nursing care for the multiple trauma victim involves, among other things (after establishing adequate ventilation and circulation), frequent and accurate observation.

Nursing care is crucial, because it is the nurse who remains with the patient and makes pertinent observations. Some observations may not be apparent during the physician's initial examination, and the nurse may note significant observations in the course of his/her care for the patient. By almost constant attention to the vital signs, one attempts to detect early warnings of impending catastrophe. The frequency of the observations is determined by the patient's condition.

The ability of the nurse to make accurate observations, to interpret observations, to record observations, and to communicate pertinent observations is without question the most important part of the nursing care for the multiple trauma patient. Early recognition of the signs and symptoms of shock and prompt treatment are necessary to ensure patient recovery.

In addition, a nurse administered 100 milligrams of Nembutal (pentobarbital) by the intramuscular route in the emergency department. This physician's order should have been questioned, because the drug is a general depressant affecting the central nervous system. This medication is generally contraindicated in patients with multiple trauma. In addition to the potential for lowering blood pressure and depressing respiration, this medication makes neurological status assessment difficult.

Patient P died from traumatic and hypovolemic shock. Had there been timely intervention, his chance of survival would have been enhanced. The plaintiff's case was based on the determination that poor nursing care and failure to recognize shock contributed to the demise of Patient P. The case settled with payment to the parents of the plaintiff.

Case 4–6

## Lower Extremity Arterial Obstruction

### Problem and Outcome

Failure to assess a 52-year-old woman's lower extremities postoperatively contributed to amputation of the left foot.

### The Patient

Patient P, an active grandmother, fell at home and injured the left hip area. X-rays revealed a comminuted intertrochanteric fracture of the left hip.

### Treatment

Patient P was admitted to the hospital, and an open reduction and internal fixation of the left hip was accomplished.

Postoperatively, the patient received physical therapy and was ambulated. Patient P was discharged home, but one day later she was readmitted to the hospital complaining of continued severe pain in the left foot. Upon examination, she had good palpable femoral, popliteal, ankle, and pedal pulses of the right lower extremity, but no palpable pulses in the left lower extremity. The left foot was cyanotic as well.

An immediate aorto-femoral arteriogram revealed atheromatous plaques in the distal abdominal aorta (proximal to the bifurcation), complete occlusion of the left common femoral artery, and a prominent mural thrombus (left) causing minimal obstruction above the knee joint. Patient P was taken to the operating room where she underwent a left common femoral thromboendarterectomy with gortex patch angioplasty and distal embolectomy.

Patient P tolerated the procedure well but did not have good resolution of the cyanosis of the distal foot and the pregangrenous changes. Postoperatively, she did demarcate the gangrenous areas to the left foot, and amputation of the foot took place. Fifteen days later Patient P was discharged from the hospital.

### Departures from the Standard of Care

Departures from prevailing professional standards of nursing care during the first hospitalization included the following:

1. Failure to assess systematically the left lower extremity

2. Failure to inform the physician of changes in the left lower extremity

3. Failure to request that the physician see the patient prior to discharge

### Discussion

Except for one nursing assessment immediately postoperatively with normal findings, there were no nursing notations regarding the status of the lower extremities until the afternoon before discharge (day nine, postoperatively, of the first hospitalization). The nurse's note read: "Severe pain in left foot; patient complains left foot cold and feels numb." The next morning, the only nurse's note charted read: "For discharge. Patient escort called."

Patient P testified that on the day of discharge she "begged" the nurses not to send her home because "my foot hurt too bad and felt funny." Patient P went on to say that "the nurse told me to go home, and if my foot wasn't better in a week, call the doctor."

Nursing assessment of lower extremity neurovascular status should have been carried out every shift postoperatively. The problems expressed by the patient the afternoon prior to discharge should have been communicated to the physician, and lower extremity neurovascular status assessment should have increased in frequency. In addition, a nurse should have requested that the physician examine the patient on the day of discharge, because the patient's condition had changed since the discharge order had been written in the early morning of the previous day.

The plaintiff's case was based on the conclusion that the departures from prevailing professional standards of nursing care caused delay in treatment of a completely occluded femoral artery and, therefore, contributed to the loss of the patient's foot. The case settled with payment to the plaintiff.

### Case 4–7

## *Pacemaker Malfunction*

### Problem and Outcome

Failure to detect a permanent pacemaker malfunction led to a persistent vegetative state in a 77-year-old man.

### The Patient

Patient J, a retired purchasing agent, was admitted to the hospital for elective mitral valve replacement because of severe mitral insufficiency and regurgitation (class four). He had a known history of rheumatic fever as a child.

### Treatment

On 1 September, Patient J underwent open heart surgery, and a #33 St. Jude mitral valve was implanted.

Postoperatively, Patient J was hemodynamically stable but pacemaker-dependent. Complete heart block developed rapidly. Attempts to wean the patient from the temporary pacemaker failed. On 7 September an experimental permanent dual-chamber rate-responsive pacemaker was implanted. The temporary epicardial pacing wires were left in place.

In the late afternoon of 7 September, malfunction of the permanent-pacer firing was evident by electrocardiogram. Patient J remained hemodynamically stable, and the physician requested close observation.

At 8:45 A.M., 8 September, a resident physician assisted by Nurse R removed the temporary epicardial pacing wires. Shortly thereafter, Patient J suffered a cardiopulmonary arrest and entered a vegetative state.

### Departures from the Standard of Care

Departures from prevailing professional standards of nursing care included the following:

1. Failure to assess the function of the permanent pacemaker prior to removal of the temporary epicardial pacer wires
2. Failure to assess hemodynamic status at least every fifteen minutes for one hour after removal of the temporary epicardial pacer wires

### Discussion

According to the medical record, no nursing assessment of permanent pacemaker function occurred after the malfunction on 7 September. Furthermore, no nursing observations were made after the removal of the temporary epicardial pacing wires on 8 September until 9:17 A.M., when it was noted that Patient J was in full cardiopulmonary arrest. Again, the functional status of the permanent pacemaker had not been ascertained by the nurse prior to the procedure. This was a very important nursing responsibility because of the malfunction the day before.

According to the medical record, a code was called at 9:17 A.M., and it was noted that pulse and blood pressure were lost for forty minutes. Patient J never regained consciousness and he became comatose.

Testimony by Nurse R revealed, "Yes, I was concerned when the doctor pulled the wires, but I just thought he knew what he was doing. . . . I guess I didn't go back to the room until someone grabbed me. You know, we were pretty busy that morning." She further testified that the pacemaker programmer was not available at the patient's bedside or in the vicinity for use during the arrest. "They had to look in the operating rooms or somewhere for it."

The plaintiff's case was based on the determination that the failure to detect an inadequate cardiac output because of lack of nursing assessment contributed to the hypoxic encephalopathy suffered by the patient. The case settled with payment to the plaintiff.


## Section Three
# Assessment of Neurological, Wound, Fluid, and Pain Status

This group of cases emphasizes assessment of neurological, wound, fluid, and pain status. Each of these cases involves a death. The causes of death were failure to detect increased intracranial pressure (Case 4–8), a cervical spine fracture (Case 4–9), hemorrhage from chest tubes (Case 4–10), a fluid excess (Case 4–11), and a myocardial infarction (Case 4–12).

### Case 4–8
### *Increased Intracranial Pressure*

**Problem and Outcome**

Undetected increased intracranial pressure resulted in brain stem herniation which caused the death of a 48-year-old man.

**The Patient**

Patient P was a hard-working man who enjoyed his job. He worked at a restaurant from 6:30 A.M. until 1:00 P.M., six days a week. Patient P was committed to his wife, fifteen years his senior. She had multiple health problems, and Patient P provided her with much assistance. This mild-mannered person was injured 27 March when he slipped and fell while cleaning floorboards at the restaurant where he was employed. He struck the right temporal area of the head and sustained a laceration on the head. He was treated at an emergency department and released. From the time of the accident, Patient P was bothered by headaches, but he was a stoical man who returned to work. On 10 May, while waiting for the bus, he experienced diplopia along with the headaches, and he did not go to work. The next day he went to work but developed a severe headache and had to be taken to an emergency department by his employer. He was examined, given 50 milligrams of Demerol (meperidine), and referred to a neurologist. He went home but did not keep the appointment because he fell asleep for the remainder of the day. His wife found him asleep when she returned home from a doctor's appointment.

### Treatment

Patient P continued to be drowsy, and he was taken to the emergency department on the afternoon of 13 May. He was admitted to the hospital and was to be observed and evaluated for a possible subdural hematoma. His condition deteriorated, and Patient P died thirteen hours after admission.

### Departures from the Standard of Care

Deviations from acceptable standards of nursing care include the following:

1. Failure to assess systematically the neurological status of the patient
2. Failure to inform the physician of a significant change in condition

### Discussion

According to the nursing admission note at 3:30 P.M. on 13 May, Patient P was alert but drowsy and was oriented to person, place, and time. His vital signs were within normal limits, and both pupils were equal and reactive to light and accommodation.

The nursing care as documented in the medical record was most incomplete and inadequate. Systematic neurological status assessments should have included response to stimuli, orientation, level of consciousness, response to commands, pupillary response, ocular movements, motor and sensory function, reflexes, pain assessment, and behavioral evaluation. These assessments should have been done at least hourly from admission until 4:00 P.M. At 4:00 P.M. the frequency of neurological status assessment should have increased because the patient's condition changed.

All of the nursing notations in the medical record for 13–14 May are listed as follows:

4:00 P.M.   Speech slurred/garbled.
7:00 P.M.   Sleepy, vital signs stable.
10:00 P.M.  Will arouse to name, shaking, and light pain. Blood pressure 150/96, pulse 44.
1:00 A.M.   Not responsive to stimuli.
3:10 A.M.   Pupils fully dilated and equal.
3:40 A.M.   Blood pressure increased to 160/110. Pulse 160 per minute.
3:50 A.M.   Blood pressure increased to 170/110. Pulse 160 per minute.
4:00 A.M.   Blood pressure suddenly dropped to 70/60. Radial pulse – none! MD called.
4:40 A.M.   MD here; patient pronounced.

Even though the nursing assessments were infrequent and incomplete, it is obvious from the medical record that Patient P had symptoms indicative of increased intracranial pressure. Any sign of increased intracranial pressure must be reported to the physician promptly, because the cranial cavity cannot expand if the brain becomes edematous or if there is intracranial bleeding. If intracranial edema or bleeding is not promptly controlled the lower portion of the brain (cerebellar tonsils) will herniate through the foramen magnum. This will then compress the brainstem causing respiratory and cardiac function to cease.

The physician was not notified of Patient P's deteriorating condition until 4:00 A.M. because "everything was normal until then," according to testimony by the attending nurse . The physician later testified that, had he been apprised of the patient's deteriorating condition earlier (by 10:00 P.M. at the latest), surgical intervention in all probability would have saved Patient P.

The plaintiff's case was based on the determination that inadequate nursing care was responsible for Patient P's death. The case settled with payment to the estate of the plaintiff.

## Case 4–9

## *Cervical Spine Fracture*

### Problem and Outcome

Failure to detect a cervical spine fracture in a timely fashion caused the death of a 69-year-old man.

### The Patient

Patient B, a retired commercial airline pilot who enjoyed leisurely travel with his wife, fell backward in the bathroom of his home while instilling eye drops. He sustained a brief loss of consciousness and was somewhat confused when he regained consciousness. Patient B's wife was concerned and took him to a hospital emergency department.

### Treatment

After an evaluation in the emergency department which included a computed tomography (CT) scan of the brain, Patient B was admitted to the telemetry unit 1 March at 9:00 P.M. with the diagnosis of syncope. Three hours after admission, Patient B became quadriplegic, and twenty days later he died.

### Departures from the Standard of Care

Significant departures from prevailing professional standards of nursing care occurred. These included the following:

1. Failure to complete an initial nursing assessment
2. Failure to make systematic nursing observations
3. Failure to contact the physician regarding a significant change in the patient's condition on 1 March by 10:15 P.M., at the latest
4. Failure to protect the patient from injury by not immobilizing Patient B by 10:15 P.M., 1 March, at the latest
5. Failure to follow the physician's orders regarding neurological checks
6. Failure to follow the written nursing care plan

### Discussion

Upon admission to the telemetry unit, Patient B was oriented to person, place, and time. He was alert, and pupillary responses were within normal limits. Motor and sensory function was also within normal limits.

By 10:00 P.M., 1 March, Patient B was described as drowsy and uncooperative. The right pupil was 4 millimeters and fixed, and the left pupil was 2 millimeters and fixed. "Mild weakness" was also noted in the right arm at this time. By midnight, Patient B could not move his arms or legs. A call was not placed to the physician regarding these observations until 8:00 A.M., 2 March.

Upon notification, the physician immediately requested neurological consultation. X-rays of the cervical spine revealed an unstable fracture of cervical vertebrae numbers three through four (C3–4). A laminectomy of C3–4 was performed, and an epidural hematoma was evacuated.

A written nursing care plan for Patient B in the medical record detailed the observations to be made for him. These observations included respiratory, circulatory, and neurological status assessments. The nursing care plan also specified that the physician be called for any significant change in the patient's condition. The nursing care plan was not followed, and the attitude of the nursing staff was exemplified by their statements that "these plans are just paperwork required by the hospital."

Patient B remained quadriplegic postoperatively. He developed adult respiratory distress syndrome and ultimately expired on 21 March.

Expert medical testimony established within reasonable medical probability that, had surgical intervention occurred soon after weakness in the limbs was noted, Patient B would not have been rendered quadriplegic and would not have suffered complications leading to death. Expert nurse testimony established that, had Patient B been observed systematically and the physician notified immediately of neurological changes, within reasonable nursing probability, surgical intervention would have occurred much earlier. The plaintiff's case was based on the determination that poor nursing care was responsible for Patient B's death. The case settled with payment to the estate of the plaintiff.

## Case 4–10
### *Excessive Chest Tube Bleeding*

#### Problem and Outcome
A six-year-old child hemorrhaged to death because chest-tube drainage was not adequately assessed.

#### The Patient
Patient M, an only child, was born with tetralogy of Fallot. He was an active child and enjoyed nursery school, but he had physical limitations because of the heart condition. He was admitted to the hospital 26 June for correction of tetralogy of Fallot not compatible with life into adulthood.

## Treatment

Upon admission, Patient M was in no acute distress and his growth and development were essentially normal. On 28 June, this child was taken to the operating room for a complete correction of tetralogy of Fallot. He tolerated the surgery well and was taken in satisfactory condition to the intensive care unit at 4:00 P.M.

Immediately following the surgery, the child's vital signs were stable. There was a problem, however, with excessive bleeding. At 2:40 A.M., 29 June, Patient M was taken back to the operating room for evacuation of hemomediastinum, hemothorax, and hemostasis. Upon his return to the intensive care unit at 5:25 A.M., Patient M's vital signs were unstable, his capillary refill was sluggish, his heart sounds were muffled, and he was unresponsive. He became mottled and exhibited bradycardia; cardiopulmonary resuscitation was instituted at 6:00 A.M. for a full cardiac arrest with complete cessation of electrical activity. After thirty minutes of resuscitation, the child responded with good return of heart rate and blood pressure. Later in the day, however, Patient M developed seizures, and neurological damage was evident. Neurological intervention was unsuccessful and Patient M died 3 July.

## Departures from the Standard of Care

Departures from prevailing professional standards of nursing care included the following:

1.  Failure to assess the patient systematically
2.  Failure to detect the patient's deteriorating condition

## Discussion

The scant information in the medical record describes a seriously ill child whose condition was deteriorating postoperatively. The nurse's notes of 28–29 June read as follows:

> 5:00 P.M.   Continues to bleed out 150 milliliters every 15 minutes.
> 6:00 P.M.   . . . continues to bleed.
> 7:00 P.M.   . . . but continues to bleed.
> 7:30 P.M.   Milked clots out – 125 milliliters out in three minutes; pulse decreasing; skin cooler.
> 8:30 P.M.   Heart sounds slightly muffled; four chest tubes draining bright red blood and being milked for large amounts; capillary refill slow.

9:30 P.M.   Heart sounds still slightly muffled . . . capillary refill sluggish; extremities cool.

10:30 P.M.   Chest tube drainage less, but still bright red; heart sounds slightly muffled; extremities cool; capillary refill sluggish.

11:30 P.M.   Heart sounds remain muffled; capillary refill sluggish; chest tube drainage is darker now but still in large amount.

12:30 A.M.   Heart sounds remain muffled, but now left tube draining bright red.

1:00 A.M.   Patient continues to bleed bright red blood.

1:30 A.M.   Capillary refill sluggish; extremities remain cool.

2:15 A.M.   Capillary refill sluggish; patient draining large amount by way of chest tube, bright red.

2:40 A.M.   Chest tube continues to drain large amount of blood; color pale; peripheral perfusion poor.

At approximately 2:25 A.M., a resident physician was "walking through" the intensive care unit and noted excessive chest tube drainage.

The actual amount of chest tube drainage never appeared in the nurse's notes. When the child was taken back to the operating room at 2:40 A.M., it was noted by the anesthesiologist that drainage from the chest tubes amounted to 3,490 milliliters in the 12-hour period. Although chest tube drainage usually does not exceed 500 milliliters per 24-hour period, children with surgery for tetralogy of Fallot experience increased sanguineous drainage. At the same time, however, the nurse should remember that hemorrhage from the chest tubes is the most common postoperative complication after this procedure.

The goal of nursing care for the child undergoing cardiovascular surgery is restoration and maintenance of optimal respiratory, cardiovascular, neurological, and renal functions. This nursing care involves, among other things, continuous and astute nursing observation to identify subtle changes that may herald impending complications. Some of the possible complications after thoracic surgery are: respiratory insufficiency, hypoxia, anoxia, hyperventilation, carbon dioxide retention, mediastinal shift, paradoxical motion, pneumothorax, hemorrhage, hemothorax, shock, hypotension, cardiac arrhythmia, myocardial infarction, respiratory arrest, cardiac arrest, pulmonary embolism, thrombophlebitis, atelectasis, pneumonia, infection, paralytic ileus, subcutaneous emphysema, and acute pulmonary edema. Furthermore, the need for intelligent assessment of children after cardiovascular surgery is intensified because of their limited physiological reserves for compensating for the physical insult of surgery.

Such basic knowledge forms the framework upon which the nurse plans and administers patient care. Thus, much of the clinical nursing care given cardiovascular surgery patients is preventive care directed at averting these complications.

No explanation was ever offered as to why the amount of chest tube drainage was never charted postoperatively. Had the nurses been assessing the amount of drainage, they would have realized that it was excessive, and that the child needed help. The situation was discovered by "accident" by Dr. H, but it was too late because hypovolemic shock was profound and irreversible.

The plaintiff's case was based on the determination that poor nursing care was responsible for Patient M's death. The case settled with payment to the child's parents.

## Case 4–11
### *Intravenous Fluid Excess*

#### Problem and Outcome
Fluid overload with a solution of 100 percent free-water (that is, dextrose 5 percent in water) caused the death of a three-year-old child.

#### The Patient
Patient S, weighing ten kilograms, had a history of tonsillitis, snoring, otitis media, cystitis, and a small urethral meatus. He was scheduled for elective surgery, but on the day before surgery his father was called out of town on urgent business. His mother called the doctor's office to reschedule the surgery, but she was told by the receptionist that it was not necessary to postpone the surgery because "it's just routine and no big deal." The parents decided to go ahead with the surgery as planned. Patient S's mother, four months pregnant, took her son to the hospital the next day.

#### Treatment
The child was admitted to the outpatient surgery unit of the hospital at 8:00 A.M., 23 February. A nurse anesthetist wrote that Patient S had nothing to eat or drink since midnight. The remarks section of the physical examination sheet was empty. Laboratory results were within normal limits and included a serum sodium concentration of 137 milliequivalents per liter (mEq/L), a normal coagulation screen, and a hematocrit of 38.5 percent.

At 9:00 A.M., Patient S was taken to the operating room for a tonsillectomy, adenoidectomy, placement of myringotomy tubes, cystoscopy, and a meatotomy. Estimated blood loss was recorded as 120 milliliters (approximately a 15-percent blood loss for a ten-kilogram child). Patient S tolerated the procedure well. He was in the recovery room for one hour and fifteen minutes before transfer to his room at 11:15 A.M. A cardiopulmonary arrest occurred at approximately 4:00 P.M. During resuscitation, the arterial blood sample sent to the laboratory was significant because the serum sodium concentration was only 111 mEq/L. The child was resuscitated but he had fixed and dilated pupils. Neurological examination demonstrated no brain stem function and flaccid paralysis with no response to painful stimuli. Patient S was pronounced dead two days later.

### Departures from the Standard of Care

Serious departures from prevailing professional standards of nursing care were evident in this case and included the following:

1. Failure to observe the patient systematically
2. Failure to administer intravenous fluids properly
3. Failure to obtain a complete intravenous infusion fluid order
4. Failure to recognize hyponatremia in a timely manner and obtain treatment
5. Failure to question the dosage of Tigan (trimethobenzamide HCL)

### Discussion

Between the operating room and admission to the recovery room, the child received 900 milliliters of 5 percent dextrose in water solution intravenously. The postoperative fluid order read: "Intravenous at 50 milliliters per hour – continue until taking fluids by mouth well." From noon through 4:00 P.M., Patient S received another 500 milliliters of 5 percent dextrose in water solution intravenously.

At 11:15 A.M., the first apical pulse rate was recorded, and the nurse noted that Patient S was "very congested bilaterally and in the upper airway." Further nursing notes at 12:00 P.M., at 1:15 P.M and at 1:40 P.M. all addressed moderate respiratory distress. The patient's mother testified that her child was "very, very restless, sleeping on and off and crying occasionally" during this time. She noted that the crying was "high pitched," and that she had never heard him cry like that before.

At 2:00 P.M. a Tigan (trimethobenzamide HCL) 100 milligrams rectal suppository was administered because of several episodes of vomiting. Testimony revealed that the child's mother questioned the use of a whole suppository by telling the nurse that she used only one-half of a suppository at home. After this, the child's mother said, Patient S fell into a "very sound sleep."

At 3:00 P.M., Patient S was noted to be diaphoretic and with "very labored respirations." The physician was called and suctioning was suggested. By 3:45 P.M., it was noted that the nurses were "unable to obtain blood pressure due to decorticate posturing." At approximately 4:00 P.M., when the child's mother summoned a nurse, Patient S was noted to be "stiff and cyanotic." A cardiopulmonary arrest was announced.

An addendum to the medical record, written the next day, states that at 3:50 P.M. the child's blood pressure (the first ever recorded in the medical record by a nurse) was "140/80, heart rate 78, and respirations 16, irregular and labored." This is inconsistent with the 3:45 P.M. note written the day before.

A very clear picture of severe acute hyponatremia from the use of a 100 percent free-water containing intravenous infusion solution was evident in this case and was the major precipitating factor in Patient S's death. An important nursing responsibility is to determine that fluid orders are complete and the type of fluid ordered is appropriate. In this tragic case, the type of intravenous infusion fluid was never specified, and the nurses continued to administer dextrose in 5 percent water in the postoperative period. It is common nursing knowledge that intravenous infusion fluid administration during and after surgery should contain sodium, because it has been demonstrated that free-water containing solutions used during and after "routine" surgery have resulted in death in several series of healthy patients, especially women and children. Furthermore, Patient S's small size and relatively large volume losses compounded the hyponatremia.

Because fluid shifts in young children can occur so rapidly, the nurse needs to be particularly careful when replacing fluid. Thus the intravenous infusion of fluid must be observed every half hour and the amount of fluid infused recorded at least every hour. In addition, drip control chambers or burettes are used with pediatric patients. Burettes permit accurate determinations of intravenous fluid infused and help prevent fluid overload by limiting the amount of fluid at one time to the amount in the drip control chamber.

Water excess was compounded by improper rate of intravenous fluid administration (greater than the prescribed 50 milliliters per hour) because testimony revealed that the "Intravenous was positional and at times a lot of fluid would run fast." Also, a burette or buretrol was not used for intravenous infusion fluid control because "one wasn't kept in our supply closet," as one nurse said. Another nurse added, "I've heard of it, but I don't know how to use it."

Correct intravenous infusion fluid administration would have prevented this tragic outcome, and systematic assessment of Patient S would have revealed early signs of fluid overload and hyponatremia. Symptoms of fluid overload that should have been recognized include increased blood pressure, bounding pulse, cough, increased urinary output, tachycardia, diaphoresis, neck-vein distention, tachypnea, dyspnea, orthopnea, rales, periorbital edema, irritability, restlessness, vomiting, convulsions, and muscle twitching.

Hyponatremia can result in cardiovascular collapse from decreased blood volume, which is one of the things that happened to Patient S. Documentation revealed a decreased hematocrit from 38.5 percent preoperatively to 26.8 percent after resuscitation.

The 3:45 P.M. description of Patient S is consistent with seizure activity. It is common nursing knowledge that seizures often occur when the serum sodium concentration falls below 120 mEq/L. An acute decrease in serum sodium concentration below 115 mEq/L is life threatening. Furthermore, the rapid fall in body osmolarity shifts massive amounts of free water to the brain, resulting in edema of the cerebral cells with rapid increase in intracranial pressure. If the pressure is not relieved, the brain stem will herniate, as it did in this case.

Finally, the order for 100 milligrams of Tigan (trimethobenzamide HCL) should have been questioned by the nurse. General dosing schedules call for 50 milligrams for children under thirty pounds. The child's mother even questioned the dosage, but the nurse went ahead and administered the medication. In addition, Tigan (trimethobenzamide HCL) is associated with seizures and hypotension in children, especially with an electrolyte imbalance. The use of this drug in a patient whose blood pressure was never taken and who was exhibiting signs of hyponatremia probably contributed to the cardiopulmonary arrest.

The plaintiff's case was based on the determination that departures from prevailing professional standards of nursing care were responsible for Patient S's death. The case settled with payment to the child's parents.

Case 4–12

## Chest Pain

### Problem and Outcome

Complaints of chest pain were ignored, and a 36-year-old woman died.

### The Patient

Patient B had been married for twenty years and had a long history of lower back problems. According to her husband, the marriage was not particularly happy because of Patient B's many hospitalizations for back and psychological problems. Approximately one month before this hospitalization, their house had burned down and they had lost everything.

### Treatment

Patient B was admitted to the hospital 20 May with the diagnosis of acute and chronic low back syndrome. She was placed on strict bed rest and medicated for pain (Demerol [meperidine] with Vistaril [hydroxyzine pamoate] and Percodan [oxycodone]), muscle spasm (Valium [diazepam]), and inflammation (Clinoril [sulindac]).

Significant past medical history revealed peptic ulcer disease, grand mal seizure disorder, migraine headaches, and three spinal fusions.

Patient B showed gradual response to the treatment for the low back syndrome. On 2 June, however, the patient complained of "epigastric distress" associated with nausea and vomiting after taking a Percodan (oxycodone) tablet. This epigastric distress was felt to be related to a recurrence of the peptic ulcer disease, and symptomatic treatment commenced. Endoscopy failed to reveal any evidence of active peptic ulcer disease.

On 8 June, Patient B suffered a cardiopulmonary arrest. Autopsy findings included status post multiple surgical procedures; severe coronary atherosclerosis; thrombo-occlusion, right coronary artery; acute posterior myocardial infarct, and status post resuscitation.

### Departures from the Standard of Care

Analysis of this tragic case reveals major departures from prevailing professional standards of nursing care as follows:

1. Failure to assess the patient systematically and in a timely fashion
2. Failure to recognize a change in the patient's condition

3. Failure to inform the physician of the complaint of chest pain

### Discussion

On 8 June in the morning, Patient B complained of "severe pain in her head" accompanied by nausea and vomiting. At 12:50 P.M., the patient was described as "sitting up in bed, hugging a pillow with head down, cigarette in hand, both hands shaking, rocking back and forth. . . . Patient states she has pain in her head, chest, and both arms." Valium (diazepam) 10 milligrams was administered by the intramuscular route. Her husband, who was visiting at this time, said that he was concerned about her condition. He stated that twice he called the chest pain to the attention of the nurse. Also, he observed that Patient B was "sweating and clammy-feeling, and when she lay down she couldn't breathe well, and this is why she was sitting up."

At 3:25 P.M., Valium (diazepam) 10 milligrams was again administered for "chest pains." Patient B continued to complain of severe chest pain, according to her husband, and at 5:00 P.M. she received Darvon Compound (propoxyphenehydrochloride) 32 milligrams by mouth. Her husband left the hospital at this time.

Patient B was found at 5:30 P.M. "sitting up in bed with arms folded across chest, lips cyanotic. Skin warm and dry, but patient unresponsive to verbal or painful stimuli. No respirations or pulse present." Cardiopulmonary resuscitation was instituted, but Patient B was pronounced dead at 6:12 P.M.

Nurses are with the patient 24-hours a day, and thus it is their responsibility to make and record detailed systematic observations of the patient's status. Testimony by some of the nurses responsible for the care of Patient B revealed that "we cared for her numerous times; she was always admitted to this unit," and that she was regarded as "a problem patient," "a chronic complainer," and "wanting pain medication to get attention." Questioning of one of the nurses caring for Patient B on the day she died revealed that "she was always complaining of pain somewhere . . . but, well you know, yes, that was the first time she complained of chest pain and arm pain. Well, her condition had changed. She was having quite a bit more anxiety, and the chest pain was new."

Patient B's complaints of chest pain were essentially ignored by the nursing staff. The only set of vital signs on the day of death prior to the arrest was taken at 8:00 A.M. The chest pain was not analyzed and documented as pain should be, according to the following: (1) *qualitative aspects* (i.e., character – e.g. burning, aching, etc.); (2) *quantitative aspects* (i.e., intensity – e.g. mild, severe) and associated symptoms (e.g., pained facial expression, restlessness); (3) *temporal aspects* (i.e., onset, duration, frequency); (4) *topographic aspects* (i.e., specific body location).

Testimony after Patient B died revealed that the nurse caring for her on the 3:00–11:00 P.M. shift was "cautioned by the hospital about charting." This nurse, who assumed the care of Patient B at 3:30 P.M., did not chart the chest pain nor the episodes of emesis because it was "incriminating." She further testified that all the charting on her shift was done approximately one hour after Patient B had expired.

Had the chest pain been recognized as a change in the patient's condition and the physician informed, perhaps the outcome for Patient B would have been different. The plaintiff's case was based on the determination that, within reasonable nursing probability, the departures from the prevailing professional standard of nursing care contributed to the death of Patient B. The case settled with payment to the estate of the plaintiff.

# Chapter 5

# Problems Associated with Communication

The malpractice cases profiled in this chapter are concerned with problems of communication between nurses and physicians. Specifically, these cases involve failure by nurses to inform physicians of a significant change in the patient's condition.

After assessing the patient systematically and charting assessments, nurses have the important obligation to communicate a change in the status of patient assessment to the physician. Communication leads to understanding, which is the foundation of appropriate medical decision-making and action.

Only the nurse remains with the patient 24 hours a day in the hospital. The nurse is the member of the health-care team entrusted with caring for the patient continuously and coordinating all elements of patient care. The hospitalized patient's well-being is wholly dependent on the nurse, since no other members of the health-care team, including physicians, are with the patient on a 24-hour basis.

Today, much of the nursing care delivered centers around systematic assessment, recording, and communication rather than the performance of a variety of technical tasks. The nurse's responsibilities have been made more difficult and complicated because patient hospital stays have become much briefer as a function of health-care economics. Hospitalized patients are sicker and require more intensive nursing assessment.

The physician, who is with the hospitalized patient for a brief time, usually is totally dependent upon the nurse to communicate changes in the patient's condition. It is not the physician's responsibility to be with the patient 24 hours a day. In each of the cases in this chapter, with one exception, the physician saw the patient each day, but a significant change in the patient's condition occurred when the physician was absent. In these situations, there was no way for the physician to know about the change in a patient's condition in a timely fashion unless he/she was informed by the nurse.

The most frequent excuse offered by the nurse during malpractice testimony for not informing the physician of a change in a patient's condition was that the nurse did not want to "disturb" the physician. This was usually in the middle of the night or on weekends.

Along the same line, observations were not communicated sometimes because a physician had the reputation of being easily upset and angered, or even of becoming verbally abusive. The nurse is not obligated to suffer verbal abuse. This problem must be corrected by reporting such behavior to the appropriate hospital authorities. Hospital policy-and-procedure manuals outline the appropriate reporting procedure for nurses within the framework of its organizational structure. It is the nurse's responsibility to communicate appropriately. Hospital administrators who are committed to excellence in patient care do take such problems seriously when there is a pattern of difficult physician behavior. It is amazing how counseling of physicians can change their behavior!

Sometimes a nurse is hesitant to communicate an observation because its significance is questionable. A discussion with a colleague is helpful in this situation. To provide safe nursing care, however, it is important to communicate even if the significance of the observation is in question. The nurse owes that duty to the patient.

In all of the cases in this chapter, the physician was named in the malpractice lawsuit along with the hospital and the nurse. In all cases except one, however, the physician was absolved of liability. One case went to trial, and the nurses as well as the hospital were held accountable for the failure to communicate a change in the patient's condition. A large jury verdict was returned in favor of the plaintiff. All of the other cases settled with payment made to the plaintiff (or his/her estate) by the malpractice insurer of the hospital.

In some of the cases, systematic assessment of the patient by the nurse was incomplete and inadequate. But even with incomplete assessment data in the medical record, the nurses did note certain changes in the patient's condition. These changes were significant, and the failure to communicate the changes to the physician resulted in injury or death to the patient. The situations involved increased intracranial pressure from meningitis, neurovascular embarrassment, respiratory distress, progressive infection, mental status deterioration, progressive lower extremity paralysis, increased intracranial pressure from a closed head injury, and the development of chest pain.

Case 5–1

## *Brain Herniation*

### Problem and Outcome

A 24-year-old man with meningitis developed cerebral edema as a result of the infection. The nurse did not communicate the signs and symptoms of increased intracranial pressure to the physician. The increased intracranial pressure went untreated, and brain stem herniation ultimately caused the patient's death.

### The Patient

Patient A had recently learned that his live-in girlfriend had become pregnant. They hurriedly made plans for a simple marriage to occur 31 October, but he was admitted to the hospital that day at 3:00 P.M., with the diagnosis of meningitis after a one-week history of vomiting, diarrhea, elevated temperature, and headache. The marriage ceremony took place at the hospital 31 October.

### Treatment

Pertinent physical findings on admission were photophobia, temperature 102.2 degrees Fahrenheit, pulse rate 120, and blood pressure 100/60 mmHg. Laboratory values of note were a white blood cell count of 26,000 per cubic millimeter with 40 percent bands, and a spinal-fluid white blood cell count of 71 per cubic millimeter with 42 percent polys, sucrose 83 milligrams per 100 milliliters, and protein 71 milligrams per 100 milliliters. Antibiotic therapy was prescribed.

On 2 November at 1:00 A.M., Patient A suffered a respiratory arrest. Massive diffuse cerebral edema was noted on computed tomography (CT) scan shortly after the arrest. In addition, a nuclear medicine examination indicated that Patient A had no blood flow to the brain. He was declared brain dead. Patient A was supported by a respirator until his family agreed to discontinue life support on 20 November.

At autopsy, there was evidence of sinusitis with subgaleal abscess and bilateral temporalis myositis. Two blood cultures grew gram-negative anaerobic rods on 3 November, and the rods were identified on 8 November as *Fusobacterium necrophorium*. This gram-negative bacillus is commonly found in the nasopharynx of persons with chronic sinusitis and exudative pharyngitis. Patient A had a history of chronic sinusitis, and it was believed that this was the likely source of infection.

## Departures from the Standard of Care

Significant departures from prevailing professional standards of nursing care contributed to the death of Patient A. They included the following:

1. Failure to assess the patient systematically
2. Failure to inform the physician of significant changes in the patient's condition starting at 10:30 A.M., 1 November, and continuing through 12:30 A.M., 2 November
3. Failure to follow the physician's orders
4. Failure to follow the written nursing care plan
5. Failure to complete the cardiopulmonary resuscitation record

## Discussion

The only neurological status nursing assessments charted in the medical record prior to the respiratory arrest were as follows:

31 October

6:40 P.M.   Oriented times three; awake and alert.


1 November

12:30 A.M.   Oriented times three; awake and alert.
2:30 A.M.   Oriented times three; awake and alert.
10:30 A.M.   Arousable; doesn't follow verbal commands.
1:30 P.M.   Oriented times two; alert; very lethargic; moves all extremities.
2:30 P.M.   Very lethargic; responds to verbal stimulation; answers questions; moves all extremities.
4:30 P.M.   Lethargic; speech slurred; restless; lethargic; reacts to pain; moves all extremities times four; pupils equal and reactive to light and accommodation.
8:00 P.M.   Will arouse only to deep pain; pupils equal and reactive to light and accommodation; moves all four extremities; lethargic; speech slurred; oriented times two.
10:00 P.M.   Restraints applied; central nervous system within normal limits; responds to verbal stimulation and painful stimulation.


2 November

12:01 A.M.   Hard to arouse; very restless to lethargic; thrashing in bed.

12:30 A.M.   Responds only to deep pain; unresponsive to verbal stimuli; coarse tremors; doctor called.

Obviously, neurological status assessment was incomplete and not carried out with the appropriate frequency demanded by the patient's condition. However, significant changes were documented. Each neurological status assessment should at least have addressed nuchal rigidity, complaints of headache, seizure activity, orientation, level of consciousness, response to stimuli, response to commands, pupillary response, ocular movement, motor function, sensory function, reflexes, and behavior change. This assessment should have been done at least every two hours, and more frequently as Patient A's condition changed.

Respiratory and circulatory status assessments were also incomplete and infrequent. The only notations in this area that appeared in the medical record prior to the respiratory arrest are presented in figure 6. Respiratory and circulatory status assessments should have included, among other things, respiratory rate, rhythm, and character; pulse rate, rhythm, and quality; skin color and temperature; and blood pressure. These assessments should have been done in concert with the neurological status assessment.

Renal status (intake and output), gastrointestinal status (appearance of abdomen, bowel sounds, and presence of nausea or vomiting), and thermoregulatory status (body temperature) assessments of Patient A were also incomplete and inadequate. The flow sheet developed and used for analysis of the actual nursing care in this case follows on pages 118–23.

| Date | 31 October | | 1 November | | | | | | 2 November | |
|---|---|---|---|---|---|---|---|---|---|---|
| Time | pm 3:07 | pm 6:30 | am 2:30 | am 8:30 | am 10:30 | pm 1:30 | pm 4:30 | pm 8:00 | am 12:00 | am 12:30 |
| Blood pressure | $\frac{110}{70}$ | $\frac{110}{70}$ | $\frac{120}{72}$ | $\frac{110}{50}$ | | $\frac{110}{70}$ | $\frac{110}{80}$ | $\frac{110}{70}$ | | |
| Pulse rate | 124 | 120 | 84 | 116 | | 124 | 112 | 80 | | |
| Respiratory rate | 18 | 20 | 20 | 32 | ok | 18 | 22 | 22 | | 49 |
| Skin color | | Good | Flushed | | Red | | | | Sweaty | |
| Skin temperature | | Warm, dry | Warm, dry | | Very hot | | | | Very warm | |

**Figure 6**  Nursing Assessment Data

## Case 5–1 Flow Sheet

**Assessment Standard for Patient**　　　　　**Minimum Frequency of Assessment**

| Assessment | Variable | 31 October 3:07 pm | 3:30 | 4:00 | 4:30 | 5:30 | 6:40 |
|---|---|---|---|---|---|---|---|
| **Neurological status** | Orientation | | | | | | oriented x3 |
| | Level of consciousness | | | | | | awake alert |
| | Response to stimuli | | | | | | |
| | Response to commands | | | | | | |
| | Pupillary response | | | | | | |
| | Ocular movement | | | | | | |
| | Motor function- strength/movement | | | | | | |
| | Sensory function | | | | | | |
| | Reflexes | | | | | | |
| | Behavioral change | | | | | | |
| | Nuchal rigidity | | | | | | |
| | Complaints of headache | | | | | | |
| | Seizure activity | | | | | | |
| **Respiratory status** | Patency of airway | | | | | | |
| | Respiratory rate | 18 | | | | | 20 |
| | Respiratory rhythm | | | | | | |
| | Respiratory character | | | | | | |
| | Breath sounds | | | | | | |
| **Circulatory status** | Pulse rate | 124 | | | | | 120 |
| | Pulse rhythm | | | | | | |
| | Pulse character | | | | | | |
| | Blood pressure | $\frac{110}{70}$ | | | | | $\frac{100}{70}$ |
| | Skin color / temperature | | | | | | good warm dry |

(entries indicate assessments that were made)

1 November

| 8:30 | 10:30 | 12:30 am | 2:30 | 4:30 | 6:30 | 8:30 | 10:30 | 11:30 | 12:30 pm | 1:30 | 2:30 |
|---|---|---|---|---|---|---|---|---|---|---|---|
|  |  | oriented x3 | oriented x3 |  |  |  |  |  |  | oriented x2 |  |
|  |  | awake alert | awake alert |  |  |  | arousable |  |  | alert | very lethargic |
|  |  |  |  |  |  |  |  |  |  | very lethargic | responds to verbal stimuli |
|  |  |  |  |  |  |  | does not follow verbal commands |  |  |  | answers questions |
|  |  |  |  |  |  |  |  |  |  |  |  |
|  |  |  |  |  |  |  |  |  |  |  |  |
|  |  |  |  |  |  |  |  |  |  | moves all extremities | moves all extremities |
|  |  |  |  |  |  |  |  |  |  |  |  |
|  |  |  |  |  |  |  |  |  |  |  |  |
|  |  |  |  |  |  |  |  |  |  |  |  |
|  |  |  |  |  |  |  |  |  |  |  |  |
|  |  |  |  |  |  |  |  |  |  |  |  |
|  |  | 20 |  |  |  | 32 |  |  |  | 18 |  |
|  |  |  |  |  |  |  |  |  |  |  |  |
|  |  |  |  |  |  |  | ok |  |  |  |  |
|  |  |  |  |  |  |  |  |  |  |  | lungs clear |
|  |  | 84 |  |  |  | 116 |  |  |  | 124 |  |
|  |  |  |  |  |  |  |  |  |  |  |  |
|  |  |  |  |  |  |  |  |  |  |  |  |
|  |  | 120/72 |  |  |  | 110/50 |  |  |  | 110/70 |  |
|  |  | flushed warm dry |  |  |  |  | very hot red |  |  |  |  |

## Case 5–1 Flow Sheet (continued)

| Assessment Standard for Patient | | Minimum Frequency of Assessment | | | | | |
|---|---|---|---|---|---|---|---|
| **Assessment** | **Variable** | 1 November 3:30 pm | 4:30 | 5:30 | 6:30 | 7:30 | 8:00 |
| **Neurological status** | Orientation | | | | | | oriented x2 |
| | Level of consciousness | | lethargic restless | | | | lethargic |
| | Response to stimuli | | reacts to pain | | | | will arouse only to deep pain |
| | Response to commands | | speech slurred | | | | speech slurred |
| | Pupillary response | | PERLA | | | | PERLA |
| | Ocular movement | | | | | | |
| | Motor function- strength/movement | | moves all ex- tremities | | | | moves all ex- tremities |
| | Sensory function | | | | | | |
| | Reflexes | | | | | | |
| | Behavioral change | | | | | | |
| | Nuchal rigidity | | | | | | |
| | Complaints of headache | | | | | | |
| | Seizure activity | | | | | | |
| **Respiratory status** | Patency of airway | | | | | | |
| | Respiratory rate | | 22 | | | | 22 |
| | Respiratory rhythm | | | | | | |
| | Respiratory character | | | | | | |
| | Breath sounds | | | | | | |
| **Circulatory status** | Pulse rate | | 112 | | | | 80 |
| | Pulse rhythm | | | | | | |
| | Pulse character | | | | | | |
| | Blood pressure | | $\frac{110}{80}$ | | | | $\frac{110}{70}$ |
| | Skin color / temperature | | | | | | |

(entries indicate assessments that were made)

| | 8:30 | 9:00 | 9:30 | 10:00 | 10:30 | 11:00 | 11:30 | 2 November 12:00 am | 12:15 | 12:30 | 12:45 | 1:00 |
|---|---|---|---|---|---|---|---|---|---|---|---|---|
| | | | | CNS-WNL | | | | hard to arouse | | | | |
| | | | | | | | | very restless to lethargic | | | | |
| | | | | responds to painful and verbal | | | | thrashing in bed | | responds to deep pain only | | |
| | | | | stimuli | | | | | | unresponsive to verbal stimuli | | |
| | | | | | | | | | | | | |
| | | | | | | | | | | | | |
| | | | | | | | | | | | | |
| | | | | | | | | | | | | |
| | | | | | | | | | | | | |
| | | | | | | | | | | | | |
| | | | | | | | | | | | | |
| | | | | | | | | | | | | |
| | | | | | | | | | | coarse tremors | | |
| | | | | | | | | | | | | |
| | | | | | | | | | | 49 | | |
| | | | | | | | | | | | | |
| | | | | | | | | | | | | |
| | | | | | | | | | | | | |
| | | | | | | | | | | | | |
| | | | | | | | | | | | | |
| | | | | | | | | | | | | |
| | | | | | | | | | | | | |
| | | | | | | | | very warm sweaty | | | | |

## Case 5–1 Flow Sheet (continued)

**Assessment Standard for Patient**               **Minimum Frequency of Assessment**

| Assessment | Variable | 31 October 3:07 pm | 7:00 | 1 November 11:00 | 3:00 am | 7:00 |
|---|---|---|---|---|---|---|
| **Renal status** | Urinary output | | | | | |
| | Character of urine | | | | | |
| **Fluid status** | Intake (amount, kind) | | | | | |
| | Intake vs. output | | | | | |
| **Gastrointes-tinal status** | Appearance of abdomen | | | | | |
| | Bowel sounds | | | | | |
| | Presence/absence nausea, emesis | emesis | | | | |
| **Thermoregu-latory status** | Body temperature | 101.3 | 99 | | 102 | 102.4 |

A team of physicians examined Patient A upon admission and again on rounds at 8:00 A.M., Saturday, 1 November. The patient's condition began to change at 10:30 A.M., 1 November, but the physicians were not notified of these changes until 12:30 A.M., 2 November.

In addition, the physicians' orders written on admission for antibiotic therapy were not executed promptly. The first dose of antibiotic was not administered until twelve hours after admission. Moreover, the medical record reflected that the nurses failed to administer some doses of the antibiotics.

Finally, the written nursing care plan in the medical record contained a list of appropriate assessments to be made, with guidelines for notifying the physician of changes, but it was not followed. Had the nursing care plan been executed as written, the departures from prevailing professional standards of nursing care could have been prevented.

The plaintiff's case was based on the determination that, within reasonable probability, the departures from prevailing professional standards

**(entries indicate assessments that were made)**

| 11:00 | 3:00 pm | 7:00 | 8:00 | 9:00 | 10:00 | 11:00 | 2 November 12:00 am | 1:00 |
|---|---|---|---|---|---|---|---|---|
| | | | | | | cumulative total 400 ml | | |
| | | | | | | | | |
| | | | | | | cumulative total 1700 ml | | |
| | | | | | | | | |
| | | | | | | | | |
| | | | | | | | | |
| | | | | | emesis 100 ml brown | | | |
| 101.3 | 99.4 | | 99.7 | | | | 104.5 | |

of nursing care contributed to Patient A's death. The case settled with payment to the estate of the plaintiff.

## Case 5–2
### *Neurovascular Embarrassment*

#### Problem and Outcome

The physician was not informed of observations indicating neurovascular embarrassment. As a result, a 26-year-old man sustained permanent damage to the right lower extremity.

#### The Patient

Patient B, the father of two children, was admitted to the hospital for elective surgery to correct a problem associated with medial compartment arthritis. This condition was related to a construction-job knee injury.

## Treatment

A right tibial osteotomy was performed and neurovascular embarrassment developed postoperatively. Patient B was eventually taken back to surgery where a fasciotomy was performed. The intervention was too late, however, and Patient B sustained a permanent partial disability of the right lower extremity which prevented his return to his occupation as a construction worker.

## Departures from the Standard of Care

Departures from prevailing professional standards of nursing care are evident in this case as follows:

1. Failure to execute the physician's order regarding circulatory assessment
2. Failure to assess systematically the right lower extremity
3. Failure to inform the physician of a change in the patient's condition

## Discussion

For the first five hours postoperatively, the nursing staff charted nothing regarding the circulatory status of the right leg despite a physician's order to "check circulation, color, sensation every two hours." At 7:00 P.M., a nurse's note states that "[Dr. G] called because the patient was having pain and was tense." Dr. G responded by ordering Valium (diazepam). By 8:30 P.M., the nurse charted "[patient] has severe pain with little relief from pain medication . . . sometimes says he has no feeling in foot then complains of a burning sensation. He always winces when toes are touched or squeezed."

As the evening progressed, signs and symptoms of increasing neurovascular embarrassment were evident by notations in the medical record as follows:

9:00 P.M.  Pain continues to be severe.
9:30 P.M.  Patient complains of pain with sometimes numbness and sometimes burning.
12:30 A.M.  Patient complains of constant bad leg pain; medicated; can't wiggle toes and they feel cooler.
3:00 A.M.  Patient still awake, complains of numb toes and pain in right leg; toes cool; blanket applied.
5:00 A.M.  Right toes and foot are cyanotic and cool to touch.

The physician was not aware of the situation until he made rounds that morning and discovered the anterior compartment syndrome.

Critical to the prevention of nursing malpractice in such a case is systematic and timely circulatory status assessment of the lower extremity. Some important observations of the right lower extremity that should have been included in the medical record are as follows:

1. Skin color
2. Temperature of the extremity
3. Presence/absence of edema
4. Peripheral pulses (femoral, popliteal, and pedal)
5. Blanching sign results
6. Sensory function
7. Motor function
8. Description of pain (qualitative, quantitative, temporal, topographic aspects)

The nurses should have assessed circulatory status in this case to detect early signs suggestive of neurovascular embarrassment. Signs of neurovascular embarrassment that the nurse should recognize include a change in skin color and/or temperature, edema, change in peripheral pulse(s), absence of blanching sign, and paresthesias in the distal portion of the extremity.

Upon recognition of the problem at 8:30 P.M., the nurse should have notified the physician immediately. Several nurses testified that Dr. G became very angry when he was called at home in the evening. The nursing staff, therefore, did not call Dr. G about any patient unless it was a "big problem, life or death." Dr. G testified that he expected the nursing staff to call when a problem developed. He further stated that had he been called, Patient B's injury could have been prevented.

It was determined at trial that, within reasonable probability, the departures from the prevailing professional standard of nursing care caused the permanent damage to the patient's right lower extremity. The jury verdict was in favor of the plaintiff.

Case 5–3

## *Respiratory Failure*

### Problem and Outcome

Patient B, a three-year-old child with wheezing, was treated in the emergency department of a hospital. Within several hours, although her condition had not improved, she was released home. She was returned to the hospital less than an hour later and died.

### The Patient

Patient B was suffering from a sore throat, ear pain, and an elevated temperature. She was admitted initially to the emergency department of a hospital at 10:45 P.M. with wheezing and shortness of breath.

### Treatment

Initial examination by the emergency department physician read "Croupy female; coarse breath sounds with wheezing; mild bilateral tympanic membrane hyperemia." A chest X-ray demonstrated "bilateral infiltrates." Medications were administered, and the child was released.

Thirty minutes after discharge from the emergency department, Patient B was brought back to the hospital. This time vital signs were absent, the skin was warm without mottling, and the pupils of the eye were dilated but reacted slowly to light. Cardiopulmonary resuscitation was instituted without success, and Patient B was pronounced dead.

### Departures from the Standard of Care

Departures from prevailing professional standards of nursing care for the first admission to the emergency department included the following:

1. Failure to assess the child comprehensively upon admission
2. Failure to assess the patient systematically for the duration of the emergency department visit
3. Failure to inform the physician that the patient did not improve after treatment

### Discussion

Vital signs on admission were temperature 100.7 degrees Fahrenheit (rectal), pulse rate 160, and respiratory rate 28. Forty-five minutes later, Bronkephrine (ethylnorepinephrine hydrochloride) 0.1 milliliter was administered subcutaneously, and the child was observed for thirty minutes. It was noted by the physician that the child had "minimal clearing" in response to the bronchodilator.

Elixir of turpenhydrate with codeine 1 milliliter, Gantrisin (sulfisoxazole) 10 milliliters, and Quibron (theophylline-glycerol guaiacolate) 10 milliliters were then administered by mouth to the child. The nurse's note at 12:30 A.M. read, "Vomiting; unable to retain medicine. Respiration increased (54), temperature 101.4 (R); wheezing with increased difficulty breathing." No further notes were made regarding the child's condition on the emergency department record by the nurse, except to state that at 1:30 A.M., "child released from emergency department."

Children with respiratory problems need skilled and competent nursing care. The symptoms of hypoxemia, a complication of respiratory problems, are often insidious. Frequently, there is peripheral vasoconstriction with accompanying skin color changes. Tachypnea, tachycardia, anxiety, and confusion may ensue. It is the nurse's responsibility to observe, evaluate, and document the patient's condition. In the emergency department, the nurse is the member of the health-care team who has the greatest contact with the patient.

The initial nursing assessment in the record was incomplete. This assessment of the child should have included such information as follows:

1. General appearance: height and weight in relation to age, development of the body, color of the skin, posture, facial expression, presence of fatigue or hyperactivity, gait, and presence/absence of apprehension
2. Neurological status: level of consciousness, signs of meningeal irritation
3. Vital signs: temperature, respiration (rate, rhythm, character), pulse (rate, rhythm, quality), and blood pressure
4. Skin: color, temperature, presence/absence of eruptions, cyanosis, erythema, icterus, petechiae, cysts, trauma, and scars
5. Developmental status
6. Disease status: breath sounds, presence/absence of congestion and/or distressed breathing, appearance of the tympanic membranes, and appearance of the throat, mouth, and nose

In addition, the nurse's notes for the entire emergency department admission were inadequate and incomplete. These notes should have reflected the execution of the physician's orders as well as pertinent nursing observations. Acceptable nursing care for children with respiratory problems involves more detailed nursing observations than those in Patient B's medical record. A nurse has the knowledge base to make and record the following nursing observations:

1. General appearance of the child (every 15 minutes)
2. Body temperature (every 30 minutes)
3. Pulse rate, rhythm, quality (every 15 minutes)
4. Respiratory rate, rhythm, character (every 15 minutes)
5. Patency of the airway (every 15 minutes)
6. Blood pressure (every 30 to 60 minutes)
7. Skin color and temperature (every 15 minutes)
8. Level of consciousness (every 15 minutes)
9. Emesis – amount, character, and frequency

Any significant change in the patient's condition (based upon nursing observation) must be promptly communicated to the physician.

The nurse should have informed the physician promptly of the 12:30 A.M. observations. These indicated that the child's condition was not improving but was, in fact, deteriorating. Obviously then, before processing the discharge order, the nurse should have communicated to the physician that the child had failed to improve with treatment.

The physician later testified that, had she known the child's condition had not improved, she would have instituted more aggressive therapy and admitted the child to the hospital. The physician further stated that, had the child been admitted to the hospital, in all probability the child would not have died.

The plaintiff's case was based on the determination that, within reasonable nursing probability, the departures from the prevailing professional standard of nursing care caused the child's death. The case settled with payment to the child's parents.

## Case 5–4

### Infection of Lower Extremity

**Problem and Outcome**

Failure of the physician to examine a 49-year-old woman each day, and failure by the nursing staff to apprise the physician of a progressing infection in the lower extremity, contributed to an above-the-knee amputation.

## The Patient

Patient I, a 49-year-old woman, was admitted to the hospital 3 June with the diagnosis of severe cellulitis of the left foot with probable early gangrene. Patient I, with known diabetes mellitus type I (insulin-dependent), had been in reasonably good health until three days prior to admission, when she developed a "bluish-colored blister" in two areas on her left foot. These lesions subsequently drained purulent material. Redness of the foot and an elevated body temperature developed. Patient I related a history of problems over a two-year period with her toenails, and an intermittent draining lesion beneath the great toe.

## Treatment

Aerobic and anaerobic cultures were obtained and appropriate antibiotic therapy commenced. The three-dose program of insulin administration (mixed/short/intermediate) that Patient I used was continued in the hospital.

Throughout the hospital stay, Patient I's temperature ranged between 98 and 102 degrees Fahrenheit. The condition of the left foot deteriorated, and she became increasingly toxic. A diagnosis of necrotizing synergistic cellulitis and gangrene of the left foot was made 8 June, and an above-the-knee amputation was performed. Physical therapy was instituted, and Patient I was discharged from the hospital on 13 July.

## Departures from the Standard of Care

During the hospitalization, departures from prevailing professional standards of nursing care were evident as follows:

1. Failure to assess systematically the infectious process
2. Failure to communicate pertinent observations to the physician

## Discussion

No nursing notations regarding Patient I's left leg were found in the medical record on the day of admission. On 4 June it was noted that "area of leg above ankle is now reddish and pink in color and tight-feeling to touch." The 5 June through 7 June nursing notations, though brief, indicated that the cellulitis was extending to the area just below the knee.

On 8 June it was noted that "leg more red to about two inches below the knee." These few notations, though incomplete, represent changes that are indicative of progressive infection.

At least every eight hours, a complete assessment should have been made regarding the infectious process in Patient I's left lower extremity. Nurses know that pain, redness, local warmth, edema, and altered function are cardinal symptoms of infection. The nurse's notes for the left lower extremity should have included among other things, a description of the following: (1) pain (qualitative, quantitative, topographic, and temporal aspects; (2) areas of redness; (3) appearance of lesions; (4) type and amount of drainage; (5) areas of local increase in temperature; (6) skin color; (7) areas of edema; (8) peripheral pulses (femoral, popliteal, and pedal); (9) sensory function ; (10) blanching sign; (11) motor function.

In addition, notation of systemic manifestations of infection (e.g., elevated body temperature, chills, diaphoresis, malaise, anorexia) should have been included each day. The nurse's notes for 3 June through 9 June did not contain these assessments. Furthermore, it is the nurse's responsibility not only to chart accurately but to inform the physician of the patient's progress, lack of progress, and/or change in condition.

The attending physician informed the nurse manager that he was traveling to a nearby town 5 through 7 June for "a long weekend." Since Patient I was his only patient in the hospital, the nurse manager was instructed to call him for "any problems or questions." He also indicated that, if necessary, he would come in during the weekend. Dr. H received no telephone calls regarding Patient I.

When Dr. H made rounds on the morning of 8 June, he found that Patient I was toxic. Severe necrotizing synergistic cellulitis and gangrene of the left foot were present. Patient I was taken to surgery immediately.

Dr. H, the attending physician, should either have seen Patient I every day or arranged for a colleague to examine her in his absence. The nurses, on the other hand, had the obligation to inform the physician that the infection was progressing.

The plaintiff's case was based on the determination that, within reasonable probability, the departures from prevailing professional standards of nursing care contributed to the above-the-knee amputation. The case settled with payment to the plaintiff.

Case 5–5

## *Mental Decompensation*

### Problem and Outcome

A 37-year-old man with the diagnosis of paranoid schizophrenia was admitted to a general hospital. He decompensated, jumped out of the window, and sustained multiple trauma.

### The Patient

Patient H was unemployed and received Social Security income because of a mental disability. He lived with his mother in a trailer. On 18 December, Patient H was admitted voluntarily to a general hospital. He presented with a diagnosis of paranoid schizophrenia. This hospital did not have a specific psychiatric unit but was licensed to have between twenty and forty-eight psychiatric beds.

### Treatment

According to the medical record, Patient H had a long history of paranoid schizophrenia and had been recently decompensating. On admission, his mental status was described as "alert, cooperative, affect inappropriate, mood-anxious, delusional with grandiose and paranoid ideation, auditory hallucinations, poor insight, and poor judgment." The plan of treatment consisted of medication, individual therapy, and milieu therapy.

According to the medical record, a significant change in Patient H's condition occurred on the morning of 5 January. He had become extremely agitated and remained that way throughout the day. The 6:20 P.M. nurse's note read: "Patient jumped out of window (third floor)." Patient H sustained multiple trauma.

### Departures from the Standard of Care

Departures from prevailing professional standards of nursing care were as follows:

1. Failure to observe the patient systematically
2. Failure to inform the physician of a change in the patient's condition
3. Failure to apply and/or secure restraints properly
4. Failure to attend a restrained patient

5. Failure to recognize lack of professional background to care for a psychiatric patient

## Discussion

Review of the physician's progress notes and the nursing notes from admission through 4 January indicates that Patient H was recurrently described as withdrawn, quiet, cooperative, anxious, nervous, seclusive, and suffering from delusions and hallucinations (auditory and visual). On 5 January, however, the 7:00 A.M. to 3:00 P.M. shift nursing note stated that Patient H was "screaming" and later "asking to be tied down." Continuing on 5 January, the nursing note at 5:25 P.M. read, "Patient agitated. Patient in bed and shaking the side rails of his bed. . . . Patient put in four-point restraints."

After Patient H was placed in four-point restraints, there were no further nursing notes for the next one and one-half hours. Patient H's hospital room had a large window with no screens, bars, or tempered glass, and his bed was next to the window. When Patient H was finally observed by a nurse, the restraints were untied, the window was open, and Patient H was lying on the ground, three storeys below the window, with people "running around." The nurse assigned to Patient H was at dinner at the time, and she testified, "I saw him fall while I was eating. I jumped up and was the first on the scene."

The nursing care that Patient H received on 5 January was incomplete and inadequate. Nursing care for psychiatric patients involves, among other factors, frequent and accurate observations. The nurse's notes should have included such observations as the following:

1. How the patient relates to peers, family, and staff
2. Recreational activities
3. Appearance (facial expression)
4. Grooming and dress
5. Body language (posture and movement)
6. Behavior
7. Communication (tone)
8. Perception and thinking (intellectual functioning, perception, thought content, thought progression)
9. Defense mechanisms utilized
10. Self-image

11. Sleep pattern
12. Nursing interventions

In addition to making and recording pertinent observations, nurses have the responsibility to communicate significant information to the physician. The nurse's notes on 5 January describe a significant change in the patient's behavior. The physician should have been informed of the change when Patient H was "screaming" and "asking to be tied down." The psychiatrist testified that constant observation was warranted at this time because of the extreme agitation, and that he would have ordered 24-hour private-duty attendants.

On 5 January, in addition, the nurse caring for Patient H on the 3:00 to 11:00 P.M. shift was not familiar with Patient H or the unit. Investigation of the case revealed that this unit was short-staffed and that this nurse had been sent to this unit from a surgical unit. The nurse testified that she had never restrained a patient before, nor had she cared for a patient in restraints. Furthermore, the nurse had not reviewed Patient H's medical record nor had she asked about his condition prior to caring for him. Thus, she was not aware that there had been a change in the patient's condition earlier that day. A nurse has the obligation to be familiar with the patient's status as well as to seek help with nursing procedures that are new and/or unfamiliar.

The plaintiff's case was based on the determination that, within reasonable probability, the departures from the prevailing professional standard of nursing care caused the patient's multiple injuries. The case settled with payment to the plaintiff.

## Case 5–6
### *Postoperative Paraplegia*

#### Problem and Outcome

A 47-year-old man developed serious neurological complications because the nurses did not report to the physician postoperative motor and sensory changes in his lower extremities.

#### The Patient

Patient T was admitted to the hospital on 7 October for low back problems. He had a history of chronic low-back pain for approximately sixteen years and had undergone multiple surgical procedures for the problem. One year prior to admission, Patient T was involved in a motor- vehicle accident. His chronic back pain decompensated into constant, severe right leg pain and weakness.

### Treatment

After orthopedic evaluation, the physician concluded that Patient T had lumbar radiculopathy secondary to lumbar stenosis of lumbar vertebrae numbers one through three (L1–3), which was a function of the previous decompressive laminectomy of lumbar vertebrae numbers four and five (L4–5) with bilateral posterolateral fusion of lumbar vertebra number four and sacral vertebra number one (L4–S1) for lumbar instability of vertebrae numbers three and four (L3–4). On 9 October, Patient T underwent a decompressive laminectomy of lumbar vertebrae numbers one through three (L1–3), reexploration of lumbar vertebrae four and five (L4–5), and bilateral posterolateral fusion of lumbar vertebrae numbers three and four (L3–4).

Later in the day, the physician discovered on postoperative rounds that Patient T was completely paraplegic with loss of rectal tone. Consultation was obtained, and a myelogram was attempted but unsuccessful. The patient was taken to the operating room the evening of 9 October for reexploration of the laminectomy, evacuation of an epidural hematoma, and intradural exploration.

Patient T's recovery after the neurological compromise was slow. His postoperative course was further complicated by a pulmonary embolus episode. At the time of hospital discharge on 2 November, Patient T was described as having "fair strength throughout the lower extremities" with sensation "approaching normal." Sphincter tone was described as improving, and he was to continue with self-catheterization for the atonic bladder condition. The physician ordered nurses for ten hours a day and daily home physical therapy.

### Departures from the Standard of Care

Serious departures from prevailing professional standards of nursing care are evident in this case and include the following:

1. Failure to assess motor and sensory function of the lower extremities

2. Failure to report a sensory alteration to the physician by 1:30 P.M. on 9 October

## Discussion

Patient T tolerated the 9 October surgical procedure well and was admitted to the recovery room at 11:00 A.M. By noon, Patient T was transferred to the surgical floor. He was noted to be "alert and moving lower extremities without difficulty."

At 1:15 P.M., 9 October, the nurse's notes included the patient's statement, "My left foot is numb." The 3:30 P.M. nurse's note reads, "Patient states legs feel a little numb. He has not voided as yet nor does he feel the urge." At 4:45 P.M. it was stated, "denies urge to void." The progressive loss of sensation in the lower extremities along with the inability to void was never reported to the surgeon by the nurses.

According to the nurse's notes, the surgeon, Dr. F, examined the patient at 5:40 P.M. on his routine postoperative rounds. The 5:45 P.M. nurse's note read, "Patient complains of total numbness of lower extremities – unable to move toes or flex calf or thigh muscles. Complains of burning with palpation of right thigh but unable to feel any sensation (sharp or dull or pressure) below right knee, but feels pressure in left thigh. Pedal and post tibial pulses palpable."

Postoperative care following spinal surgery is directed at preventing complications, preventing further spinal injury, and providing an opportunity for the surgical site to heal. Among other things, the postoperative nursing care for Patient T should have included more frequent evaluation of motor and sensory function in the lower extremities. The alteration of sensory function at 1:15 P.M. required intensive nursing assessment. The alteration not only persisted but progressed. The situation, indicative of possible spinal cord edema or a hematoma compressing the spinal cord, was not reported to the physician. Furthermore, Patient T was at increased risk for developing a hematoma because he had had a spinal fusion as opposed to a laminectomy alone.

Patient T needed active nursing intervention at 1:15 P.M. on 9 October. Fortunately for the patient, the physician discovered the problem on his rounds. The intervention was too late, however, to prevent neurological complications.

The plaintiff's case was based on the determination that, within reasonable probability, the departures from prevailing professional standards of nursing care caused these neurological complications. The case settled with payment to the plaintiff.

## Case 5–7
*Increased Intracranial Pressure*

### Problem and Outcome

This tragic case involves a closed head injury. Nursing assessments, indicating increased intracranial pressure, were not communicated to the physician in a timely manner, and this contributed to the death of a 14-year-old girl.

### The Patient

Patient H, at approximately 3:30 P.M. on 18 May, fell from a swimming pool sliding board and struck the right side of her head on the side of a concrete pool. An emergency fire-rescue unit was summoned and, according to the report at 3:50 P.M., the patient was complaining of dizziness, nausea, and vomiting. At the scene of the accident, she was described as lying beside the pool, conscious but lethargic with a blood pressure of 110/60 mmHg, pulse rate of 88, and respiratory rate of 12.

### Treatment

Patient H was transported to the hospital and admitted to the emergency department at 4:00 P.M. She was found to have blood streaks in both nostrils, a small superficial laceration anterior to the right ear, an ecchymotic right eye, and periorbital edema. The right tympanic membrane was injected, the right pupil was 4 millimeters in size and reacted briskly to light while the left pupil was 2.5 millimeters and reacted briskly to light. A right, third nerve paresis was also present. Patient H's level of consciousness was described as "conscious but very quiet – will respond to questions if prodded to do so." Several episodes of vomiting were recorded. Vital signs in the emergency department were stable with the blood pressure ranging from 110/60 mmHg to 120/80 mmHg, pulse rate 80 to 92, and respiratory rate of 16 to 20. Skull X-rays revealed clouding of the sphenoid sinus and linear lucency in the right temporoparietal area. The physician's clinical impression was that the patient had a probable right temporal skull fracture and a closed head injury (cerebral concussion with probable right temporal lobe contusion). Epidural hematoma and direct global trauma could not be ruled out.

The patient was admitted to the intensive care unit where she deteriorated neurologically. She was taken to the operating room 19 May, and an epidural hematoma was evacuated. She failed to improve, and on 22 May she was pronounced dead. At autopsy, the cause of death was stated as epidural hematoma due to a fractured skull.

### Departures from the Standard of Care

Numerous departures from prevailing professional standards of nursing care occurred as follows:

1. Incomplete assessment of pain and numbness
2. Failure to monitor vital signs as ordered
3. Failure to inform the physician of complaints of headache and numbness
4. Failure to describe accurately a change in the level of consciousness on 19 May at 6:00 A.M.
5. Failure to inform the physician of the change in the level of consciousness on 19 May at 6:00 A.M.
6. Failure to inform the physician of a change in pupils on 19 May at 8:00 A.M
7. Failure to inform the physician of multiple neurological status changes on 19 May at 10:00 A.M.
8. Failure to inform the physician of further changes in the level of consciousness after a call was placed on 19 May at 10:00 A.M.
9. Failure to inform the physician as requested when the computed tomography (CT) scan was completed
10. Failure to administer 20 percent mannitol solution
11. Failure to make detailed nurse's notes between 10:00 P.M. and midnight on 19 May
12. Failure to inform the physician of neurological status changes in the early morning of 20 May

### Discussion

At 9:15 P.M., 18 May, the patient was admitted to the intensive care unit from the emergency department. According to the admission nursing note, the patient was in "no acute distress" and was "awake, alert, and oriented." The patient was "moving all extremities to command, strongly." Vital signs were stable and both pupils were "small and reactive normally to light." Patient H did complain of pain on the right side of her face.

The description of the pain lacks information regarding the qualitative, quantitative, topographic, and temporal aspects. The physician's admission orders were executed with the exception of vital signs every half-hour for six times. The nurses recorded vital signs hourly.

At 3:00 A.M., 19 May, Patient H complained of a "headache" and "numbness on the right side of the face." Again, the nurse's notes do not adequately describe the pain or numbness. The nurse's note also states that the urinary output was "0 at this time – [Dr. Z] notified of the decreased urinary output." The nurse failed to inform the physician of the complaints of headache and numbness of the face.

On 19 May at 6:00 A.M., the nurse's note states, "becoming restless – level of consciousness lighter . . . still complains of headache and numbness on right side of face." Patient H apparently had a change in the level of consciousness, but from this poor description one cannot judge what was taking place. The physician should have been informed of this change in level of consciousness.

Vital signs remained stable, but the neurological status continued to change during the early morning of 19 May. At 8:00 A.M., 19 May, the right pupil was now 3 millimeters in size and reacted briskly to light while the left pupil was 7 millimeters and nonreactive to light. The patient was described as "very lethargic and drowsy – falls asleep quickly and easily." Ptosis of the right eyelid was also described for the first time. The nurses should have informed the physician of these changes immediately. The nurses did not contact Dr. Z regarding these changes until 10:00 A.M., 19 May, and only a "non-urgent" message was left with his service.

The patient's neurological status continued to deteriorate that morning. By 11:00 A.M., Patient H was described as "very difficult to arouse . . . it takes repeated stimuli to awake patient." The physician had not responded to the previous message. He should have been called again at this time. At 12:00 noon, Patient H was still "difficult to arouse," but by 1:00 P.M., she was described as "still unable to arouse." At 2:00 P.M., the nurses were still "unable to arouse patient." Patient H then displayed "decorticate movement of the left arm and decerebrate movement of the right arm." Both right and left pupils were noted to be 5 millimeters in size and reacting sluggishly to light. After 2:00 P.M. the physician returned the call placed at 10:00 A.M., and he ordered a computed tomography (CT) scan of the brain.

The computed tomography (CT) scan was performed at 3:00 P.M., 19

May, and it revealed a large right-sided epidural hematoma. The patient was returned to the intensive care unit at 3:45 P.M. The nursing staff was instructed to call Dr. Z immediately with the results of the CT scan, but Dr. Z was not called until 5:35 P.M. because of the shift change.

An order for the intravenous administration of 20 percent mannitol solution at 35 milliliters per hour for three hours and then 15 milliliters per hour appeared on the chart 19 May (no time was indicated). According to the testimony of Dr. Z, he wrote the order at about 12:30 P.M. But the telephone order written for the computed tomography (CT) scan appears before this order. According to the medical record, the nurses never executed the order for the mannitol.

At 7:00 P.M., 19 May, Patient H was taken to the operating room where a right superior temporal craniotomy was performed, and the acute epidural hematoma was evacuated. It was noted that the patient was moving purposefully upon reversal of the anesthesia. Patient H was taken back to the intensive care unit at 9:40 P.M. There were no nurse's notes in the chart from 10:00 P.M. until midnight.

Between midnight and 4:00 A.M., 20 May, the only notations in the chart were "decorticate movement of the left arm; right pupil 6 millimeters and nonreactive to light; left pupil 3 millimeters and nonreactive to light; patient stuporous and patient will arouse to light pain (the reaction is appropriate)." The nurses did not inform the physician of these observations.

By 8:00 A.M., Patient H was exhibiting "restlessness" and was "not reacting to painful stimuli." Decerebrate reaction to stimuli was noted at 10:00 A.M., and by 11:00 A.M. both pupils were nonreactive to light, the right pupil was 6 millimeters, and the left was 5 millimeters. The nurses did not inform Dr. Z of these changes until 11:00 A.M.

At 11:55 A.M., the nurses noted that the "patient began having snoring-type respirations with labored breathing; increased secretions; increased heart rate 170s." Dr. Z was called again, and he arranged for an anesthesiologist to intubate the patient.

According to the progress note by Dr. Z on 20 May, there was a "sudden turn for the worst this A.M." At 1:30 P.M., Patient H was taken to the operating room again, where an anterior temporal lobectomy with brain stem decompression was performed. An intracranial pressure monitor was also placed at this time, with "tremendous increased intracranial pressure" noted. The patient was returned to the intensive care unit and never regained consciousness. The physicians later concluded that Patient H satisfied the criteria of the Harvard Committee for Brain Death. She was pronounced dead at 7:45 P.M. on 22 May.

Throughout this short hospitalization, Patient H exhibited significant neurological changes. The nurses, however, did not inform the physician of the changes in a timely fashion.

The plaintiff's case was based on the determination that, within reasonable probability, the departures from the prevailing professional standard of nursing care contributed to the demise of Patient H. The case settled with payment to her parents.

## Case 5–8
## *Chest Pain*

### Problem and Outcome

A 60-year-old lady died of a myocardial infarction fourteen hours after admission to the hospital. Nurses appropriately assessed complaints of chest pain, but never informed the physician of the situation.

### The Patient

Patient J was admitted to the hospital 19 October at 5:15 P.M. with the diagnosis of pleural effusion. This illness began several days before while the patient was working in the yard. When bending over, the patient developed severe pain in the left flank area. Prior to this, Patient J was in good health, with the exception of obesity.

### Treatment

Dyspnea and pain in the left flank was present upon admission. Throughout the fourteen-hour hospitalization, the patient complained of increasing pain. She was medicated frequently during the night for the pain, with some relief. At 7:15 A.M. on 20 October, the nurse's note reads "patient unresponsive; cyanotic; no vital signs; pupils fixed." Patient J. was pronounced dead at 7:30 A.M., on 20 October.

### Deviations from the Standard of Care

Serious departures from prevailing professional standards of nursing practice are evident in this case as follows:

1. Failure to assess systematically the patient, particularly

with regard to the respiratory and circulatory status

2. Failure to execute the order for Lanoxin (digoxin)
3. Failure to inform the physician of the chest pain

## Discussion

Vital signs were taken on admission. No other notations of vital signs appeared in the medical record. The nurses should have taken the vital signs of this patient at least every four hours.

According to the medical record, Patient J. was "medicated for pain on admission." She was described as "resting and offering no complaints" until 12:30 A.M. on 20 October, with the noted complaint of "pain along left side and down left arm." At 12:45 A.M., it was noted "complains of severe sharp pain under breastbone (more toward left side) radiating down left arm. Not relieved by position change and extra pillows. Medicated." Systematic assessment of the patient should have occurred at 12:30 A.M., with particular attention paid to circulatory and respiratory status. The frequency of assessment should have increased with the complaint of left arm pain, and if the pain did not improve within 10–15 minutes, the nurses should have notified the physician.

Complaints of pain after this were present in the medical record throughout the night and read: 1:30 A.M. "Same pain as above [12:45 A.M.] but less intense," and at 2:30 A.M., "As above but medication no longer effective. Pain is severe again." The last note in the medical record before Patient J was found without vital signs appears at 3:45 A.M. It read, "medicated for same pain as above." The nurses did not inform the physician of the continuing significant complaints of pain.

Patients such as Patient J are admitted to a hospital for systematic observation and prompt intervention if a problem should occur. Although the nurses did not provide adequate systematic assessment, they did observe that Patient J had chest pain radiating down the left arm. Unfortunately, they did not inform the physician of this development. Patient J was found dead fourteen hours after admission. Autopsy revealed a myocardial infarction.

The plaintiff's case was based on the determination that, within reasonable probability, the departures from the prevailing professional standard of nursing care contributed to the death of Patient J. The case settled with payment to the estate of the plaintiff.

# Chapter 6

# Problems Associated with a Physician's Departure from the Standard of Care

Nursing malpractice can occur when nurses fail to take action in situations where the care provided by physicians departs from prevailing professional standards of practice. The discussion and case studies presented in this chapter relate to situations where inadequate care was rendered by the physician.

Many years ago, when a nurse observed poor care provided by a physician, little if anything was done. The nurse was not expected to speak up or to obtain help for a patient not receiving proper care. More recently, the observation of poor care provided by a physician fell into a gray area for the nurse. That is, the nurse was taught that failure to provide proper care should be called to the attention of "appropriate authorities." In reality, most of the time nothing was done to solve the problem of poor care, and sometimes the nurse, if he/she spoke up appropriately, was labeled as a "troublemaker."

Today this has changed. The nurse is held accountable for failure to act when a physician departs from the standard of care. The courts consistently hold the nurse responsible for protecting the patient. Nurses possess a sophisticated knowledge base as a function of contemporary educational programs. Today's nurse is expected to recognize patient-care problems and to accept the responsibility for active intervention, so that help can be obtained for the patient. The nurse, though not qualified nor expected to practice medicine, is obligated, through the application of knowledge, to recognize inadequate care provided by a physician. Case 6–3 (Postoperative Abdominal Sepsis) was one of the pioneer cases in Florida in which it was determined that the nurse had the responsibility for the safety and welfare of the patient in the presence of inadequate medical care.

A disturbing element of the nursing testimony in these cases was the hesitancy of the nurse to do anything about inadequate patient care by physicians. In some instances, when a nurse informed the physician of a patient-care problem, and no action was taken by the physician, the nurse also took no further action. The nurses in this situation basically testified that the physician was informed, and that was all one could do.

In other instances, when a physician was informed of a patient-care problem and nothing was done, the nurse did inform the immediate supervisor (head nurse, charge nurse, nurse manager, nursing supervisor) that a problem existed. Testimony revealed a disturbing pattern on the part of the nurse's superior in these situations. The superior did not pursue the matter and only reassured the nurse that enough was done by contacting the physician.

In all the cases discussed in this chapter, the hospital policy-and-procedure manual outlined clearly what was to be done when a patient was not receiving adequate care. Generally, the nurse was advised to go through the chain of command, pursuing the inadequate patient-care situation to the level where action would be taken. In these cases, however, the nurses did not follow these directions.

In the cases that follow, the patient was assessed and the physician was made aware of the problem(s). The treatment plan was not altered, however, and nothing more was done to address the problem(s). These selected cases illustrate the failure of the nurse to obtain help for a patient when he/she realized that a patient was bleeding excessively from chest tubes, extubated prematurely, was failing to progress normally from an elective cholecystectomy, and was manifesting signs of increased intracranial pressure.

In each instance, a substantial award was made to the plaintiff or his/her estate. The hospital and nurses involved were held accountable to the standard that the patient was entitled to proper care and that the nurse under these circumstances was obligated to take the necessary actions to obtain this care.

## Case 6–1
### *Excessive Chest Tube Bleeding*

**Problem and Outcome**

Excessive bleeding from chest tubes was observed in the postoperative period. Lack of action, however, led to the development of hypovolemic shock, which later caused a cardiopulmonary arrest. The arrest in turn resulted in anoxic brain syndrome and the ultimate death of a 56-year-old man.

### The Patient

This case involves Patient H, a prominent architect admitted to the hospital for elective surgery. Patient H was married with four children. He was the sole support of his immediate family and of his mother, who was also a dependent in his home. Family life was complicated by the fact that one son had been born profoundly developmentally disabled. By the time this child was fourteen years old, adequate home care could no longer be provided by the family. Because the child was totally dependent for all activities of daily living, institutionalization was necessary. This was an agonizing decision for the family. The private institutional care was not covered by health insurance, and this was an added financial burden for the family.

### Treatment

Patient H was admitted to the hospital with the diagnosis of an anterior mediastinal mass. Diagnostic studies were completed, and it was agreed that surgical exploration and excision of the mass was necessary. Patient H was taken to the operating room on 10 June. He tolerated the procedure well, but excessive bleeding from the chest tubes occurred. Hypovolemic shock developed, and at 10:30 P.M. on the day of surgery, Patient H was found to be without pulse or respiration. After cardiopulmonary resuscitation with difficulty, Patient H was taken back to the operating room for reentry of the median sternotomy because of the bleeding. Patient H never regained consciousness after this occurrence, and his condition continued to deteriorate until death on 27 June.

### Departures from the Standard of Care

Departures from prevailing professional standards of nursing care were as follows:

1. Failure to assess the patient systematically
2. Failure to inform the nursing supervisor of the patient's deteriorating condition in order to obtain additional care for the patient's benefit

## Discussion

After surgery, Patient H was admitted to the intensive care unit at 9:45 A.M. Vital signs were stable initially, but by 1:15 P.M., Patient H had a blood pressure of 90/50 mmHg, a pulse rate of 85, and a respiratory rate of 22. Vital signs continued to deteriorate. All vital signs charted for the first twelve hours of the postoperative period are presented on the flow sheet on pages 146–53.

Patient H's central venous pressure and urinary output were also abnormal during this period. The only central venous pressure notations in the medical record were: 2:00 P.M., 7.5 cmHOH; 9:00 P.M., 5.0 cmHOH; 9:15 P.M., 12 cmHOH; and 10:00 P.M., 13 cmHOH. Urinary output was recorded only at 4:00 P.M. and 5:00 P.M. and was 300 milliliters and 20 milliliters, respectively.

Chest tube drainage was markedly abnormal. At 12:15 P.M. it was 700 milliliters; by 4:30 P.M. it was 1,600 milliliters, with a cumulative total of 2,647 milliliters recorded by 8:00 P.M. Between 8:00 P.M. and 10:00 P.M., another 500 milliliters of chest tube drainage was noted.

Patient H's condition continued to deteriorate, and at 10:30 P.M. on 10 June, he was found without pulse or respiration. It was noted in the medical record that six calls regarding vital signs and chest tube drainage were placed to the surgeon between 1:00 P.M. and the time of the cardiopulmonary arrest.

Testimony by the nurse involved in the care of this patient revealed that "all of us [the nurses] in the unit [intensive care unit] were concerned about [Patient H]. Things weren't right, but we called the doctor frequently. . . . He said everything was OK and that he [Patient H] would stabilize eventually. . . . Yes, we [the nurses in the intensive care unit] talked it over, and we kept calling the doctor. He was informed."

Nursing care for the thoracic surgery patient involves, among other elements, frequent and accurate observation because a variety of complications can occur, such as respiratory insufficiency, hypoxia, anoxia, hyperventilation, carbon dioxide retention, mediastinal shift, paradoxical motion, pneumothorax, hemorrhage, hemothorax, shock, hypotension, cardiac arrhythmias, myocardial infarction, respiratory arrest, cardiac arrest, pulmonary embolism, thrombophlebitis, atelectasis, pneumonia, infection, paralytic ileus, subcutaneous emphysema, and acute pulmonary edema. This basic knowledge forms the framework within which the nurse plans and administers patient care. Thus, much of the clinical

## Case 6–1 Flow Sheet

**Assessment Standard for Patient**                        **Minimum Frequency of Assessment**

| Assessment | Variable | 10 June 9:45 am | 10:00 | 10:15 | 10:30 | 10:45 | 11:00 |
|---|---|---|---|---|---|---|---|
| **Respiratory status** | Patency of airway | | | | | | |
| | Respiratory rate | 20 | 18 | 18 | 20 | 26 | 25 |
| | Respiratory rhythm | | | | | | |
| | Respiratory character | | | | | | |
| | Depth of respiration | | | | | | |
| | Breath sounds | equal bilateral | | | | | |
| | Appearance of chest | | | | | | |
| **Circulatory status** | Heart rate | 95 | 85 | 85 | 75 | 78 | 80 |
| | Heart rhythm | NSR | | | | | |
| | Pulse quality | | | | | | |
| | Blood pressure | $\frac{180}{100}$ | $\frac{145}{80}$ | $\frac{138}{80}$ | $\frac{120}{70}$ | $\frac{128}{70}$ | $\frac{120}{75}$ |
| | Skin temperature | | | | | | |
| | Skin color | | | | | | |
| | Nailbed appearance | | | | | | |
| | Central venous pressure (cm HOH) | | | | | | |

**(entries indicate assessments that were made)**

| 11:15 | 11:30 | 11:45 | 12:00 pm | 12:15 | 12:30 | 12:45 | 1:00 | 1:15 | 1:30 | 1:45 | 2:00 |
|---|---|---|---|---|---|---|---|---|---|---|---|
|  |  |  |  |  |  |  |  |  |  |  |  |
| 20 | 32 | 22 | 22 | 25 | 25 | 22 | 22 | 22 | 20 | 20 | 20 |
|  |  |  |  |  |  |  |  |  |  |  |  |
|  |  |  |  |  |  |  |  |  |  |  |  |
|  |  |  |  |  |  |  |  |  |  |  |  |
|  |  |  |  |  |  |  |  |  |  |  |  |
| 80 | 80 | 85 | 85 | 85 | 85 | 80 | 80 | 85 | 85 | 85 | 110 |
|  |  |  |  |  |  |  |  |  |  |  |  |
| $\frac{118}{70}$ | $\frac{110}{70}$ | $\frac{115}{70}$ | $\frac{110}{72}$ | $\frac{120}{70}$ | $\frac{110}{75}$ | $\frac{115}{72}$ | $\frac{115}{72}$ | $\frac{90}{50}$ | $\frac{105}{60}$ | $\frac{92}{68}$ | $\frac{90}{55}$ |
|  |  |  |  |  |  |  |  |  |  |  |  |
|  |  |  |  |  |  |  |  |  |  |  |  |
|  |  |  |  |  |  |  |  |  |  |  |  |
|  |  |  |  |  |  |  |  |  |  |  | 7.5 |

## Case 6–1 Flow Sheet (continued)

**Assessment Standard for Patient**          **Minimum Frequency of Assessment**

| Assessment | Variable | 10 June 2:15 pm | 2:30 | 2:45 | 3:00 | 3:15 | 3:30 |
|---|---|---|---|---|---|---|---|
| **Respiratory status** | Patency of airway | | | | | | |
| | Respiratory rate | | | | | | 35 |
| | Respiratory rhythm | | | | | | |
| | Respiratory character | | | | | | |
| | Depth of respiration | | | | | | |
| | Breath sounds | | | | | | |
| | Appearance of chest | | | | | | |
| **Circulatory status** | Heart rate | 95 | 100 | 105 | 100 | | 100 |
| | Heart rhythm | | | | | | |
| | Pulse quality | | | | | | |
| | Blood pressure | $\frac{95}{55}$ | $\frac{92}{50}$ | $\frac{70}{40}$ | $\frac{95}{50}$ | $\frac{100}{50}$ | $\frac{90}{50}$ |
| | Skin temperature | | | | | | |
| | Skin color | | | | | | |
| | Nailbed appearance | | | | | | |
| | Central venous pressure (cm HOH) | | | | | | |

**(entries indicate assessments that were made)**

| 3:45 | 4:00 | 4:15 | 4:30 | 4:45 | 5:00 | 5:15 | 5:30 | 5:45 | 6:00 | 6:15 | 6:30 |
|---|---|---|---|---|---|---|---|---|---|---|---|
| | | | | | | | | | | | |
| 38 | 38 | 38 | 30 | 30 | 30 | 28 | | | 18 | 22 | 18 |
| | | | | | even | | | | | | |
| | | | | | unlabored | | | | | | |
| | | | | | | | | | | | |
| | | | | equal bilateral | | good lung sounds | | equal bilateral | | | |
| | | | | | | | | | | | |
| 100 | 102 | 100 | 105 | 105 | 105 | 220 | 216 | 208 | 208 | 196 | 221 |
| | | | | | ST | NSR | ST | ST | | | |
| | | | | | full | | full | full | | | |
| $\frac{90}{50}$ | $\frac{95}{50}$ | $\frac{85}{52}$ | $\frac{95}{52}$ | $\frac{95}{52}$ | $\frac{95}{52}$ | $\frac{80}{58}$ | $\frac{70}{46}$ | | $\frac{94}{59}$ | $\frac{79}{44}$ | |
| | | | | | cool | cool moist | | cool | | | |
| | | | | | pale | pale | | pale | | | |
| | | | | | | | | | | | |
| | | | | | | | | | | | |

## Case 6–1 Flow Sheet (continued)

**Assessment Standard for Patient**                    **Minimum Frequency of Assessment**

| Assessment | Variable | 10 June 6:45 pm | 7:00 | 7:15 | 7:30 | 7:45 |
|---|---|---|---|---|---|---|
| **Respiratory status** | Patency of airway | | | | | |
| | Respiratory rate | | | 24 | | |
| | Respiratory rhythm | | | | | |
| | Respiratory character | | | | | |
| | Depth of respiration | | | | | |
| | Breath sounds | | | | | |
| | Appearance of chest | | | | | |
| **Circulatory status** | Heart rate | 146 | 110 | 222 | 128 | |
| | Heart rhythm | ST | | ST | | |
| | Pulse quality | | | | | |
| | Blood pressure | $\frac{68}{46}$ | $\frac{69}{37}$ | $\frac{64}{40}$ | | |
| | Skin temperature | | | cool diaphoretic | | |
| | Skin color | | | | | |
| | Nailbed appearance | | | | | |
| | Central venous pressure (cm HOH) | | | | | |

**(entries indicate assessments that were made)**

| 8:00 | 8:15 | 8:30 | 8:45 | 9:00 | 9:15 | 9:30 | 9:45 | 10:00 | 10:15 | 10:30 |
|------|------|------|------|------|------|------|------|-------|-------|-------|
|      |      |      |      |      |      |      |      |       |       |       |
| 22   |      |      |      | 45   |      |      |      |       |       |       |
|      |      |      |      |      |      |      |      |       |       |       |
|      |      |      |      | difficult breathing |  |  |  |       |       |       |
|      |      |      |      |      |      |      |      |       |       |       |
|      |      |      |      |      |      |      |      |       |       |       |
|      |      |      |      |      |      |      |      |       |       |       |
| 123  |      |      |      | 135  |      |      | 154  | 72    |       |       |
|      |      |      |      | ST   |      |      |      |       |       |       |
|      |      |      |      |      |      |      |      |       |       |       |
| $\frac{95}{51}$ |  |  |  | $\frac{76}{42}$ |  |  |  |       |       |       |
|      |      |      |      |      |      |      |      |       |       |       |
|      |      |      |      |      |      |      |      |       |       |       |
|      |      |      |      |      |      |      |      |       |       |       |
|      |      |      |      | 5    | 12   |      |      |       |       | 13    |

## Case 6–1 Flow Sheet (continued)

**Assessment Standard for Patient**          **Minimum Frequency of**

| Assessment | Variable | 10 June 10:00 am | 11:00 | 12:15 pm | 1:00 |
|---|---|---|---|---|---|
| **Wound status** | Condition of dressing | dressing dry | | dressing dry | |
| | Chest tube drainage-amount | some | | 700 ml | |
| | Chest tube drainage-character | bloody | | | |
| **Renal status** | Urinary output | | | | |
| | Character of urine | | | | |
| **Fluid status** | Intake | | | | |
| | Estimated fluid loss | | | | |
| | Intake vs. output | | | | |
| **Neurological status (when awake)** | Level of consciousness | awake | | awake | |
| | Orientation | responding verbally | | | |
| **Pain status** | Qualitative aspects | | | | |
| | Quantitative aspects | | | | |
| | Topographic aspects | | | | |
| | Temporal aspects | | | | |
| **Gastrointes-tinal status** | Appearance of abdomen | | | soft | |
| | Bowel sounds | | | absent | |
| **Thermoregula-tory status prn** | Body temperature | 98.6 | | | |

## Assessment (entries indicate assessments that were made)

| 2:00 | 3:00 | 4:30 | 5:00 | 6:00 | 7:00 | 8:00 | 9:00 | 10:00 |
|---|---|---|---|---|---|---|---|---|
|  | dressing dry |  | bright red blood |  |  |  |  |  |
|  |  | 1600 ml |  | 50 ml |  | cumulative total 2647 ml | 230 ml | 270 ml |
|  | bloody |  |  |  | bloody |  |  |  |
|  |  | 300 ml | 20 ml |  |  |  |  |  |
|  |  | amber |  |  |  |  |  |  |
| ÷ unit PC | ÷ unit PC | 1630 ml | total 3100 ml | ÷ unit PC | ÷ unit PC | 2000 ml + ÷ unit PC | 2100 ml + ÷ unit PC |  |
|  |  |  |  |  |  |  |  |  |
|  |  |  |  |  |  |  |  |  |
|  |  |  | awake alert | awake alert | alert |  |  |  |
|  |  |  |  | oriented x3 |  |  |  |  |
|  |  |  |  |  |  |  |  |  |
|  |  |  |  |  |  |  |  |  |
|  |  |  |  |  |  |  |  |  |
|  |  |  |  |  |  |  |  |  |
|  |  |  | soft | soft |  |  |  |  |
|  |  |  | absent | absent |  |  |  |  |
|  |  |  | 97.2 |  |  | 98 |  |  |

nursing care given thoracic surgery patients is preventive care directed at averting these complications.

In addition to observation, nurses have the responsibility to communicate assessment information to the physician and to expect appropriate intervention when necessary. The nursing staff, according to testimony, knew that Patient H was not receiving appropriate care from his physician. The nurses in the intensive care unit discussed this situation but did not notify the nursing supervisor or anyone else of their concern. The information in the medical record describes a seriously ill man whose condition was deteriorating. The nurses placed numerous calls to the surgeon, but the treatment plan was not modified. Patient H continued to bleed abnormally from the chest tube. The nursing staff recognized this, but failed to take appropriate action to secure help for Patient H.

The plaintiff's case was based on the determination that, within reasonable probability, the departures from the prevailing professional standard of nursing care contributed to the death of Patient H. The case settled with payment to the estate of the plaintiff.

### Case 6–2
## *Premature Extubation*

### Problem and Outcome

Premature extubation by a physician led to the death of a 43-year-old man. The physician was known to the nursing staff for performing this procedure prematurely.

### The Patient

Patient C, a self-employed certified public accountant with a wife and two children, was admitted with chest pain to the hospital 10 September.

### Treatment

Patient C underwent cardiac catheterization and was noted to have normal left ventricular function, segmental 80 percent obstruction of the proximal left anterior descending artery, and diffuse irregularities of the right coronary artery. The attending physician concluded that percutaneous transluminal coronary angioplasty was risky for this patient and that surgery was preferable.

On 17 September, Patient C was taken to the operating room for coronary artery bypass graft (CABG) surgery. He tolerated the procedure well and was taken to the intensive care unit at 12:30 P.M. At 2:23 P.M., Patient C suffered a cardiac arrest and was pronounced dead at 3:40 P.M.

## Departures from the Standard of Care

Departures from prevailing professional standards of nursing care in this case were as follows:

1. Failure to make systematic and timely nursing assessments of respiratory status
2. Failure to obtain timely arterial blood gas analysis after extubation
3. Failure to detect profound hypoxia in a timely manner
4. Failure to obtain adequate physician care for the patient
5. Failure to institute ventilatory support in a timely manner

## Discussion

Upon admission to the intensive care unit at 12:30 P.M., vital signs and arterial blood gasses were within normal limits. At 1:15 P.M., Patient C was described as "pretty asleep" and arterial blood gasses were pH 7.25; $pCO_2$ (mmHg) 55.8; $pO_2$ (mmHg) 86.4; and BE -3.0. His vital signs at this time were blood pressure 160/69 mmHg, a heart rate of 93 with sinus tachycardia, and a respiratory rate of 19 with shallow breathing and "a lot of grunting." At 1:25 P.M., Patient C was extubated by the anesthesiologist, and at 1:30 P.M. vital signs were noted as blood pressure 203/72 mmHg, heart rate of 123 with sinus tachycardia, and a respiratory rate of 28 with grunting.

The next notation on the chart was not until 2:00 P.M., and it revealed blood pressure 178/82 mmHg; heart rate 123 and irregular; respiratory rate 34 with grunting; pH 7.15; $pCO_2$ (mmHg) 65.9; and BE -1.8. The anesthesiologist was called at 2:00 P.M., and at 2:10 P.M. it was noted, "patient ambued." The anesthesiologist did not arrive until 2:15 P.M. He reintubated Patient C at 2:20 P.M., and at 2:23 P.M. Patient C suffered a cardiac arrest. After unsuccessful cardiopulmonary resuscitation, Patient C was pronounced dead at 3:40 P.M.

Testimony by the nurse involved in the care of Patient C revealed that the anesthesiologist was "well known to us to extubate too early, disappear, and leave us with a difficult patient." In essence, she knew better but did not act with appropriate decisiveness. She further stated, "It's up to the doctor," when she was questioned about extubation. She did not communicate her concern about this physician to anyone at the hospital, with tragic consequences. When this nurse was questioned as to why nothing was done for the patient between 1:25 P.M. and 2:00 P.M., her answer was, "Well, you know, we were really busy with a lot of sick patients."

The plaintiff's case was based on the determination that, within reasonable probability, the departures from the prevailing professional standard of nursing care contributed to the death of Patient C. The case settled with payment to the estate of the plaintiff.

## Case 6–3

## *Postoperative Abdominal Sepsis*

### Problem and Outcome

This case involves Patient L, a 45-year-old man who developed an intra-abdominal infection after a cholecystectomy. The infection was not adequately treated, and he died.

### The Patient

Patient L, a war hero, was a retired colonel from the U.S. Marine Corps. While attending college on a football scholarship, he married and withdrew from college to "go fly" in the Marine's cadet program. He became a flight instructor and then served in Vietnam four times. As a fighter pilot, he was known as "Bear." Patient L was the commanding officer of a F-4 phantom fighter squadron. He commanded 36 officers and 400 enlisted personnel. He was awarded the Silver Star, Purple Heart, and Legion of Merit and he was designated a Marine Corps Aviator of the Year. An auditorium was named after Patient L at the base which he formerly commanded.

### Treatment

Patient L was admitted to a hospital 26 February with a history of vomiting and with pain in the upper abdomen that later localized between the shoulders. One year prior to admission, Patient L had a Bjork-Shiley aortic valve implantation for repair of an ascending aortic aneurysm, along with bypass of the coronary arteries. After this procedure, Patient L was described as being in good health.

Patient L was evaluated, and an oral cholecystogram revealed a one-centimeter gallstone. On 28 February, a cholecystectomy with common bile duct exploration, duodenotomy, and dilatation of the ampulla of Vater was performed.

Several hours after surgery, Patient L was hypotensive and had temperature elevation of 104 degrees Fahrenheit (rectally). During the postoperative period, Patient L continued to have temperature elevations and became markedly icteric. Liver failure ensued. At the request of his family, Patient L was transferred to another hospital on 19 March.

Upon admission to the second hospital, Patient L was described as "extremely ill." He was somewhat somnolent but responsive and oriented. The admitting physician said, "He smelled so bad. He had a massive infection, and the area around the incision was black. It was the rottenest-looking wound I've ever seen. He was premoribund, had a God-awful infection, and had almost total body anasarca." The white blood cell count was 3,500 per cubic millimeter of blood. The physician concluded that Patient L had an intra-abdominal abscess with inadequate drainage. Under local anesthesia, a Chaffin-Pratt tube was inserted into the abscess region. By 20 March, Patient L's condition was "somewhat stabilized."

A T-tube cholangiogram revealed the T-tube to be in the common bile duct with the distal end of it partway through the sphincter of Oddi. Some extravasation of dye occurred lateral to the entry of the T-tube into the common bile duct. Gastrograffin studies via the nasogastric tube revealed a duodenal leak. The patient was taken to surgery 22 March, with the significant problems of sepsis and coagulopathy. At surgery, multiple drains were inserted and the wound was left open.

Postoperatively, hematologic problems persisted along with the sepsis. Patient L continued to bleed briskly from his wound sites. Disseminated intravascular coagulation was suspected. Even with supportive blood component therapy and antibiotics, Patient L's condition deteriorated. On 25 March, the patient demonstrated multiple one- to three-centimeter circular skin lesions consistent with ecthyma gangrenosum. Blood cultures along with wound and skin lesions grew out *Pseudomonas aeruginosa* and *Escherichia coli*.

On 27 March, Patient L started to bleed massively from the nasogastric tube. Supportive blood component therapy was instituted, and he was taken to surgery. An ulcer of the antrum of the stomach was found and repaired. Complicating the surgery was a cardiac arrest, but a normal sinus rhythm was restored by closed chest massage and cardioversion. Patient L began to hemorrhage extensively again on 28 March, this time from all drainage sites. At 8:15 P.M., Patient L had another cardiac arrest and expired.

Gross and microscopic findings at autopsy demonstrated bacterial and fungal dissemination throughout the body. The etiology of the microorganisms was felt to be related to one of the surgical intra-abdominal procedures. There was also acute inflammation and necrosis of the pancreas, probably caused by pancreatic duct obstruction from mechanical or inflammatory causes. Evidence of terminal shock included centrilobular necrosis of the liver, early acute tubular necrosis, and necrotizing enteropathy. Intra-abdominal hemorrhage (3,000 milliliters) and gastrointestinal hemorrhage correlated with the premortem-disseminated intravascular coagulopathy.

The cause of death was due to bacterial and fungal infection with bacterial sepsis and intra-abdominal hemorrhage, complicating a cholecystectomy.

### Departures from the Standard of Care

Serious departures from prevailing professional standards of nursing practice occurred during the entire admission to the first hospital. These deviations from the standard of care are listed by preoperative and postoperative period and include the following:

A. Preoperative period
   1. Failure to complete a comprehensive nursing history and nursing assessment
   2. Failure to observe the patient systematically
B. Postoperative period (intensive care unit)
   1. Failure to observe the patient systematically
   2. Failure to inform the physician of significant changes in the patient's condition
   3. Failure to question certain medication orders
C. Postoperative period (surgical unit)
   1. Failure to observe the patient systematically
   2. Failure to inform the physician of changes in the patient's condition
   3. Failure to test nasogastric drainage and stools for the presence of blood

4. Failure to summarize numerous laboratory results into a workable flow sheet
5. Failure to question certain medication orders
6. Failure to detect severe candidiasis of the oropharynx
7. Failure to obtain treatment for the candidiasis
8. Failure to prevent decubitus ulcers
9. Failure to inform the nursing supervisor and/or hospital authorities of the patient's deteriorating condition in order to obtain additional care for the patient's benefit.

## Discussion

This case analysis is confined to the admission to the first hospital. Preoperatively, a thorough nursing assessment with a nursing history did not appear in the medical record. This nursing assessment and history for Patient L should have included the following:

1. Chief complaint (onset of illness, complete description of symptoms and condition)
2. Past medical history
3. Social and family history
4. Mental status
5. Respiratory status
6. Circulatory status
7. Neurological status
8. Body temperature
9. Renal function and fluid status
10. Gastrointestinal status
11. Weight and height

This nursing assessment and history would have provided the necessary data base for the nursing care plan, which was also absent from the medical record.

During this preoperative period of 26 through 28 February, no nursing notations were made in reference to Patient L's presenting problem. Notes for each shift should have included such data as presence/absence of abdominal pain; presence/absence of jaundice; appearance of stools; and characteristics of the abdomen along with food intolerance, nausea and/or vomiting. Complete and accurate nursing notes would have provided important data to the entire health-care team. For example, there

## Case 6–3 Flow Sheet

| Assessment Standard for Patient | | Date/Time | |
|---|---|---|---|
| | | 28 February | 29 February |
| Assessment | Variable | 2:30 pm-12:00 am | 12:00 am-1:00 pm |
| **Respiratory status** | Patency of airway | every hour | every hour |
| | Respiratory rate | every 10-15 min. | every 5-10 min. |
| | Respiratory rhythm | every 10-15 min. | every 5-10 min. |
| | Respiratory character | every 10-15 min. | every 5-10 min. |
| | Breath sounds | every 1-2 hours | every 1-2 hours |
| **Circulatory status** | Pulse rate | every 10-15 min. | every 5-10 min. |
| | Pulse rhythm | every 10-15 min. | every 5-10 min. |
| | Pulse quality | every 10-15 min. | every 5-10 min. |
| | Blood pressure | every 10-15 min. | every 5-10 min. |
| | Skin temperature | every 10-15 min. | every 5-10 min. |
| | Skin color | every 10-15 min. | every 5-10 min. |
| | Central venous pressure | not applicable | not applicable |
| | Presence/absence edema | one time | one time |
| | Nailbed appearance | every hour | every hour |
| **Neurological status** | Level of consciousness | every hour | every hour |
| | Orientation | every hour | every hour |
| | Behavioral changes | every hour | every hour |
| **Wound status** | Amount/character of wound drainage | every hour | every hour |
| | Skin color/temperature around wound | when dressed | when dressed |
| **Pain status** | Pain assessment | every hour | every hour |
| **Gastro-intestinal status** | Appearance of abdomen | every 30 min. | every 30 min. |
| | Bowel sounds | one time | one time |
| | Nasogastric tube drainage amount and description | every hour | every hour |
| | T-tube drainage amount and character | every 2 hours | every 2 hours |
| | Appetite | not applicable | not applicable |
| | Weight | not applicable | one time |
| **Renal status** | Urinary output amount and character | every hour | every hour |
| **Fluid status** | Fluid intake amount and type | every hour | every hour |
| **Thermo-regulatory status** | Body temperature | every 2 hours | every 2 hours |

| 29 February | 1 March | | 2 March | 3 March | 4 March |
|---|---|---|---|---|---|
| 1:00 pm-12:00 am | 12:00 am-11:00 am | 11:00 am-12:00 am | all day | all day | until transfer |
| every 2 hours | every 2 hours | every 4 hours | every 8 hours | every 8 hours | every 8 hours |
| every 30 min. | every 30 min. | every hour | every hour | every 2 hours | every 2 hours |
| every 30 min. | every 30 min. | every hour | every hour | every 2 hours | every 2 hours |
| every 30 min. | every 30 min. | every hour | every hour | every 2 hours | every 2 hours |
| every 30 min. | one time | one time | every 8 hours | every 8 hours | every 8 hours |
| every 30 min. | every 30 min. | every hour | every hour | every 2 hours | every 2 hours |
| every 30 min. | every 30 min. | every hour | every hour | every 2 hours | every 2 hours |
| every 30 min. | every 30 min. | every hour | every hour | every 2 hours | every 2 hours |
| every 30 min. | every 30 min. | every hour | every hour | every 2 hours | every 2 hours |
| every 30 min. | every 30 min. | every hour | every hour | every 2 hours | every 2 hours |
| every 30 min. | every 30 min. | every hour | every hour | every 2 hours | every 2 hours |
| every hour | every hour | every hour | every hour | every 2 hours | every 2 hours |
| one time | one time | one time | every 8 hours | every 8 hours | every 8 hours |
| every 2 hours | every 4 hours | every 6 hours | every 8 hours | every 8 hours | every 8 hours |
| every 2 hours | every 4 hours | every 4 hours | every 4 hours | every 8 hours | every 8 hours |
| every 2 hours | every 4 hours | every 4 hours | every 4 hours | every 8 hours | every 8 hours |
| every 2 hours | every 4 hours | every 4 hours | every 4 hours | every 8 hours | every 8 hours |
| every 2 hours | every 4 hours | every 4 hours | every 4 hours | every 4 hours | every 4 hours |
| when dressed | when dressed | when dressed | when dressed | when dressed | when dressed |
| every hour | every hour | every 2 hours | every 4 hours | every 4 hours | every 4 hours |
| every hour | every hour | every 2 hours | every 4 hours | every 4 hours | every 4 hours |
| one time | one time | one time | every 8 hours | every 8 hours | every 8 hours |
| every hour | every hour | every 2 hours | every 6 hours | every 6 hours | every 6 hours |
| every 2 hours | every 4 hours | every 4 hours | every 6 hours | every 6 hours | every 6 hours |
| not applicable | not applicable | not applicable | not applicable | not applicable | not applicable |
| not applicable | one time | not applicable | every 24 hours | every 24 hours | every 24 hours |
| every hour | every hour | every hour | every 6 hours | every 6 hours | every 6 hours |
| every hour | every hour | every hour | every hour | every hour | every hour |
| every 2 hours | every 2 hours | every 2 hours | every 2 hours | every 4 hours | every 4 hours |

was considerable confusion in the medical record as to whether jaundice existed preoperatively. Accurate nursing observations would have settled this issue.

Postoperatively, because of the heart condition, Patient L was admitted to the intensive care unit as a precaution. The postoperative nursing care that Patient L received (as reflected in the medical record) was seriously below accepted nursing standards. Postoperative nursing care for patients that have had major abdominal surgery involves, among other things, systematic nursing assessment.

Upon admission to the intensive care unit on 28 February, Patient L's blood pressure was considerably lower than it had been preoperatively and intraoperatively. Vital signs remained "somewhat variable." Between 3:50 P.M. and 11:35 P.M., the patient's pulse rate, respiratory rate, and body temperature increased significantly while the blood pressure decreased. Laboratory studies were indicative of metabolic acidosis. It was also noted that Patient L was restless. The nurses should have informed the physicians of this situation.

The patient's condition continued to deteriorate 29 February. Between 1:00 A.M. and 6:30 A.M., Patient L's respiratory rate and pulse rate continued to increase while the blood pressure decreased. His body temperature continued to be elevated, and no urinary output was recorded. The medical record reflected that the only time a physician was notified about the patient's condition was at 3:40 A.M. The physician did not provide any additional orders.

The type and frequency of nursing care that Patient L should have received while in the intensive care unit (based upon his changing condition) is outlined on the preceding flow sheet (see pages 160–61). All nursing actions should have been executed and documented. A physician's order was not necessary for any of the specified nursing actions. A competent nurse has the knowledge base to determine the kind and frequency of nursing actions needed.

While Patient L was in the intensive care unit, the nurses should have questioned the adequacy of his fluid orders, because it is common nursing knowledge that such patients can have large fluid losses due to nasogastric suction, among other things. Nurses also know the signs of hypovolemia (e.g., decreased blood pressure, oliguria or anuria, poor skin turgor), and they should have discussed this with the physicians. The nurses should also have questioned the order for Lasix (furosemide) on 29 February, in light of the patient's fluid status.

The nursing care that Patient L received after he was transferred out of the intensive care unit to a surgical floor continued to be inadequate. The nurse's notes for each shift from 4 to 18 March should have included at least the following observations:

1. Vital signs
    a. Body temperature
    b. Pulse (rate, rhythm, quality)
    c. Respiration (rate, rhythm, character)
    d. Blood pressure
2. Skin: color and temperature
3. Presence or absence of peripheral edema
4. Neurological status
    a. Level of consciousness
    b. Orientation
    c. Behavioral changes
5. Wound status
    a. Character of drainage
    b. Amount of drainage
    c. Condition of surgical wound, dressings, and suture lines
6. Renal status
    a. Urinary output
    b. Character of urine
7. Fluid status
    a. Intake (amount, kind, route, rate)
    b. Intake vs. output
    c. Estimated or actual fluid loss
8. Pain status
    a. Qualitative aspects
    b. Quantitative aspects
    c. Topographic aspects
    d. Temporal aspects
    e. General level of comfort
9. Gastrointestinal status
    a. Appearance of abdomen
    b. Bowel sounds
    c. Presence/absence of nausea, emesis
    d. Amount and character of nasogastric tube drainage
    e. Amount and character of T-tube drainage

  f. Character of stools

  g. Testing nasogastric drainage and stools for blood, when indicated

  h. Presence/absence of jaundice

 10. Nutritional status

  a. Appetite

  b. Daily weight

The nurse's notes were incomplete in relation to these observations. The frequency with which these observations are made each shift is determined by the patient's condition.

In addition to the incomplete nurse's notes, other inappropriate nursing actions were noted. These included the following:

1. *4 March* "Small amount red-brown drainage from T-tube." According to this description, the drainage was possibly abnormal and the physician should have been notified.

2. *5 March* "Dark black stool." The color of the stool is possibly related to gastrointestinal bleeding; the stool should have been tested for blood (guaiac), charted, and if positive, called to the attention of the physician.

3. *5 March* "Slightly confused this evening." This change in the patient's condition should have been communicated to the physician.

4. *7 March* "Patient pulled intravenous out." Was this related to the mental status change?

5. *7 March* "Abdomen softly distended; T-tube dark-brownish liquid; exertional dyspnea." These significant changes were not reported to the physician.

6. *8 March* "More confusion today, disoriented, diaphoretic." These phrases speak to the deteriorating condition of Patient L, and the nursing supervisor should have been notified in order to obtain help for patient.

7. *9 March* "Very lethargic and icteric; incontinent of urine; bloody drainage at T-tube; patient is breathing rapid and shallow." Nothing was done to obtain help for Patient L.

8. *10 March* "Abdomen distended; incontinent; diaphoretic; expelling gas per puncture site of T-tube; confused; icteric; short of breath." Nothing was done to obtain help for Patient L.

9. *11 March* "Confused and disoriented; extremely jaundiced; abdomen more distended; large and foul-smelling drainage; air

bubbling out of T-tube puncture site; incontinent." This certainly is not the expected course of a cholecystectomy in a healthy patient.

10. *12 March* "Large amounts of drainage from dressings; suture line open in center; condition remains poor." Nothing was done to obtain help for Patient L.

11. *13 March* "Abdomen remains distended; large amount of drainage and foul-smelling; condition remains guarded." The nurses still did not seek help for Patient L.

12. *15 March* "Disoriented; icteric; ankles edematous; respirations rapid and shallow; dyspnea on exertion." Patient L needed help by a physician.

13. *16 March* "T-tube draining green fluid; clear liquid seeping from sores on buttocks; black stool." The nurses continued to do nothing to help Patient L.

In addition, many of Patient L's numerous laboratory studies were abnormal. The nursing staff made no attempt to organize the studies into a useful format.

There were also problems regarding medication. As noted on 10 March, there was a physician's order for Luminal (phenobarbital) 30 milligrams by mouth three times a day. The nurses should have questioned this order in light of the patient's condition in general and the possibility of hepatic encephalopathy. It was noted that Patient L was more alert when this drug was discontinued at the second hospital. Patient L was also on Solu-Medrol (methylprednisolone sodium succinate) from 29 February until discharge from the first hospital. This is another medication that the nurses should have questioned, in light of the patient's condition. There was no rationale for the use of steroids in this case. In addition, it is well known by nurses that steroid therapy can lower an individual's resistance to infection because of its immunosuppressive action, and can mask early signs of infection. It is likely that the administration of steroids contributed to Patient L's septic course.

Finally, at the second hospital, Dr. F noted on 18 March that Patient L had "severe Candidiasis of the oropharynx and tonsillar pillar regions." No notation as to this condition was found in the medical record from the first hospital. If nurses had been giving mouth care, this would certainly have been discovered and treated. It is gross laxity for the nursing staff to neglect such basic hygienic measures and to let such a condition develop unmentioned. Furthermore, extensive decubitus ulcers were described upon admission to the second hospital. The admitting physician said: "It looked like he had lain in bed on his back on a standard mattress for a long time and had probably failed to receive proper back care." Decubitus ulcers are preventable by proper nursing care and should not occur.

The nursing staff at the first hospital did chart data that indicated a deteriorating postoperative course. It was interesting to note that none of the physicians' progress notes in the medical record acknowledged or addressed such a state. As a matter of fact, the surgeon, Dr. M, made only four brief entries (28 February, 3, 10, 17 March) in the progress notes, each stating: "Patient doing well."

The nursing staff caring for Patient L recognized that he was failing to improve after a "common" surgical procedure, but they failed to take action to secure appropriate help for him. Nurse S, who cared for Patient L, testified:

> He was sick, very jaundiced, bloated, in pain. . . . Well, from a nursing stand-point, he did not appear to be improving on a day-to-day basis. . . . The incision site deteriorated. . . . A very sick, near-death man . . . he was jaundiced, bloated. He had drainage that was foul-smelling. He was weak . . . and if you really want to know what he looked like, I've never seen a living person in my whole life who looked so nearly gone, even beyond jaundiced and green.

Nurse S also stated that one day she found "no code" written on Patient L's kardex card. She erased the "no code" notation because there was no physician's order for it, nor was there any basis for such an action.

Certainly the seriousness of Patient L's condition was documented again when he was transferred to the second hospital at the request of his family. Nurses have an important responsibility to the patient and need to take action when they feel the care provided by a physician is not adequate.

The plaintiff's case was based on the determination that, within reasonable probability, the departures from the prevailing professional standard of nursing care contributed to the death of Patient L. The case settled with payment to the estate of the plaintiff.

## Case 6–4

# *Increased Intracranial Pressure*

### Problem and Outcome

Patient F, a 51-year-old man, was involved as a pedestrian in a motor-vehicle accident. He developed an intracerebral hematoma which was not treated promptly. The patient remained neurologically impaired.

### The Patient

Patient F was hit in the right flank by a mirror on a moving motor vehicle and was knocked to the ground. At the time of the accident, he was suffering from acute alcoholic intoxication. He had been drinking alcoholic beverages all day because it was his day off, according to his wife. Patient F was attended by a fire-rescue unit and refused to be taken to the hospital. Later that evening, at 11:37 P.M. on 11 March, he was brought to the emergency department because of hematemesis and a syncopal episode.

### Treatment

According to the emergency department record, Patient F was still under the influence of alcohol, very restless, ataxic, and dysarthric. There were two abrasions on the right flank, the abdomen was soft and flat, and vital signs were stable. Bloody material and alcohol were obtained from the stomach by nasogastric tube.

Patient F was admitted to the intensive care unit and he was described as intoxicated. His condition did not improve over time. Forty-eight hours later, Patient F was comatose and vital signs were unstable. At this time (on 13 March at 7:30 P.M.), Patient F was taken to the operating room. A left frontal temporal parietal craniotomy was performed, and an intracerebral hematoma of approximately 60 to 70 milliliters was evacuated. In addition, a left frontal burr hole was made for placement of a Richmond subarachnoid screw to monitor intracranial pressure. The patient tolerated the procedure well and was returned to the intensive care unit.

Postoperatively, Patient F slowly regained consciousness and was noted to have a right hemiparesis, right hemiplegia, and global aphasia. Speech, occupational, and physical therapies were instituted. On 24 March, Patient F was transferred to a medical-surgical floor with 24-hour private-duty nurses. In early May, a postoperative computed tomography (CT) scan demonstrated evidence of developing hydrocephalus. On 10 May, a ventriculoperitoneal shunt was placed.

From the time of the first surgery on 13 March through discharge from the hospital on 15 June, Patient F remained neurologically impaired. During this period of time, nurses frequently utilized the following descriptors: confused; disoriented as to time, place, and person; incoherent babbling; inappropriate responses; violent behavior; agitated; restless; cooperative at times; uncooperative and combative.

At the time of discharge, Patient F was completely aphasic. In addition, he had a right hemiparesis resulting in difficulty in walking and he was totally dependent for all activities of daily living .

### Departures from the Standard of Care

Serious departures from prevailing professional standards of nursing care occurred and included the following:

1. Failure to complete an initial nursing history and nursing assessment
2. Failure to assess the patient systematically from 1:00 A.M., on 12 March through 7:30 P.M. on 13 March
3. Failure to inform the physician of important changes in the patient's condition
4. Failure to inform the nursing supervisor of the patient's deteriorating condition so care could be obtained for the patient's benefit
5. Failure to provide continuity and reinforcement of the physical, speech, and occupational therapies

### Discussion

The nursing care for Patient F, as documented in the medical record for the first forty-eight hours, was inadequate. The initial nurse's note for Patient F was incomplete. A thorough nursing assessment with a nursing history should appear in the medical record. The nursing assessment and history provide the necessary data base for proper formulation of the nursing care plan.

In addition, the nursing history and assessment should have addressed Patient F's alcoholic intoxication. It would have been very helpful to have ascertained from his wife if this intoxicated state was an isolated incident or a chronic problem. Patient response to alcohol differs as to whether consumption is occasional and social, or chronic. This information was not present in the medical record.

Ongoing systematic nursing assessments were incomplete and inadequate. Patient F was admitted to the intensive care unit at 2:00 A.M. on 12 March. At this time, he was described as combative and intoxicated. Vital signs were temperature 99 degrees Fahrenheit (rectal), pulse rate 72, respiratory rate 18, and blood pressure 130/80 mmHg.

Eight hours later he was described as extremely lethargic and unable to follow simple commands. Vital signs were temperature 101.3 degrees Fahrenheit (rectally), pulse rate 76, respiratory rate 24, and blood pressure 140/90 mmHg. Pupils were equal and reactive to light. A physician evaluated Patient F at this time, and he attributed Patient F's condition to "acute alcoholic intoxication."

Twenty-four hours after admission to the hospital, Patient F's condition was essentially unchanged. The lethargy and inability to follow simple commands were again attributed by the physician to acute alcoholic intoxication.

By 7:00 A.M. on 13 March, Patient F's condition began to deteriorate even more. At this time, his pupils became unequal in size, and he was unable to move his right arm or leg. His condition continued to deteriorate until he became comatose with unstable vital signs. The flow sheets developed for analysis of the actual nursing care in this case follow on pages 170–74.

The ability of the nurse to make accurate observations, interpret observations, record observations, and communicate observations is without question the most important element in caring for seriously ill patients. The nurse is the person who remains with the patient to observe for pertinent physiological alterations. The frequency with which nursing observations are made is determined by the patient's condition. The nurse must notify the physician immediately of any significant changes in the patient's condition and must expect the physician to take appropriate action. Early recognition of signs of increased intracranial pressure related to the head injury and/or internal bleeding demand prompt treatment. Alcoholic intoxication complicates nursing assessment, but mental status alterations and physiological alterations must not be attributed to alcoholic intoxication without the careful exclusion of all other causes.

During the first forty-eight hours, the nurses called the physician eight times to inform him of "concerns" regarding Patient F's condition. For each phone call, the physician attributed the neurological status changes to "alcoholic intoxication and alcoholic coma." On admission Patient F had a blood alcohol level of 0.07 grams percent (gm%). If the rate of metabolism of

## Case 6–4 Flow Sheet

**Assessment Standard for Patient**   **Minimum Frequency of Assessment**

| Assessment | Variable | 12 March 1:00 am | 2:00 | 2:15 | 2:30 | 2:45 | 3:00 | 4:00 |
|---|---|---|---|---|---|---|---|---|
| **Neurological status** | Response to stimuli | | | restrained | | | | restrained |
| | Orientation | | | | | | | |
| | Level of consciousness | | | arousable lethargic | | | lethargic | |
| | Response to commands | | combative | | unable to follow simple command | | | |
| | Pupillary response | | | | | | | |
| | Ocular movements | | | | | | | |
| | Motor and sensory function | | | | | | | |
| | Behavioral changes | | intoxicated | | intoxicated | | restless | |
| | Headache and/or seizure | | | | | | | |
| **Respiratory status** | Patency of airway | | | | | | | |
| | Respiratory rate | | 18 | 18 | 18 | | | 22 |
| | Respiratory rhythm | | | regular | | | | |
| | Respiratory character | | | non-labored | | | | |
| | Breath sounds | | | | | | | |
| **Circulatory status** | Heart rate | | 72 | 64 | 64 | | | 84 |
| | Heart rhythm | | | NSR | | | | NSR |
| | Pulse quality | | | | | | | |
| | Blood pressure | | $\frac{130}{80}$ | $\frac{150}{95}$ | $\frac{150}{90}$ | | | $\frac{160}{110}$ |
| | Skin color / temperature | | | hot dry | warm | | | |
| **Renal status** | Urinary output | | | 50 ml | | | | |
| | Character of urine | | | clear yellow | | | | |
| **Fluid status** | Intake-amount and kind | | | | | | | |
| **Thermoregulatory status** | Body temperature | | 99 | 100 | 100 | | | 101 |
| **Gastrointestinal status** | Presence/absence nausea/emesis | | | small amount emesis | | | | |
| | Appearance of abdomen and bowel sounds | | | | | | | |

**(entries indicate assessments that were made)**

| 5:00 | 6:00 | 7:00 | 8:00 | 9:00 | 10:00 | 11:00 | 12:00 pm | 1:00 | 2:00 | 3:00 | 4:00 | 5:00 |
|---|---|---|---|---|---|---|---|---|---|---|---|---|
| | | | | | | restrained | restrained | | | | | |
| | | | | | | | | | | | | |
| | | | | | lethargic | drowsy | | | | | | |
| | | | | | unable to follow simple commands | | | no response to commands | | responds to name | | |
| | | | | | PERLA | | | | | | | |
| | | | | | | | | | | | | |
| | | | moves all extremities | | | | | | | | | |
| intoxicated | | | | | | restless | | restless | | restless combative | | |
| | | | | | | | | | | | | |
| | | | | | | | | | | | | |
| | 20 | | | | 24 | | 24 | | 24 | | 24 | |
| | | | | | | | | | | | | |
| | | | | | | | | | | | | |
| | | | | | | | | | | | clear bilateral | |
| | 80 | | | | 76 | | 72 | | 70 | | 82 | |
| | NSR | | | | NSR | | NSR | | NSR | | NSR | |
| | | | | | | | | | | | | |
| | 160/90 | | | | 140/90 | | 140/80 | | 140/80 | | 130/80 | |
| | | | | | | | | | | | warm dry | |
| | | | | | | | | | | | 500 ml | |
| | | | | | | | | | | | dark amber concentrated | |
| | | | | | | | | | | | | |
| | 101.4 | | | | 101.3 | | 100.8 | | | | 100.6 | |
| | | | | | | small amount emesis | | | | | | |
| | | | | | | | | | | | soft present | |

## Case 6–4 Flow Sheet (continued)

**Assessment Standard for Patient**          **Minimum Frequency of Assessment**

| Assessment | Variable | 12 March 6:00 pm | 7:00 | 8:00 | 9:00 | 10:00 | 11:00 | 12:00 am |
|---|---|---|---|---|---|---|---|---|
| Neurological status | Response to stimuli | | | | | restrained | | opens eyes |
| | Orientation | | | | | | | |
| | Level of consciousness | | | | | | | lethargic |
| | Response to commands | | | | | | | no verbal response |
| | Pupillary response | | | | | | | R=6 mm L=5 mm |
| | Ocular movements | | | | | | | |
| | Motor and sensory function | | | | | | | moves all 4 ex-tremities |
| | Behavioral changes | | | | | restless combative | | |
| | Headache and/or seizure | | | | | | | |
| Respiratory status | Patency of airway | | | | | | | |
| | Respiratory rate | 28 | | 28 | | 28 | | 26 |
| | Respiratory rhythm | | | | | | | regular |
| | Respiratory character | | | | | | | |
| | Breath sounds | | | | | | | R=clear L= rhonchi |
| Circulatory status | Heart rate | 86 | | 76 | | 86 | | 76 |
| | Heart rhythm | NSR | | NSR | | NSR | | NSR |
| | Pulse quality | | | | | | | |
| | Blood pressure | $\frac{140}{90}$ | | $\frac{150}{90}$ | | $\frac{150}{90}$ | | $\frac{138}{84}$ |
| | Skin color / temperature | | | | | | | |
| Renal status | Urinary output | | | | | | | 200 ml |
| | Character of urine | | | | | | | dark amber |
| Fluid status | Intake-amount and kind | | | | | | | |
| Thermoregulatory status | Body temperature | 99.6 | | 101.2 | | 99 | | 101.1 |
| Gastrointestinal status | Presence/absence nausea/emesis | | | | | | | |
| | Appearance of abdomen and bowel sounds | | | | | | | soft hyper-active |

**(entries indicate assessments that were made)**

| 13 March | 1:00 | 2:00 | 3:00 | 4:00 | 5:00 | 6:00 | 7:00 | 8:00 | 9:00 | 10:00 | 11:00 | 12:00 pm | 1:00 |
|---|---|---|---|---|---|---|---|---|---|---|---|---|---|
| | | | | up in bed | | | | | | | | | |
| | | | | | | | | | | | | | |
| | | | | | | | | drowsy | | | | alert | |
| | | | | | | | | does not follow commands | | | | | |
| | reactive equal | | | | | unequal | | unequal | | | | R=4 mm L=2 mm | |
| | | | | | | | | | | | | | |
| | | | | less move-ment R arm + leg | | unable to move right arm and leg | | | | | | unable to move right arm + leg | |
| | | | restless | | | | | restless | | restless | | restless | |
| | | | | | | | | | | | | | |
| | | | | | | | | | | | | | |
| | | 28 | | 32 | | 36 | | 32 | | 34 | 34 | 36 | |
| | | | | | | | | | | | | | |
| | | | | | | | | bilateral rhonchi | | | | | |
| | | 80 | | 82 | | 115 | | 98 | | 96 | | 100 | |
| | | NSR | | NSR | | ST | | NSR | | NSR | | NSR | ST |
| | | | | | | | | | | | | | |
| | | 142/84 | | 148/86 | | 170/102 | | 170/100 | 140/100 | 160/90 | | 170/100 | |
| | | | | | | | | warm dry | | | | | |
| | | | | | | 50 ml | | 50 ml | | | | | |
| | | | | | | dark amber | | dark yellow | | | | | |
| | | | | | | | | | | | | | |
| | | 100.4 | | 100.7 | | 100.4 | | 98.8 | | 100 | | 101.3 | |
| | | | | | | | | | | | | | |
| | | | | | | | | soft active | | | | | |

**Assessment Standard for Patient**      **Minimum Frequency of Assessment**

| Assessment | Variable | 13 March 2:00 pm | 3:00 | 4:00 | 5:00 | 6:00 | 7:00 | 7:30 |
|---|---|---|---|---|---|---|---|---|
| **Neurological status** | Response to stimuli | | | responds to pain only | | | | |
| | Orientation | | | | | | | |
| | Level of consciousness | very lethargic | | comatose | | comatose | | |
| | Response to commands | | | | | | | |
| | Pupillary response | | | R=4 mm L=2 mm | | R=3 mm L=3 mm | fixed | |
| | Ocular movements | | | | | | | |
| | Motor and sensory function | | | moves left side only | | unable to grade | | |
| | Behavioral changes | | | | | | | |
| | Headache and/or seizure | | | | | | | |
| **Respiratory status** | Patency of airway | | | | | | | |
| | Respiratory rate | 36 | | 40 | | 36 | unstable | |
| | Respiratory rhythm | | | | | | | |
| | Respiratory character | | | labored | | | | |
| | Breath sounds | | | bilateral rales | | | | |
| **Circulatory status** | Heart rate | 116 | 120 | 124 | | 100 | unstable | |
| | Heart rhythm | ST | ST | ST | | ST | | |
| | Pulse quality | | | unstable | | | | |
| | Blood pressure | 160/90 | 150/80 | 170/90 | | 160/100 | unstable | |
| | Skin color / temperature | | | flushed warm dry | | | | |
| **Renal status** | Urinary output | | | | | | | |
| | Character of urine | | | | | | | |
| **Fluid status** | Intake-amount and kind | | | | | | | |
| **Thermoregulatory status** | Body temperature | 101 | | 101.3 | | | 101.8 | |
| **Gastrointestinal status** | Presence/absence nausea/emesis | | | | | | | |
| | Appearance of abdomen and bowel sounds | | | distended | | | | |

alcohol had been considered, it would have been obvious to the nursing staff that, after a maximum of five hours, Patient F would have metabolized the alcohol. Thus, his neurological status changes could no longer be attributed to this etiology.

In addition, the physician only saw Patient F eight hours after admission and two hours prior to the first surgery. Testimony by the physician revealed that he did not see Patient F the next day after admission because "the patient was obviously intoxicated; it was Saturday and I usually don't see patients that aren't sick. . . . I had family commitments . . . it was my son's birthday."

Patient F should have been seen by a physician at the latest on 13 March at 7:00 A.M., with active intervention instituted. When a physician is informed of a problem, appropriate intervention is expected. The nursing staff felt that Patient F was not receiving adequate care from his physician, but they did not notify the nursing supervisor. The nursing staff failed to take appropriate action to secure additional help for Patient F when he needed it.

Finally, while Patient F was receiving postoperative intensive physical, occupational, and speech therapies, there was no mention of how the nurses were incorporating these prescriptions into daily care. The nurse has an important responsibility to reinforce these therapies by incorporating specific activities throughout the day, and then to record the patient's progress.

The plaintiff's case was based on the determination that, within reasonable probability, the departures from the prevailing professional standard of nursing care contributed to the permanent neurological impairment suffered by Patient F. The case settled with payment to the plaintiff.

## Case 6–5

### *Torn Thoracic Aorta*

#### Problem and Outcome

Patient C, a twelve-year-old girl, died from an undiagnosed torn thoracic aorta. Excessive chest tube bleeding was "watched" by the child's physician and nurses. Intervention was not attempted until it was too late.

#### The Patient

Patient C was brought to the emergency department on 4 May at 8:30 P.M. after a motor-vehicle accident. She was a passenger in the front seat of a vehicle that was struck broadside by a second vehicle. Patient C was not wearing a seat belt.

## Treatment

After evaluation in the emergency department, it was determined that Patient C had a possible closed head injury, multiple lacerations of the scalp and face including the periorbital areas, a compound fracture of the nasal bone, a fracture of the clavicle, multiple bony injuries to the pelvis, and a fracture of the shaft of the femur. Peritoneal lavage was positive for red blood cells. An intravenous pyelogram (IVP) and cystogram revealed a ruptured bladder.

After administering five liters of fluid and three units of packed red blood cells intravenously, the patient's blood pressure was stabilized to 140/80 mmHg, and Patient C was taken to the operating room for an exploratory laparotomy and repair of the bladder. When the abdomen had been closed, the nasal fracture was reduced and facial lacerations were repaired. During the later part of the procedure, the anesthesiologist had some difficulty in bagging the patient and a stat chest X-ray was obtained. This revealed a large left hemothorax, and a chest tube was placed with immediate evacuation of 1,200 milliliters of blood. No active bleeding was noted.

The patient was transferred to the recovery room at 1:15 A.M. Hypotension became a problem along with a "large" right hemothorax. Patient C expired at 6:00 A.M. on 5 May. Autopsy revealed that Patient C had a torn thoracic aorta.

## Departures from the Standard of Care

Departures from prevailing professional standards of nursing care were evident and included the following:

1. Failure to perform systematic nursing assessments
2. Failure to inform the nursing supervisor or another physician on the team of the patient's deteriorating condition

## Discussion

Patient C was transferred to the recovery room at 1:15 A.M., where Buck's extension traction was applied for stabilization of the femur fracture. The patient became very hypotensive at 1:30 A.M. Also noted at this time was the fact that the right breast and subcutaneous tissue were quite indurated when compared with the left side. At 1:45 A.M., a stat chest X-ray indicated a large hemothorax, this time on the right side. A chest tube was placed, and 2,500 milliliters of blood "spurted out." Vital signs continued to deteriorate.

The postoperative nursing care that Patient C received was inadequate and incomplete. Testimony by the nurse caring for Patient C revealed that a family practice physician was in attendance constantly from 1:30 A.M. on 5 May. The physician was aware that the left chest tube was "draining a substantial amount, like 2,000 milliliters" in addition to the 2,500 milliliters that "spurted out" of the right chest tube upon insertion. The nurse further testified that the physician "reassured me" and said that the patient "only needs more fluid." This nurse admitted that she was aware that the chest tube drainage was excessive, and that she was concerned, but she made no attempt to contact the nursing supervisor and/or another physician regarding the situation. The family-practice physician did not call a thoracic surgeon until 3:30 A.M. By this time, Patient C's condition was such that she was no longer stable for surgery.

In addition, the nurse testified that hourly nursing assessments were sufficient in the recovery room for this patient "because the doctor was here." The nurse should have performed neurological, respiratory, circulatory, renal, fluid, wound, and gastrointestinal status assessments at least every fifteen minutes, based upon the data in the chart. She further testified that "90 percent of the nurse's notes were written after [Patient C] died because we didn't have time."

Analysis of the case by physician experts revealed that timely diagnosis and repair of the torn thoracic aorta would have given Patient C a greater than 50 percent chance of surviving the accident.

The plaintiff's case was based on the determination that, within reasonable probability, the departures from the prevailing professional standard of nursing care contributed to the death of Patient C. The case settled with payment to the parents.

## Chapter 7

# Problems Associated with Nosocomial Infection

The hospital environment harbors a large number of virulent microorganisms that are frequently resistant to antibiotics. Infection not found to be present or incubating at the time that a patient is admitted to the hospital is classified as a hospital-acquired or nosocomial infection.

Despite hospital and government regulations designed to control infection, nosocomial infections still remain a serious threat to hospitalized patients. Patients entering the hospital are at an increased risk of acquiring an infection, not only because of the increased variety and increased concentration of microbial agents but because of decreased patient resistance to infection as a function of illness, invasive procedures, and invasive treatments. Nosocomial infections cause discomfort, extend the length of hospitalization, increase a patient's time away from work and family, cause disability, and even result in death. Nosocomial infections also increase the cost of health care.

Nurses are responsible for providing a safe biological environment for the hospitalized patient by eliminating reservoirs of infection, controlling portals of exit and entry, and avoiding actions that transmit microorganisms. Principles and practices of medical and surgical aseptic technique are fundamental to the nurse's effort to provide a safe biological environment.

In many instances, nosocomial infections can be totally prevented by good nursing care. Defenses against infection, among other things, include scrupulous hand-washing, aseptic technique, maintenance of the integrity of the skin, and preventing the introduction of microorganisms in wounds or during invasive treatments.

The nurse is responsible for a number of treatments and procedures that are invasive. It is essential that the prevention of infection be utmost in the nurse's mind. Maintaining invasive venous, arterial, and central lines, for example, is exclusively a nursing responsibility. The patient is totally dependent on the nurse to provide appropriate care to prevent infection. On occasion, failure of prevention has tragic consequences. In Case 3–1 (Infection of Intravenous Infusion Site) Patient B developed an intravenous infusion site infection because of poor nursing care. Intravenous infusion catheter changes were omitted, and intravenous infusion site care was not provided. The infection was severe; a bacteremia developed which ultimately caused the death of a 46-year-old man.

The two cases in this chapter are concerned with infections that could have been prevented by proper nursing care.

## Case 7–1

### *Infection of Intravenous Infusion Site and Amputation*

#### Problem and Outcome

An above-the-knee amputation in a 57-year-old woman was the result of an infected intravenous infusion site.

#### The Patient

Several episodes of transient weakness and numbness of the extremities over a two-day period prompted Patient V to seek medical attention. Past medical history revealed chronic atrial fibrillation and hypertension.

#### Treatment

Patient V was admitted to the hospital on 24 April with the diagnosis of transient ischemic attacks. A computed tomography (CT) scan demonstrated only cortical atrophy, but Patient V was, nonetheless, started on full-dose heparin.

On 28 April, while in the echocardiogram laboratory, Patient V developed a rapid heart rate which degenerated into ventricular tachycardia and then into ventricular fibrillation with cardiac arrest. Resuscitation efforts were successful, and the patient was transferred to the coronary care unit.

On this day, sometime after the cardiac arrest, it was noted that the patient's right lower extremity was cold to touch, mottled, blue, and pulseless. It was believed that an embolus from a thrombus, visualized earlier in the left ventricle of the heart, migrated to the right lower extremity. A vascular surgery consultation was obtained. The patient's right lower extremity improved with return of color and doppler ultrasound pulses.

On 1 May, phlebitis of the right arm at the intravenous infusion site and an elevated body temperature were added to the problem list. On 2 May, Patient V embolized again to the right lower extremity. This time, surgical intervention was necessary. A right femoral artery embolectomy for a thrombus to the common femoral artery was performed on 2 May.

Postoperatively, an infection in the anterior compartment of the right leg developed, but after treatment with antibiotics, Patient V was discharged from the hospital on 4 June.

Patient V presented to the emergency department of the hospital at 1:00 A.M. on 8 June with an elevated temperature and a right lower extremity with fluid and fluctuance in the anterior compartment, along with the lower aspect of the extremity draining hemopurulent fluid. She was admitted to the hospital and taken to the operating room on 8 June for an incision and drainage of the infected anterior compartment of the right leg.

On 17 June, redebridement of the right leg was performed. Involvement of the posterior and lateral compartments with extensive myonecrosis was also evident during this surgical procedure. An above-the-knee amputation of the right leg was performed on 18 June. Rehabilitation was initiated, and Patient V was discharged home on 2 July.

### Departures from the Standard of Care

Serious departures from prevailing professional standards of nursing care existed during Patient V's two hospitalizations. The deviations that occurred from 25 April through 4 June include the following:

1. Failure to record the site, size, and type of intravenous infusion catheters inserted
2. Failure to observe systematically the intravenous infusion sites
3. Failure to change systematically the intravenous infusion administration tubing
4. Failure to clean systematically the intravenous infusion sites and to change dressings
5. Failure to change the intravenous infusion catheter and sites after the maximum of 72 hours
6. Failure to observe systematically the infected right arm
7. Failure to observe systematically the infected right lower extremity
8. Failure to observe systematically the embolectomy incision site
9. Failure to prevent a decubitus ulcer

Deviations that occurred from 8 June through 2 July include the following:

1. Failure to care systematically for the intravenous infusion site
2. Failure to observe systematically the right lower extremity
3. Failure to administer an antibiotic continuously

### Discussion

On 1 May, it was noted in the medical record that "fever and phlebitis" were added to the problem list. Antibiotic therapy commenced on this day. By 2 May, it was noted that the elevated temperature was in fact secondary to the "phlebitis in the right arm at the intravenous infusion site." Blood cultures grew *Staphylococcus aureus*.

The percutaneous insertion of a plastic catheter in a vein breaks the integrity of the skin. Because of this, Patient V was at increased risk for iatrogenically induced problems such as nosocomial infection, infiltration, and inflammation.

The nurse is responsible for the safety of parenteral infusions via intravenous catheters as well as for the comfort of the patient. The safety of an intravenous infusion depends on surgical asepsis in the placement and maintenance of the catheter, accuracy of administration, early detection of complications (e.g., inflammation, infection, infiltration), and preservation of the patient's usable veins.

Review of the medical record revealed that an intravenous infusion was started in the emergency department on 24 April. The site was the "right arm." This intravenous infusion catheter and site was not changed until 1 May, when the "phlebitis" was noted. It is common nursing knowledge that the risk of infection with the plastic indwelling venous catheter increases with the duration of the catheterization, and that the risk of bacteremia secondary to an infected catheter may be as high as 2 percent. *Staphylococcus aureus* is the most common pathogen isolated from catheter tips and from bacteremias related to catheterization. *S. aureus* can disseminate from local lesions by invasion of the bloodstream with spread to any tissue or organ of the body, where it can then produce abscesses.

In addition, prior to 1 May, only one notation was entered in the medical record (on 27 April) regarding intravenous infusion–site care and site appearance; this read, "site OK." No notations were made in reference to intravenous infusion tubing changes.

Scrupulous nursing care of the intravenous infusion site must be rendered to control contamination and prevent the introduction of microorganisms into the bloodstream. Acceptable nursing care for Patient V should have included the following:

1. Use of sterile technique for the insertion of the intravenous infusion catheter along with documentation of the date, time, and type of catheter inserted
2. Observation of the intravenous infusion site at least every eight hours for catheter-related problems along with documentation
   a. Palpation of site for tenderness and/or pain
   b. Observation of site and areas along the course of the vein for redness, swelling, and increased skin temperature
3. Securing the intravenous infusion catheter as needed to decrease motion, which could injure the vein or allow entry of microorganisms into the wound
4. Changing the intravenous infusion administration tubing every 24 hours, along with documentation
5. Observing and recording the amount of fluid infused, kind of fluid infused, and the rate of fluid flow
6. Cleansing the intravenous infusion catheter site every 24 hours, or sooner if the dressing is wet or soiled, and documentation
7. Documentation and changing of the intravenous infusion catheter and its site every 48 to 72 hours (removal of the catheter is mandatory after 72 hours) provided there are no catheter-related complications (the catheter and site are changed at the earliest sign of malfunction or catheter-related complication)
8. Notifying the physician of any signs of infection or inflammation at the intravenous infusion catheter site

During the first hospitalization, only two nursing notations were present in the medical record concerning intravenous infusion-site care and maintenance. During the second hospitalization, there were only six such notations for the entire hospital stay.

Routine wound care of the surgical incision of 2 May (right femoral artery embolectomy) was not described in the nurse's notes. A notation regarding the incision site at least every shift is expected. The only notation was 5 May, which read, "Right groin site with staples—leg red, swollen, hot, tender."

In addition, there were departures from prevailing professional standards of nursing practice related to the assessment of the infectious process in the right arm and right leg. At least every eight hours, a complete and systematic nurse's note should have been written regarding the infectious process in Patient V's right arm and right lower extremity. Nurses know that pain, redness, local warmth, edema, and altered function are cardinal symptoms of infection. The note about the infected extremities should have included a description of the following:

1. Pain (qualitative, quantitative, topographic, and temporal aspects)
2. Areas of redness
3. Appearance of lesions
4. Type and amount of drainage
5. Areas of local increase in temperature
6. Skin color
7. Areas of edema
8. Peripheral pulses (femoral, popliteal, and pedal)
9. Sensory function
10. Blanching sign
11. Motor function

In addition, systemic manifestations of infection, including elevated temperature, chills, diaphoresis, malaise, and anorexia should have been noted each day. Only three and five notations, respectively, for the first and second hospital admissions appeared in the record regarding the infections, and they were incomplete.

Poor nursing care is also reflected by a notation written on 1 June that reads, "broken skin on the heel, appears to be a decubitus." A decubitus ulcer does not develop with proper nursing care.

Finally, on 15 June, Patient V did not receive four doses of Prostaphlin (oxacillin sodium). The medication sheet read "Medication not reordered by physician yet." Patient V had a serious infection, and it was the nurses' responsibility to secure prompt orders so that the antibiotic administration was not interrupted.

The plaintiff's case was based on the determination that, within reasonable probability, proper care of the intravenous infusion site during the first hospitalization would have prevented the infection in Patient V's right arm. It was further determined by an infectious-disease specialist that the infection at the intravenous infusion site caused the infection in the right lower extremity which ultimately led to the above-the-knee amputation. The case settled with payment to the plaintiff.

Case 7–2

## *Infection of Intramuscular Injection Site*

### Problem and Outcome

Failure to use proper sterile technique in the administration of two intramuscular injections in the right, upper, outer quadrant of the gluteus muscle resulted in a severe infection in a 26-year-old woman.

### The Patient

Patient P was admitted to the hospital overnight for observation because of excessive bleeding after a dilatation and curettage. Except for "spotting between periods," Patient P was in excellent health.

### Treatment

The dilatation and curettage was performed on 9 May for diagnostic purposes, and "abnormal" postoperative bleeding was noted. Patient P was admitted to the hospital for observation. Bleeding was within normal limits by 10 May, and Patient P was discharged from the hospital. On the day of discharge, Patient P noticed a red area at each preoperative medication injection site. She informed the nurse and was told that the injection sites were "perfectly normal."

During the next two weeks, Patient P experienced a gradual increase in the size of the area of redness at the injection sites. She also noticed stiffness and soreness in her right leg.

Patient P was readmitted to the hospital on 25 May. Intravenous antibiotic therapy was started, and Patient P was taken to the operating room for an incision and drainage of the infected injection sites. Debridement of the area became essential several days later. Corrective plastic surgery was necessary after the infection was controlled.

### Departures from the Standard of Care

The departure from prevailing professional standards of nursing care in this case was failure to administer the intramuscular injections using proper sterile technique.

### Discussion

Testimony by the nurse, who administered both preoperative injections, confirmed that proper sterile technique was not utilized. Only one needle was used to give both injections. Nurse L said that "the pharmacy had forgotten to send our needles, and there was only one left. . . . Yes, I gave that woman the first shot, and since she had to have another one, I took the needle off the first syringe and put it on the next one and injected it. It's not like I was using a needle from another patient for her."

The plaintiff's case was based on the determination that, within reasonable probability, the failure to utilize proper sterile technique in the administration of the intramuscular injections was the source of the infection. The infection caused Patient P to suffer permanent scarring at the injection sites along with residual pain that radiated down the right leg. The case settled with payment to the plaintiff.

# Chapter 8

# Problems Associated with Equipment and Products

Problems associated with equipment and products are not uncommon in hospitals today, and nurses must be knowledgeable about new and changing technologies. Hospitals make increasing use of sophisticated instrumentation such as bedside hemodynamic monitoring devices and a wide variety of complex equipment. Injury or death to the patient may result from misuse or careless use of equipment and products, or from the use of malfunctioning or poorly maintained equipment. For safe patient care, equipment must be maintained and utilized properly. Nursing education programs provide basic instruction about equipment and products, but it is the nurse's responsibility to learn about new and unfamiliar equipment and products. In addition to periodicals and textbooks, hospital inservice education programs and information furnished by manufacturers provide the necessary resources for the acquisition of this knowledge.

The cases in this chapter illustrate that improper use of standard equipment and products can have catastrophic consequences. A *Chux* pad caused suffocation; a cartridge-needle unit led to severe patient injury; a heating pad caused second- and third-degree burns; and a cardiac monitor did not sound an alarm when asystole occurred. Each of these incidents could have been prevented by the proper use of equipment and products.

## Case 8–1
### *Suffocation*

**Problem and Outcome**

The improper use of a *Chux* pad (a light paper pad with a plastic lining) caused a three-month-old child to suffocate.

**The Patient**

Patient K, an only child, developed tracheobronchitis. The child's parents were relieved when the physician suggested that she should be admitted to the hospital. This child was very special to her parents because the mother had difficulty becoming pregnant. The parents wanted Patient K to have the "best care possible, taking no chances."

## Treatment

Patient K was admitted to a hospital with the diagnosis of tracheo-bronchitis and a rash on the trunk of the body. The infant responded well to treatment over four days and was ready to be discharged home the next morning.

The afternoon before discharge (at 2:30 P.M.), the "infant was found with a *Chux* pad wrapped around the face." The child "was unwrapped" and noted to be "cyanotic and not breathing." Cardiopulmonary resuscitation was instituted but was unsuccessful. The cause of death according to the medical examiner was suffocation due to mechanical airway obstruction.

## Departures from the Standard of Care

Obvious departures from prevailing professional standards of nursing care were evident and included the following:

1. Failure to provide a safe environment
2. Failure to utilize a product properly

## Discussion

The mother had remained at the bedside of Patient K almost continuously each day during the hospitalization. On the day of the incident, however, she left the hospital about noon to go shopping because she was happy her child had recovered and was coming home the next day. When she returned to the hospital at approximately 3:30 P.M., Patient K was dead.

By the time the father arrived at the hospital, around 4:00 P.M., his wife was hysterical. She not only had to cope with the tragic loss of their daughter, but she had to face criticism from the head nurse. Nurse N testified that she was "upset by the event" because "they're [the parents] supposed to notify me when they leave and we would have looked in on the baby more, knowing the mother wasn't there. It's her [the mother's] fault."

Nurses are taught that accidents are the leading cause of death in children and that suffocation is the most frequent accident in children under one year of age.

Investigation of the matter by the medical examiner revealed that the use of a *Chux* pad was a common practice by the nursing staff on this unit to protect linens and "prevent bed changes." The nursing staff placed patients on *Chux* pads who were likely to soil the linens.

This death could have been prevented by the use of appropriate protective padding. A rubberized flannel pad is safe for use with infants and is designed to protect linens for a longer period of time than a *Chux* pad, which is disposable and is designed to be used to protect linens only temporarily, for example, during a short procedure. Furthermore, the use of a light plastic-lined pad for an infant not under continuous observation is totally unacceptable. In this case, it was fatal. Plastic is nonporous, and suffocation can take place in minutes.

The plaintiff's case was based on the determination that the departures from the prevailing professional standard of nursing care caused the death of Patient K. The case settled with payment to the child's parents.

## Case 8–2
## *Amputation*

### Problem and Outcome

A physician ordered an intramuscular injection for an 18-month-old child. Because the nurse used an adult-size cartridge-needle unit, the medication was injected intra-arterially. This ultimately necessitated the partial amputation of the right foot.

### The Patient

Patient M, a child who suffered many upper respiratory infections, was admitted to the hospital on 21 June for outpatient surgery. The diagnosis was chronic bilateral serous otitis media.

### Treatment

The child was taken to the operating room on the day of admission for an adenoidectomy and bilateral myringotomy with tubes. She tolerated the procedure well.

Patient M was taken to the recovery room, and at 8:22 A.M., C-R Bicillin (penicillin G benzathine and penicillin G procaine suspension) was administered "intramuscularly" as ordered. Following the injection, it was noted at 8:40 A.M. that the right lower leg became white and the upper thigh to the groin area became bluish and mottled. Patient M was seen by physicians immediately, and Solu-Cortef (hydrocortisone sodium succinate) and Benadryl (diphenhydramine hydrochloride) was ordered and administered. Patient M was transferred by helicopter to a children's hospital that day at 11:17 A.M.

The child was evaluated, and by 5:30 P.M. the ischemic changes appeared to be progressing. The judgment was that Patient M had a closed compartment syndrome, and she was taken to the operating room for a fasciotomy of the right leg and thigh. The injection site was inspected during surgery and found to be extremely ecchymotic with necrotic muscle.

Postoperatively, the ischemic changes in the right lower extremity had improved, but the toes remained dusky and somewhat cool. Ultimately, Patient M had to have the right toes amputated as well as a portion of the dorsum of the right foot.

### Departures from the Standard of Care

Departures from prevailing professional standards of nursing care in this case included the following:

1. The use of an adult-size cartridge-needle unit for administration of medication in a child
2. Insufficient knowledge of the medication administered
3. Incorrect site and technique of intramuscular injection

### Discussion

During the fasciotomy, the injection site was inspected. Dr. S, the surgeon, testified that the area of injection was in the vastus intermedius muscle. Nurse H testified "I gave it in the anterior lateral aspect of the child's thigh." According to this description, the rectus femoris muscle would have been penetrated. This is incorrect, for the vastus lateralis muscle should be utilized in this procedure for an 18-month-old child.

The vastus lateralis muscle is thick and is free of major nerves and blood vessels. Nurse H did not use the correct procedure for the location of this injection site. According to testimony, she did not utilize the greater trochanter and patella as landmarks, nor did she divide the thigh into thirds. She should have drawn two lines, one down the middle of the anterior thigh, and the other down the midline of the lateral thigh. Had this been done, the correct injection site would have been located in the middle third of the thigh, between these two areas.

Dr. S also noted, during visual inspection of the injection area at surgery, that "It's very suspicious for injection of the profunda femoral artery or superficial femoral . . . because of the location and the amount of bleeding into the muscle. . . . It was deep. It was medial." Nurse H testified that "you hold the injection at an angle of anywhere between 60 or 80 degrees." This is incorrect, because the needle (of appropriate length) must be injected at a 90-degree angle to ensure intramuscular penetration.

Nurse H also stated that "in a small child you usually do not use the whole needle, because some of the kids are so small that the needle would be too big, so you put it in as far as you deem necessary." Even the head nurse of the unit stated, "I wouldn't push the needle in all the way and I wouldn't inject the needle quite straight." This again represents an error in technique because needles come in various lengths and gauges, and one must use the size necessary for a particular type of injection. It is unsafe to utilize a needle that is too long and to guess at the depth of penetration. A medication can easily be withdrawn from a Tubex Cartridge-Needle Unit and placed in a syringe with a needle length and gauge appropriate for administration.

When questioned about potential complications of C-R Bicillin (penicillin G benzathine and penicillin G procaine suspension), Nurse H testified, "The only complication I knew about, if the patient was allergic to penicillin." In addition, Nurse H stated that she was not aware of the risks associated with the intra-arterial injection of C-R Bicillin (penicillin G benzathine and penicillin G procaine suspension). Lack of knowledge about the medication was evident. It is an important responsibility for the nurse to be knowledgeable about a medication before it is administered. Nurse H testified that a *Physicians Desk Reference (PDR)* was available to her in the recovery room. The *PDR* specifies the site for injection of this medication in children and calls attention to the dangers of intravenous and intra-arterial injection, as well as injection into or near major peripheral nerves or blood vessels.

The intra-arterial administration of the C-R Bicillin (penicillin G benzathine and penicillin G procaine suspension) could have been avoided by proper injection technique, which includes accurate location of the injection site, use of the proper length of needle, accurate angle of needle penetration, and aspiration before injecting the contents of the syringe.

The plaintiff's case was based on the determination that, within reasonable nursing probability, the departures from the prevailing professional standard of nursing care caused the injury to the right leg of Patient M. The case settled with payment to the child's parents.

Case 8–3

## *Burn*

### Problem and Outcome

A five-month-old child suffered second- and third-degree burns of his buttocks while in the recovery room.

### The Patient

Patient C, the last-born child among three siblings, was admitted to the hospital for elective surgical correction of a left inguinal hernia. The child's health was excellent, and growth and development were within normal limits.

### Treatment

Patient C was taken to the operating room for a herniorrhaphy on 10 July, and he tolerated the procedure well. While in the recovery room, the child was placed on a heating pad because of "shivering." Later in the day, during a diaper change, large blisters on Patient C's buttocks were noted by the nurse. The child was examined by the physician and deep second- and third-degree burns were diagnosed on both buttocks. Plastic surgery and skin grafts were ultimately required to treat the burns.

### Departures from the Standard of Care

Failure to use equipment (a heating pad) properly was the departure from the prevailing professional standard of nursing care in this case.

### Discussion

The nurse caring for Patient C in the recovery room testified that the infant was "shivering" and she wanted to "warm him fast." She further stated, "We want our patients to be comfortable. With the air conditioning and all, people get cold, and I always use heating pads to get people warmed up."

The use of a standard heating pad under a five-month-old infant is inappropriate because it is not designed for this use. The heating pad in this case even carried a warning label that read: "Caution do not use on an infant, invalid, or a sleeping or unconscious person." Obviously, the use of a blanket or a warmed blanket would have prevented the situation.

The plaintiff's case was based on the determination that the departure from the prevailing professional standard of nursing care caused the burns. The case settled with payment to the child's parents.

## Case 8–4
### *Cardiac Asystole*

### Problem and Outcome

A 52-year-old man was rendered comatose after elective surgery because cardiac monitor alarms were not activated.

### The Patient

Patient J was admitted to the hospital for an elective cholecystectomy. He presented with a history of Grade II mitral valve regurgitation and atrial fibrillation.

### Treatment

Patient J went to surgery on 4 September. He tolerated the procedure well and was taken to the recovery room at 10:30 A.M. As a precaution, because of the heart problem, the physician ordered cardiac monitoring. Upon admission to the recovery room, vital signs were within normal limits, and Patient J was described as awake.

At 12:10 P.M., the charge nurse of the recovery room noticed from the nurses' station that Patient J's cardiac monitor was displaying a flat line. Cardiopulmonary resuscitation commenced, but Patient J remained ventilator-dependent and comatose.

### Departures from the Standard of Care

Departures from prevailing professional standards of nursing care in this case included the following:

1. Failure to activate the alarm system on the cardiac monitor
2. Failure to assess the patient systematically

### Discussion

Patient J was placed on the cardiac monitor promptly upon admission to the recovery room. Vital signs and level of consciousness were assessed every fifteen minutes for the first hour (10:30 A.M. through 11:30 A.M.). During this time, Patient J was "awake but sleepy." Vital signs were stable and within normal limits.

At approximately 11:30 A.M., the nurse assigned to Patient J went to lunch. There were no nursing notes or vital signs in the medical record for the next forty minutes. At 12:10 P.M., the head nurse "glanced at [Patient J's] scope" and noticed that the cardiac monitor was displaying a flat line. She went to Patient J's bedside "to check the leads," but found that he was not breathing and was cyanotic.

No alarm had sounded on the cardiac monitor because the alarm was turned off. Testimony by the recovery room nurse caring for Patient J revealed that "the alarms are routinely turned off because we watch our patients so constantly and alarms aren't necessary. They just make unnecessary work and noise."

The plaintiff's case was based on the determination that, within reasonable probability, the departures from the prevailing professional standard of nursing care contributed to the anoxic brain damage. The case settled with payment to the plaintiff.

# Chapter 9

# Problems Associated with
# Nursing Treatments and Procedures

Nursing malpractice cases occur when nursing treatments or procedures
are omitted or are executed incorrectly. Even mistakes or lapses in such
basic procedures and treatments as turning/positioning or skin care can
create major problems. Basic procedures are frequently regarded as "routine" or "unimportant," and are thus performed with less care and less
understanding than are more complex nursing procedures and treatments.

Many treatments and procedures are *independent* nursing actions. That
is, they are initiated by the nurse and do not require a physician's order
or direction. Systematic nursing assessment, the maintenance of intravenous infusions, skin care, and the provision of patient comfort measures are examples of nursing treatments and procedures that are
independent actions. Nursing knowledge determines the type and frequency of independent nursing treatments and procedures necessary for
patient care. On the other hand, *dependent* nursing actions require a physician's order or supervision. Examples of treatments and procedures that
are dependent actions include intravenous infusion therapy prescription,
urinary catheterization, heating pad application, and medication prescription.

Seven of the eight cases discussed in this chapter required independent nursing interventions in the form of a nursing procedure or treatment. A physician's order or direction was not necessary. Basic nursing
care was at issue. Four of these seven cases involved turning/positioning
and skin care, while the other three cases were concerned with the maintenance of immobilization, proper suctioning, and preventing intravenous
infusion infiltration. The one case that did require a physician's order for
a nursing procedure concerned tracheotomy care.

Case 9–1
## *Sciatic Nerve Injury*

### Problem and Outcome

A 53-year-old woman sustained a sciatic nerve injury while in the intensive care unit. This resulted in a permanent partial disability in the form of chronic pain and a limp.

### The Patient

Patient B, a schoolteacher, was admitted to the hospital with the diagnosis of coronary artery disease. Prior to admission she had suffered an acute anterior wall myocardial infarction and was "not well in general."

### Treatment

Cardiac catheterization revealed arteriosclerotic coronary artery disease, a subtotal occlusive lesion of the anterior descending branch of the left coronary artery, and an occlusive lesion of the proximal right coronary artery. A double aortic coronary artery bypass was performed, and the patient tolerated the procedure well.

Postoperatively, Patient B progressed uneventfully from the cardiac surgery, but she developed left hip pain, decreased ability to move the left leg, and left leg numbness. These abnormal sensory and motor functions of the left leg persisted, and Patient B was discharged from the hospital with a limp and chronic pain in that extremity.

### Departures from the Standard of Care

Review of the case revealed the following departures from prevailing professional standards of nursing care:

1. Failure to execute the physician's order to turn the patient every two hours postoperatively
2. Failure to position the patient properly in the intensive care unit

### Discussion

On the second postoperative day, when Patient B was ambulatory, a problem with the left leg was evident. A number of consultants attended Patient B and evaluated the left lower extremity. The problem was diagnosed as that of sciatic nerve injury. Injection was ruled out as a cause of the sciatic nerve injury because Patient B had not received any intramuscular injections in the buttocks prior to the problem. A fall or preexisting injury was also ruled out, and the left sciatic nerve injury (left sciatic palsy) was ultimately attributed to prolonged pressure over the sciatic nerve region. Improper positioning of the patient and/or maintaining a particular position for an extended period of time will create pressure and may cause such a nerve injury.

Careful positioning of the patient for surgery is particularly important because the anesthetic agent renders the patient unconscious. During normal sleep (nonanesthesia-induced), if the blood supply to a nerve is decreased due to pressure, the sleeper awakens or changes position during sleep. For surgery, special attention must be directed to the patient's proper body alignment, minimizing pressure over bony prominences and preventing unnecessary compression of tissues. Detailed documentation by the circulating nurse was present in the medical record regarding patient-positioning and protection of pressure points in the operating room. The operating room was, therefore, ruled out as the source of injury to Patient B.

Positioning of the patient during the postanesthesia period is also very important. A patient may not change position because of pain or altered consciousness, and unrelieved pressure over time may cause nerve injury. Postoperative cardiac surgery patients should be turned slowly and gently and repositioned at least every two hours.

The nurse caring initially for Patient B testified that she did not take the surgery "pull sheets" out from under the patient until the end of the shift (eight and one-half hours after surgery). Furthermore, in response to a question, this nurse stated that the sheets under the patient were "of course, wrinkled and wadded up." Wrinkled sheets under a patient may not only cause generalized discomfort, but they may exert undue pressure on tissues and thereby decrease circulation. This may lead to ischemia in the surrounding structures.

The physician wrote an order that Patient B was to be turned every two hours postoperatively. The medical record, however, contained no documentation regarding turning and positioning of Patient B. The nurse caring for Patient B on the next shift stated, "We do not routinely turn any of the open-heart patients." This statement was in conflict with acceptable standards of nursing care as well as with the physician's order. In this case, it was not necessary for the physician to write an order for such basic nursing care. He did, however, but the patient still did not receive the proper nursing care.

The plaintiff's case was based on the determination that within reasonable nursing probability, the departures from the prevailing professional standard of nursing care caused Patient B's permanent partial disability. The case settled with payment to the plaintiff.

## Case 9–2
### *Decubitus Ulcer*

#### Problem and Outcome
A 54-year-old woman developed a large sacral decubitus ulcer postoperatively. Multiple surgical procedures were required to correct the defect caused by the decubitus ulcer.

#### The Patient
Patient L had successfully raised three children as a single parent. She also had founded and was running a thriving catering business based in her home.

#### Treatment
On the evening of 30 October, Patient L experienced severe abdominal pain and was taken to the hospital emergency department. Prior to this, she was in excellent health except for obesity (height 5 feet 6 inches and weight 195 pounds). After evaluation, she was admitted in critical condition with the diagnosis of a strangulated umbilical hernia that had perforated the bowel. Emergency surgery was performed, and she tolerated the procedure well.

After spending five days in the intensive care unit, Patient L was transferred to a surgical floor. At this time, the nurse's note stated that there was an eight-centimeter-by-eight-centimeter area of excoriation in the sacral area. This area subsequently became severely infected and necessitated multiple surgical procedures for correction. Patient L was not discharged from the hospital until 5 December.

#### Departures from the Standard of Care
Departures from prevailing professional standards of nursing care in this case involved the following:

1. Failure to turn and position the patient every two hours in the intensive care unit
2. Failure to maintain the integrity of the skin

## Discussion

According to the medical record, Patient L was not turned on a regular basis while in the intensive care unit. Special attention should have been directed at maintaining the integrity of the skin, because Patient L was a prime candidate for the development of decubitus ulcers owing to (1) the large abdominal incision restricting movement, and (2) profound obesity.

According to testimony by the intensive care unit nurses, they experienced "great difficulty in turning or moving [Patient L] because of the obesity, and she didn't want to move." Given this condition, the nurses should have placed Patient L on an alternating-pressure mattress and should have formulated a plan for turning the patient at regular intervals as well as an intensive plan for systematic skin care. There was no documentation in the medical record regarding skin care or the use of a specialized mattress to relieve pressure points. Only one notation was made regarding turning and repositioning the patient.

The area of excoriation in the sacral region was not noted until Patient L was transferred to the surgical unit (five days postoperatively). It was also noted that this finding was new because, according to the initial nursing admission assessment, Patient L did not have any prior skin lesions. Again, on the surgical unit, the medical record did not include a plan of nursing care for systematic treatment of the area of excoriation.

Three days after admission to the surgical unit, the nurse's notes read, "Area of skin breakdown much larger, very red, and draining purulent-like material." The infection became severe, prolonging hospitalization and necessitating multiple corrective surgical procedures.

This situation caused the patient a lot of anxiety, not only because of the decubitus ulcer but because of lost business. Patient L was most concerned about her business because, as she stated, "Thanksgiving and Christmas are my busiest times. And you know, when I do a good job for someone at this time, they call me back to make parties the rest of the year. They tell their friends. That's the way I get a lot of work."

The decubitus ulcer could have been prevented by good nursing care. "Decubitus ulcer" should be a term found only in nursing history texts, for one should never see such a lesion today.

The plaintiff's case was based on the determination that, within reasonable nursing probability, the departures from the prevailing professional standard of nursing care caused the decubitus ulcer. The case settled with payment to the plaintiff.

## Case 9–3
### *Paraplegia*

### Problem and Outcome

Failure to maintain immobilization of the spine resulted in a 32-year-old man becoming paraplegic.

### The Patient

Patient R was involved in a motorcycle accident on 19 March. He was brought to the hospital on a backboard with his head sandbagged, and he was admitted to the emergency department at 7:15 P.M. He had sustained multiple injuries, including facial, neck, and chest abrasions and lacerations; fractures of ribs 8–12; multiple pelvic fractures; and compound fractures of both arms.

### Treatment

After evaluation, Patient R was taken to the operating room at 10:45 P.M. for repair of facial lacerations, open reduction with internal fixation of the arm fractures, and chest tube placement. From there, he was admitted to the intensive care unit. By 11:15 A.M. on 20 March, Patient R was paraplegic. Immediate neurosurgical evaluation and spinal X-rays revealed comminuted fractures of thoracic vertebrae five and six (T5–6). Spinal stabilization was accomplished, but Patient R remained paraplegic.

### Departures from the Standard of Care

Departures from prevailing professional standards of nursing care included the following:

1. Failure to maintain immobilization of the patient, until spinal injury was ruled out
2. Failure to make a systematic and complete initial nursing assessment and history
3. Failure to make systematic nursing observations from 7:15 P.M. on 19 March through 11:15 A.M. on 20 March

## Case 9–3 Flow Sheet

| Assessment Standard for Patient | | Minimum Frequency of Assessment | | | | | |
|---|---|---|---|---|---|---|---|
| **Assessment** | **Variable** | 19 March 7:15 pm | 7:30 | 7:45 | 8:00 | 8:15 | 8:30 |
| **Respiratory status** | Patency of airway | | | | | | |
| | Respiratory rate | 28 | | 28 | | 24 | 24 |
| | Respiratory rhythm | | | | | | |
| | Respiratory character | | | | | | |
| | Breath sounds | decreased breath sounds | | | | | |
| | Chest tube drainage (amount/character) | NA | NA | NA | bloody | | bloody |
| **Circulatory status** | Heart rate | 113 | 108 | 101 | 96 | 97 | 101 |
| | Heart rhythm | | | | | | |
| | Pulse quality | | | | | | |
| | Blood pressure | $\frac{127}{68}$ | $\frac{105}{71}$ | $\frac{104}{71}$ | $\frac{143}{72}$ | $\frac{130}{68}$ | $\frac{134}{70}$ |
| | Skin color/temperature | | | | | | |
| | Central venous pressure (cmHOH) | NA | NA | 2.5 | | | |
| | Forearm circulation | good | | | | | |
| **Neurological status** | Response to stimuli | | | | | | |
| | Orientation | confused | | | | | |
| | Level of consciousness | awake | | | | | |
| | Response to commands | | | | | | |
| | Pupillary response | PERL | | | | | |
| | Ocular movement | | | | | | |
| | Motor function | | | | | | |
| | Sensory function | | | | | | |
| | Behavioral changes | | | | | | |

| 8:45 | 9:00 | 9:15 | 9:30 | 9:45 | 10:00 | 10:15 | 10:30 | 10:45 | In OR | to ICU 1:00 am | 20 March 1:15 |
|---|---|---|---|---|---|---|---|---|---|---|---|
| | | | | | | | | | | | |
| 22 | | 20 | 28 | | 32 | | 32 | | | 16 | |
| | | | | | | | | | | | |
| | | | | | | | | | | | |
| | | | | | | | | | | | |
| | | | | | | | | | 300 ml | | |
| 101 | 108 | 108 | 110 | | 59 | | 114 | 113 | | 90 | |
| | | | | | | | | | | | |
| | | | | | | | | | | | |
| $\frac{118}{59}$ | $\frac{125}{60}$ | $\frac{120}{58}$ | $\frac{104}{49}$ | | $\frac{80}{64}$ | $\frac{129}{59}$ | $\frac{124}{57}$ | $\frac{139}{78}$ | | $\frac{130}{70}$ | |
| | | | | | | | | | | | |
| | | | | | re-inserted | | | | | | |
| | | | | | | | | | | | |
| | | | | | unre-sponsive | | | | | | |

## Case 9–3 Flow Sheet (continued)

**Assessment Standard for Patient**  **Minimum Frequency of Assessment**

| Assessment | Variable | 20 March 1:30 am | 1:45 | 2:00 | 2:15 | 2:30 | 2:45 |
|---|---|---|---|---|---|---|---|
| **Respiratory status** | Patency of airway | intubated | | | | | |
| | Respiratory rate | 20 | | 12 | | | |
| | Respiratory rhythm | | | | | | |
| | Respiratory character | | | | | | |
| | Breath sounds | rales rhonchi | | | | | |
| | Chest tube drainage (amount/character) | large amount blood | | | sero-sanguinous | | |
| **Circulatory status** | Heart rate | 90 | | 96 | | | |
| | Heart rhythm | NSR ST | | | | | |
| | Pulse quality | | | | | | |
| | Blood pressure | $\frac{130}{80}$ | | $\frac{119}{93}$ | | | |
| | Skin color/temperature | pale | | | | | |
| | Central venous pressure (cmHOH) | | | | | | |
| | Forearm circulation | good | | | | | |
| **Neurological status** | Response to stimuli | unre-sponsive | | | | | |
| | Orientation | | | | | | |
| | Level of consciousness | | | | responsive | | |
| | Response to commands | | | | answers questions appropriately | | |
| | Pupillary response | PERL | | | | | |
| | Ocular movement | | | | | | |
| | Motor function | moving arms + legs | | | | | |
| | Sensory function | normal | | | | | |
| | Behavioral changes | | | | | | |

(entries indicate assessments that were made)

| 3:00 | 3:30 | 4:00 | 4:30 | 5:00 | 5:30 | 6:00 | 6:30 | 7:00 | 7:30 | 8:00 | 8:30 |
|---|---|---|---|---|---|---|---|---|---|---|---|
| | | | | attempting to pull out ET tube | | | | intubated | | | |
| | | 16 | | 14 | | 12 | | | | $\frac{0}{12}$ | |
| | | | | | | | | | | | |
| | | | | | | | | | | | |
| | | | | | | | | bilateral rales & rhonchi | | | |
| | | | | | | total 500 ml | | | | | |
| 88 | | 90 | | 82 | | 84 | | | | 82 | |
| | | | | | | | | RSR | | | |
| | | | | | | | | | | | |
| $\frac{88}{50}$ | $\frac{88}{50}$ | $\frac{110}{70}$ | | $\frac{110}{60}$ | | $\frac{110}{70}$ | | | | $\frac{96}{74}$ | |
| | | | | | | | | | | | |
| 2.5 | | | | | pulled out | | | | | | |
| good | | good | | good | | | | good | | good | |
| | | | | | | | | lethargic | | | |
| | | | | | | | | | | | |
| | | | | | | | | awake | | | |
| | | answers questions appropriately | | | | | | | | | |
| | | | | | | | PERLA | | | | |
| | | | | | | | | | | | |
| | | | | | | | good | | | | |
| | | | | | | | good | | | | |
| | | | | agitated | | agitated | | | | | |

## Case 9–3 Flow Sheet (continued)

**Assessment Standard for Patient**     **Minimum Frequency of Assessment**

| Assessment | Variable | 20 March 9:00 am | 9:30 | 10:00 | 10:30 | 11:00 | 11:15 |
|---|---|---|---|---|---|---|---|
| **Respiratory status** | Patency of airway | | | | | | |
| | Respiratory rate | $\frac{0}{12}$ | | $\frac{0}{12}$ | | $\frac{0}{12}$ | |
| | Respiratory rhythm | | | | | | |
| | Respiratory character | | | | | | |
| | Breath sounds | | | | | | |
| | Chest tube drainage (amount/character) | | | | | | |
| **Circulatory status** | Heart rate | 108 | | 86 | | 84 | |
| | Heart rhythm | | | RSR | | | |
| | Pulse quality | | | | | | |
| | Blood pressure | $\frac{98}{70}$ | | $\frac{80}{62}$ | $\frac{92}{66}$ | $\frac{82}{60}$ | |
| | Skin color/temperature | | | | | | |
| | Central venous pressure (cmHOH) | | | | | | |
| | Forearm circulation | | | | | | |
| **Neurological status** | Response to stimuli | | | | | | |
| | Orientation | | | | | | |
| | Level of consciousness | | | | | | |
| | Response to commands | | | | | | |
| | Pupillary response | | | | | | |
| | Ocular movement | | | | | | |
| | Motor function | | | | | | unable to move legs |
| | Sensory function | | | | | | no sensation below nipples |
| | Behavioral changes | | | | | | |

## Discussion

According to the medical record, Patient R was transported to the hospital on a backboard, and he remained on it in the emergency department. But by the time Patient R had been admitted to the intensive care unit, the backboard had disappeared. There was no further reference to it. Testimony by Nurse G of the intensive care unit read, "We discussed whether spinal precautions should be taken but we decided it wasn't necessary because there was no backboard. He was moving everything fine so it wasn't really necessary." If the medical record had been reviewed by the nurse caring for Patient R, the missing backboard would have been evident. The backboard issue then could have been clarified with the physician.

In addition, Nurse G stated that she was told in report by Nurse B, the emergency department nurse, that she "felt" there was no spinal cord injury. Later, Nurse B testified that she said this in report because she was told "by someone" that cervical spine X-rays were within normal limits. The cervical, thoracic, and lumbar spinal X-rays ordered by the physician in the emergency department were in all probability never done. No spinal X-rays from that evening were ever found. In addition, the patient's name appeared in the radiology log book for skull, chest, extremity, and pelvic X-rays, but not for spinal X-rays.

Throughout the night of 19 March, the nurses charted that Patient R was "restless and sitting up in bed." Neurological status assessments were inadequate. The flow sheet developed and used for analysis of the actual nursing care in this case is on pages 200–4 and 206–7. The head of bed had been elevated 30 degrees throughout the night, and there were two references to Patient R "trying to get out of bed." At 8:00 A.M. on 20 March the nurses charted that Patient R was "found sitting on the side of the bed kicking his legs." Vital signs and a complaint of pain were the only other nursing notations in the chart until 11:15 A.M. when the nurse noted, "[Dr. S] visited—states patient is paraplegic. Patient unable to move lower extremities and has no sensation below nipples."

During the discovery period in litigation, it was revealed by the hospital that the neurological watch sheets were mysteriously missing from the chart. Testimony by the involved nurses, however, indicated that special neurological watch sheets were not in use at that hospital until after Patient R had been discharged. Nursing testimony also indicated that the attending physician's admission order sheet was a copy of the original because it had no addressograph stamp, and it was not signed off by the nurse who transcribed all the orders (from other physicians) that evening.

## Case 9–3 Flow Sheet (continued)

**Assessment Standard for Patient**  **Minimum Frequency of Assessment**

| Assessment | Variable | 19 March 7:15 pm | 7:30 | 7:45 | 8:00 | 9:00 | 10:00 |
|---|---|---|---|---|---|---|---|
| **Wound status** | Description of trauma | multiple lacerations and abrasions of face, chest, neck | | | | | |
| | Character of drainage | | | | | | |
| | Amount of drainage | | | | | | |
| | Condition of dressings/ suture lines | | | | | | |
| **Renal status** | Urinary output | | 250 ml | | | | |
| | Character of urine | | clear | | | | |
| **Fluid status** | Intake-amount/kind | 1000 ml LR ↑ | 1000 ml LR ↑ | 1000 ml LR ↑ | 1000 ml LR ↑ | 1000 ml LR ↑ | 1000 ml LR ↑ wide open |
| | Intake vs. output | | | | | | |
| | Estimated fluid loss | | | | | | |
| **Pain status** | Qualitative aspects | | | | | | |
| | Quantitative aspects | | | | | | |
| | Topographic aspects | | | | | | |
| | Temporal aspects | | | | | | |
| | General level of comfort | | | | | | |
| **Gastrointestinal status** | Appearance of abdomen | | | | abdominal girth 31¾" | | |
| | Bowel sounds | | | | | | |
| | Presence/absence nausea, emesis | | | | | | |
| | Nasogastric tube drainage | | | | bloody | | |
| **Thermoregulatory status** | Body temperature | | | | | | |

**(entries indicate assessments that were made)**

| In OR | 20 March 1:00 am | 2:00 | 3:00 | 4:00 | 5:00 | 6:00 | 7:00 | 8:00 | 9:00 | 10:00 | 11:00 |
|---|---|---|---|---|---|---|---|---|---|---|---|
| | ecchymosis both eyes | | severe scrotal edema | | severe scrotal edema | | ecchymosis face, chest neck | | | | |
| | | | | | | | | | | | |
| EBL= 150 ml | | | | | | | | | | | |
| | lacerations cleaned | | | | | | | | | | |
| | 50 ml | 130 ml | 120 ml | 440 ml | 420 ml | 200 ml | | | | | |
| | concentrated amber | | yellow | | | | | | | | |
| | 75 ml | | | | 300 ml | 200 ml | | | | | |
| | | | | | | | | | | | |
| | | | | | | | | | | | |
| | complains of pain | | | | | | | | complains of pain | | |
| | | | | | | | | | | | |
| | right hand | | | | | | | | generalized | | |
| | | | | | | | | | | | |
| | | | | | restless | restless | | | restless | | |
| | soft nondis-tended | | | | | | soft flat | | | | |
| | present | | | | | | faint | | | | |
| | | | | | | | | | | | |
| | small amount brown | | | | | | positive for occult blood | | | | |
| | 97.8 | 97 | | | 99 | | | 99.4 | | | |

A physician's order to maintain the backboard was written on it by the attending physician.

The nurse is a key person when caring for the multiple injured patient. The first twenty-four hours are critical for the spinal-cord–injured patient, because damage can be prevented, arrested, or reversed. The simple task of maintaining spinal immobilization for "potential" spinal cord injury was not accomplished.

The plaintiff's case was based on the determination that within reasonable probability, the departures from the prevailing professional standard of nursing care caused Patient R to become paraplegic. The case settled with payment to the plaintiff.

## Case 9–4
### *Decubitus Ulcers*

#### Problem and Outcome

Patient H, a 68-year-old woman, was another unfortunate patient who developed decubitus ulcers. In this case, the physician wrote specific orders for skin care, but they were not executed. Patient H required complex skin grafting to correct the damage done by the ulcers.

#### The Patient

Patient H was admitted to the hospital for treatment of a spiral fracture of the right femur. Her medical history was complex because she suffered from hypertension, chronic obstructive pulmonary disease, atrial fibrillation, and type I diabetes mellitus.

#### Treatment

The fracture of the femur was treated successfully with Bucks extension traction followed by surgery. Patient H developed sacral decubitus ulcers, however, which required skin grafting, prolonging her hospitalization.

#### Departures from the Standard of Care

Departures from prevailing professional standards of care were as follows:

1. Failure to maintain the integrity of the skin
2. Failure to follow the physician's orders regarding skin care

## Discussion

The physician caring for Patient H noted, "Patient susceptible to the formation of decubitus ulcers." He wrote orders directed at this concern which read, "Turn patient every two hours. Massage pressure points when turning. Report any areas of redness at pressure points."

Review of the medical record disclosed that the nurses did not execute the physician's orders regarding skin care. Furthermore, there was no nursing notation in the record regarding skin care, turning, or skin condition until there was actual skin breakdown. The nurses caring for Patient H were of the opinion that the physician's orders had been executed and that the development of the decubitus ulcers was "sudden." The staff nurses' attitude was indicated in testimony of the charge nurse that "skin care is always given, but my nurses are too busy to chart insignificant routine stuff."

Again the development of the decubitus ulcers should have been prevented. In this case, the physician actually prescribed the proper nursing care to prevent decubitus ulcers, but the prescription was ignored by the nursing staff. A physician should not have to write orders for basic nursing care, for that is a primary nursing responsibility.

The plaintiff's case was based on the determination that the departures from the prevailing professional standard of nursing care caused the decubitus ulcers. The case settled with payment to the plaintiff.

## Case 9–5
### *Tracheal Stenosis*

#### Problem and Outcome

Failure to deflate the cuff on a tracheotomy tube resulted in necrosis, infection, and tracheal stricture. Because of the stricture, a 40-year-old man must live with a permanent tracheotomy.

#### The Patient

Patient H, a store clerk, was admitted to the hospital for a tonsillectomy, uvulectomy, and pharyngoplasty to treat sleep apnea syndrome. The patient was obese (weight 275 pounds, height 5 feet 5 inches) and had a history of type II diabetes mellitus and intermittent asthma.

### Treatment

Surgery, including a prophylactic tracheotomy, was performed on 26 August. Subsequently, the tracheotomy site became infected, and tracheal stenosis developed. Surgical interventions to correct the tracheal stenosis were unsuccessful because of severe tissue damage from the infection. Patient H remains today with a permanent tracheotomy.

### Departures from the Standard of Care

Departures from prevailing professional standards of nursing care in this case included the following:

1. Failure to assess tracheotomy cuff pressure
2. Failure to deflate the tracheotomy cuff in a timely manner
3. Failure to perform tracheotomy care at least every eight hours
4. Failure to inform the physician of a significant change in the patient's condition

### Discussion

Postoperatively, Patient H was admitted to the intensive care unit with a tracheotomy. The cuff on the tracheotomy tube was inflated. By 6:00 P.M. on the day of surgery (26 August), Patient H was awake, alert, and able to handle secretions. At this point, it was safe to deflate the cuff of the tracheotomy tube. If necessary, it is a nursing responsibility to seek a physician's order to deflate the cuff. The cuff, however, was not attended to nor deflated until four days postoperatively. During this entire time, there was no documentation in the nurse's notes regarding assessment of tracheotomy cuff pressure nor regular tracheotomy care.

On 28 August, a nurse's note read, "thick, yellowish, foul-smelling secretion from tracheotomy. . . . Patient complains of pain around tracheotomy." The physician was not informed of these observations, and he did not note such an observation until 30 August.

The stricture of the trachea did not develop at the tracheotomy site, but below it, at the location of the cuff of the tracheotomy tube. Expert testimony by a physician determined the cause of the stricture to be "from excessive inflation of the cuff for a protracted period of time, causing ischemia of the tracheal mucous membrane."

The plaintiff's case was based on the determination that the departures from the prevailing professional standard of nursing care caused the tracheal stricture. The case settled with payment to the plaintiff.

Case 9–6

## *Decubitus Ulcers*

### Problem and Outcome

A 72-year-old man developed decubitus ulcers because of poor nursing care.

### The Patient

Patient W, a semi-retired real estate broker, was injured in a motor-vehicle accident on 17 September. Patient W sustained an acute left acetabular and right femoral neck fracture. Significant past medical history revealed coronary artery disease.

### Treatment

Patient W was admitted to the coronary care unit and placed on bed rest in bilateral Buck's extension traction. On 22 September, an open reduction and internal fixation of the hip was accomplished. Patient W developed severe decubitus ulcers on the heels of both feet and the right buttock. The decubitus ulcers ultimately required skin grafting and prolonged the hospitalization.

### Departures from the Standard of Care

Failure to provide proper skin care constituted the departure from prevailing professional standards of nursing care in this case.

### Discussion

No notation was made on the nursing admission assessment to indicate any preexisting abnormal condition of the skin. The first notation of any heel problem was made on 18 September and read, "slight ecchymosis noted at heel sites bilaterally." A physician's order of 18 September read, "Please remove traction boots for five minutes every shift to inspect skin." A note on 30 September read, "Broken skin areas on both heels and right buttock."

Skin care for the heels was mentioned sporadically in the nurse's notes, but the actual frequency and type of care was not documented. In addition, regular (at least every two hours for the first ten days of hospitalization) attention to repositioning the patient (consistent with the injury) was not addressed in the medical record.

The problem of preventing pressure sores on patients in traction is a serious responsibility for nurses. Traction seems to predispose patients to pressure sores because mobility is restricted. An important concept in patient care with traction is that the patient should not suffer from lack of any kind of nursing care because of the immobilization. In addition, advanced age predisposes one to skin breakdown. Elderly patients often have dry, tender skin, and protective fat pads are frequently absent from bony prominences. Nutrition in the elderly is at times inadequate, particularly regarding protein and vitamin C, both of which are important elements for promoting tissue health.

It is important for nurses to recognize such predisposing factors. The prevention of pressure sores is clearly the responsibility of the nurse. Fundamental to all treatment is the removal of pressure. Meticulous preventive skin care by the nurse is required for all patients and especially for the elderly, immobilized patient. The skin must be thoroughly inspected for signs of breakdown (at least three times per twenty-four hours). Subtle change in skin color is the forerunner of skin breakdown. Nursing interventions to reduce pressure must be instituted at the first sign of a problem in order to prevent actual skin breakdown.

Patient H's prolonged hospitalization would have been prevented with proper attention to skin care.

The plaintiff's case was based on the determination that the departure from the prevailing professional standard of nursing care caused the decubitus ulcers. The case settled with payment to the plaintiff.

## Case 9–7
### *Airway Obstruction*

#### Problem and Outcome

A sixteen-year-old adolescent was admitted to the hospital for elective maxillofacial surgery. The surgery was successful but the young man suffered anoxic brain damage.

#### The Patient

Patient M was an academically talented high-school student with special interests in computers. He was admitted to the hospital during summer vacation for elective surgery to correct "buck teeth." The surgery was necessary because the condition interfered with mastication and was cosmetically unacceptable to Patient M.

## Treatment

Patient M tolerated the surgical procedure well and was transferred to the intensive care unit with an endotracheal tube in place at 1:30 P.M. on 9 July. At 3:45 P.M., it was noted that he was cyanotic. A full cardiopulmonary arrest occurred at 3:50 P.M. Resuscitation was successful but Patient M suffered anoxic brain damage. Patient M was left with a severe permanent neurological deficit and requires 24-hour care.

## Departures from the Standard of Care

Departures from prevailing professional standards of nursing care were as follows:

1. Failure to maintain a patent airway
2. Failure to suction the patient properly and in a timely manner
3. Failure to assess the patient systematically

## Discussion

Patient M was not adequately assessed or suctioned. No respiratory status assessments, including patency of the airway, were present in the medical record. Only one notation regarding suctioning was made at 3:15 P.M., and it read, "Attempted suctioning but unsuccessful in passing catheter." Difficulty or inability to pass a suction catheter in an endotracheal tube is a cause for alarm for the nurse. According to testimony, a nurse stated that no further attempts were made at suctioning because "he was not in any distress."

During the cardiopulmonary resuscitation, the endotracheal tube was changed because of "obstruction by viscous secretions," and it was further noted by the anesthesiologist that the patient was "ventilating well now."

The plaintiff's case was based on the determination that the departures from the prevailing professional standard of nursing care allowed secretions to accumulate gradually and thicken, thereby obstructing the endotracheal tube. This tragic incident could have been prevented by frequent suctioning. The case settled with payment to the plaintiff's parents.

Case 9–8

## Intravenous Infusion Infiltration

### Problem and Outcome

A 57-year-old woman suffered a myocardial infarction. She recovered rapidly from the myocardial infarction but sustained permanent damage to the right lower arm from an intravenous infusion.

### The Patient

Patient T, an executive secretary for the chief executive officer of a large company, suffered chest pains at work. She was taken to the hospital by a fire-rescue unit.

### Treatment

The patient was evaluated and stabilized in the emergency department. Because the blood pressure remained low, an Intropin (dopamine hydrochloride) drip was started. Patient T was then transferred to the coronary care unit.

Patient T made an uneventful recovery from the myocardial infarction, but she sustained a severe injury to the right lower arm. The injury was caused by infiltration of the intravenous infusion of Intropin (dopamine hydrochloride). Permanent scarring to the patient's dominant arm resulted in disfigurement and limitation of motion. When Patient T returned to work, the injury interfered with her typing duties and her handling of a computer keyboard.

### Departures from the Standard of Care

Departures from prevailing professional standards of nursing care included the following:

1. Failure to place the intravenous infusion catheter for the Intropin (dopamine hydrochloride) drip in a large vein
2. Failure to assess systematically the intravenous infusion sites
3. Failure to follow the hospital procedure manual regarding the administration of an Intropin (dopamine hydrochloride) infusion

### Discussion

The intravenous infusion catheter for the Intropin (dopamine hydrochloride) drip was placed in a small vein of the right wrist by the emergency department nurse. Intropin (dopamine hydrochloride) must be infused into a large vein whenever possible to prevent extravasation into adjacent tissue. Less suitable sites should only be used in an emergency, and it is a nursing obligation to move the intravenous infusion site to a larger vein as soon as possible.

An Intropin (dopamine hydrochloride) infusion must be monitored continuously, because the infusion rate is determined by the patient's blood pressure. The nurse should not leave the patient unattended. Signs of infiltration must be detected promptly because extravasation into the tissues can cause local vasocontriction. If this is allowed to continue, it may result in ischemia, necrosis, and sloughing.

No notations were made in Patient T's medical record regarding the Intropin (dopamine hydrochloride) infusion site until sixteen hours after it was started. The notation read, "Right lower arm bluish in color, swollen, painful with a large blistered area around intravenous site. [DR. G] here. Ordered intravenous infusion discontinued and treatment with Regitine." Regitine (phentolamine) treatment, in order to be effective in preventing tissue damage, must commence within a maximum of twelve hours after recognition of infiltration. The infiltration was not detected promptly, and severe tissue damage occurred.

The plaintiff's case was based on the determination that the departures from the prevailing professional standard of nursing care caused the scarring, disfigurement, and limitation of motion to Patient T's right arm. The case settled with payment to the plaintiff.

Chapter 10

# Problems Associated with Medication Administration

Accurate and safe administration of medication is a fundamental nursing responsibility. Nonetheless, medication errors are not uncommon in a hospital setting because principles of safe medication administration are at times ignored. I cannot begin to recount the instances when I have observed a nurse administering a medication to a patient with no attempt to identify that patient properly, nor how often I have encountered a situation where a nurse was completely unfamiliar with various medications being administered.

A valid, complete, accurate, and legible physician's order is the first step in avoiding medication errors. The medication order must be compared with the medical record and then evaluated for appropriateness in the context of the patient's history and current treatment. If an order is ambiguous or seemingly erroneous, the physician must be contacted and the order must be reaffirmed, clarified, or revised. If the patient's condition changes, or if the patient questions a medication, the order must be reviewed.

Safe administration of medication involves, among other things, reading a medication label multiple times when preparing/pouring a medication, possessing a thorough knowledge about the medication, and respecting the "five rights" of medication administration (the right patient, the right medication, the right route, the right dose, and the right time). In addition, the patient's response to a medication must be evaluated along with observation for untoward effects. Because many patients receive multiple medications, the potential for drug interactions must be considered.

Many times I have heard testimony by nurses that these principles are important, but that they generally do not apply beyond academic nursing-school practice. The predominant attitude in their testimony is that when one graduates, in reality, one does not have the time to observe the "five rights," to look up unfamiliar medications, to identify a patient properly by wrist band, etc.

This attitude probably accounts for the numerous medication errors that appear in medical records. In at least 75 percent of the medical records that I have reviewed, medication errors were present. Fortunately, in a good number of cases, the medication error did not cause or contribute to patient injury.

The cases presented in this chapter involve medication errors that, in and of themselves, actually caused patient injury or death. Departures from prevailing professional standards of nursing care in these cases include failure to question a medication order, failure to administer a medication correctly (that is, the wrong patient, wrong medication, wrong dose, wrong route, and/or wrong time), and failure to execute a medication order correctly.

## Case 10–1
## *Narcotic-Induced Respiratory Depression*

### Problem and Outcome

A 42-year-old man developed respiratory depression because of a narcotic overdose. Failure to detect the respiratory depression and then to institute treatment resulted in death.

### The Patient

Patient F, a divorced father of two children, was admitted to the hospital at 7:00 A.M. on 30 July with the diagnosis of intractable lumbar pain. Past medical history revealed that Patient F had sustained an employment-related low back injury some years before. After four lumbar laminectomies, the patient was still unable to return to his job as a postman.

### Treatment

The purpose of this hospital admission was to perform an epidural morphine nerve block for treatment of the pain. Patient F was to remain hospitalized for observation for twenty-four hours after the nerve block. The nerve block was completed by 12:30 P.M. on 30 July. At 4:25 A.M. on 31 July, Patient F was found in full cardiopulmonary arrest. Patient F was resuscitated but remained in a vegetative state.

### Departures from the Standard of Care

Departures from prevailing professional standards of nursing care were as follows:

1. Failure to assess respiratory rate, rhythm, and character along with level of consciousness at appropriate intervals
2. Failure to question the order for Demerol (meperidine)
3. Failure to assess pain properly
4. Failure to detect respiratory depression in a timely manner
5. Failure to follow hospital policy regarding documentation of "patient progress, routine care, treatments, changes in condition"

### Discussion

At 12:10 P.M. the epidural morphine block was performed and 10 milligrams of Duramorph (morphine) were instilled. After a short stay in the recovery room, Patient F was returned to the surgical floor at 12:55 P.M. Postoperative orders were as follows: vital signs every two hours, Demerol (meperidine) 100 milligrams intramuscularly every four hours as needed, and Urecholine (bethanechol chloride) 25 milligrams by mouth three times a day.

The usual dose of Duramorph (morphine) for an epidural nerve block is 2 through 5 milligrams. Patient F received the maximum recommended dose of 10 milligrams. With this dosage, and because of the danger of respiratory depression, Patient F needed to be assessed systematically at least every hour for twenty-four hours. The only postoperative vital signs and nursing assessments charted prior to the cardiopulmonary arrest include the following:

12:55 P.M.   Blood pressure 126/90; respiratory rate 16; pulse rate 68.
2:00 P.M.   Patient complains of pain – Demerol 100 milligrams intramuscular.
4:00 P.M.   Blood pressure 140/80; respiratory rate 20; pulse rate 80.
6:00 P.M.   Patient complains of pain—Demerol 100 milligrams intramuscular.
8:00 P.M.   Blood pressure 150/80.
4:25 A.M.   Patient unresponsive; code called.

The nurse on the 3:00 to 11:00 P.M. shift testified, when asked why Patient F was not observed, "He was sleeping soundly after I gave the 6:00 P.M. injection and, you know, he needed to rest and I didn't want to bother him." The nurse responsible for Patient F on the 11:00 P.M. to 7:00 A.M. shift, when asked the same question, responded, "I see all my patients at least every hour . . . but I don't chart normal stuff because, you know, we are very busy." When this nurse was further questioned about Patient F's condition, she stated, "I don't remember him at all. . . . Gee, it was so long ago. I guess I don't know because I don't see anything written here."

In addition, the administration of Demerol (meperidine) at 2:00 P.M. and 6:00 P.M. was totally inappropriate. The order should have been questioned in light of the Duramorph (morphine) administration; moreover, the physician should have been notified regarding complaints of postoperative pain. Deposition testimony on the part of the physician revealed that he did not intend for the patient to receive Demerol (meperidine) intramuscularly postoperatively. He stated that the Demerol (meperidine) order was an error and said, "I would expect a nurse to call me about such an order."

Finally, hospital policy was violated. The procedure manual specified for nurses that "all vital signs be taken and documented as ordered and/or as determined by R.N. . . . Fully document nursing actions taken for patient care in areas of patient assessment, continuing observation. . . . Nurse's notes should reflect your care and observation fully and include notes on actions you take to maintain your responsibility for patient care and safety. . . . When taking the pulse, record the rate, rhythm, and character, and for respiration, record the rate, rhythm, and depth." The nurses caring for Patient F did not document care according to hospital policy.

The plaintiff's case was based on the determination that the departures from the prevailing professional standard of nursing care caused the patient's death. The case settled with payment to the estate of the plaintiff.

## Case 10–2
### *Medication Allergy*

#### Problem and Outcome

A 68-year-old man, hospitalized for an infected foot, suffered a life-threatening duodenal ulcer hemorrhage precipitated by the administration of pain medication.

#### The Patient

Patient R was admitted to the hospital with a diagnosis of cellulitis of the left foot. Patient R had injured his foot on his son's boat. Prior to this, the patient was in excellent health except for a history of duodenal ulcer disease.

### Treatment

The cellulitis, treated by intravenous antibiotics, responded well. Patient R, however, suffered a life-threatening duodenal ulcer hemorrhage that required surgical intervention. The duodenal ulcer hemorrhage was attributed to Percodan (oxycodone) administration. Patient R had received this medication for foot pain every four to six hours for ten days.

### Departures from the Standard of Care

Departures from prevailing professional standards of nursing care were as follows:

1. Failure to complete a comprehensive nursing assessment and history on admission
2. Failure to respect the allergy status of the patient
3. Failure to question the Percodan (oxycodone) order

### Discussion

The admission note by the physician stated that Patient R had a long history of duodenal ulcer disease. In addition, hypersensitivity to acetylsalicylic acid (ASA) was noted. This information was available to the nursing staff.

An admission nursing history and a nursing assessment form was present in the medical record but was void of any entries. The nursing staff would have been aware of Patient R's medical history and allergy status had this part of the medical record been completed. The order for Percodan (oxycodone) would have been questioned, because the nursing implications would have been obvious. Patient R received Percodan (oxycodone) every four to six hours consistently for ten days.

The physician testified that, had he been "reminded" about the patient's allergy to acetylsalicylic acid, he would have prescribed another medication. In addition, Patient R's son, a physician, testified that he told the nurses on several occasions that his father should not be receiving Percodan (oxycodone) because of the duodenal ulcer disease. This information was ignored by the nursing staff.

The plaintiff's case was based on the determination that, within reasonable nursing probability, the departures from the prevailing professional standard of nursing care contributed to the duodenal ulcer hemorrhage. The case settled with payment to the plaintiff.

Case 10–3

## *Intravenous Fluid Excess*

### Problem and Outcome

A six-year-old child suffered a head injury and died from massive cerebral edema as a result of intravenous fluid overload.

### The Patient

Patient W was Christmas-shopping with her grandmother. In the shopping-center parking lot, she was struck by a slow-moving truck. The child lost consciousness for a brief period of time, and her grandmother brought her to a hospital emergency department.

### Treatment

The child had sustained a laceration on the right cheek. This was repaired. Neurological evaluation was within normal limits except for a notation that the child "appeared lethargic." Skull X-rays were negative for fracture. Patient W was admitted to the hospital at 11:45 A.M. on 23 December for "24-hour observation." Initial vital signs as recorded were temperature 100.2 degrees Fahrenheit (rectally), pulse rate 84, and blood pressure 120/70 mmHg.

Less than twenty-four hours later, Patient W died. The report of the medical examiner stated that the patient's brain weighed 1420 grams. The brain of a six-year-old, 22.73-kilogram child should weigh approximately 700 grams. The massive cerebral edema caused uncal and tonsillar herniation of the brain stem, and death.

### Departures from the Standard of Care

Departures from prevailing professional standards of nursing care included the following:

1. Failure to administer intravenous infusion fluids properly
2. Failure to assess the patient systematically

### Discussion

The physician ordered an "intravenous infusion of 5 percent G/E 48 or equivalent every eight hours." The order did not specify the amount of fluid the child was to receive. The nurses did not contact the physician regarding this incomplete order and administered the fluid at a rate

of greater than 300 milliliters every hour. The amount of fluid administered was greatly in excess of the requirements for a child of this age and
weight. Fluid status assessment was recorded only every four hours.

According to the medical record, vital signs were ascertained only every
four hours. Interestingly, there was little if any variance in the recorded
vital signs from the time of admission until Patient W's death. Neurological status assessments for the entire hospitalization of 23–24 December were as follows:

1:00 P.M.   Received on unit in state of unconsciousness
3:00 P.M.   Condition has not changed since admission
6:00 P.M.   Sleeping at long intervals; family in [to visit]

No other neurological assessments appeared in the record. The only
other nursing notation in the entire record was dated 24 December at
12:20 A.M., and read, "Patient not breathing – cardiopulmonary resuscitation unsuccessful."

Ongoing systematic nursing assessments were incomplete and inadequate. Patient W was, in fact, admitted to the hospital for observation.
The nurse who remains with the patient is responsible for observing pertinent physiological alterations. The frequency and type of nursing observations are determined by the patient's condition. A minimum of hourly
assessment was essential, with increasing frequency as Patient W's condition changed. In addition, the physician should have been notified
immediately of significant changes in the patient's condition.

Increased intracranial pressure demands early recognition and prompt
treatment. Massive fluid overload with accompanying increased intracranial pressure was not detected in this tragic case.

The plaintiff's case was based on the determination that, within reasonable probability, the departures from the prevailing professional standard of nursing care caused the death of Patient W. The case settled with
payment to the child's parents.

## Case 10–4

### *Intramuscular Injection: Incorrect Angle*

#### Problem and Outcome

A 10-year-old child suffered left sciatic nerve neuropathy and secondary
reflex sympathetic dystrophy from an intramuscular injection. The needle was inserted at an incorrect angle (45 degrees), causing this injury.

## The Patient

Patient W, a tall and slender child, was at the neighborhood playground with friends from school. The children were playing basketball and occasionally teasing the "neighborhood dog." Patient W was bitten by the dog.

## Treatment

Patient W was taken to the emergency department for treatment. A 3-centimeter laceration on the leg was sutured, and the child was given a tetanus-diphtheria booster immunization. Six days later the sutures were removed and the wound was healing well.

One month after the dog bite, Patient W was admitted to the hospital for evaluation of progressive weakness, pain, and edema of the left lower extremity. A diagnosis of left sciatic nerve neuropathy and secondary reflex sympathetic dystrophy was made. The patient received physical therapy and used a transcutaneous electrical nerve stimulator for pain control. Improvement was noted, but contractures in the gastrocnemius muscle and Achilles tendon required surgery.

It was the opinion of the attending physician that the left sciatic nerve injury was attributed to the tetanus-diphtheria injection that Patient W received in the left buttock.

## Departures from the Standard of Care

The departure from the prevailing professional standard of nursing care in this case was failure to insert a hypodermic needle into the patient at the appropriate angle.

## Discussion

Review of the medical record revealed that Patient W received "pediatric diphtheria and tetanus toxoid 0.5 milliliters intramuscular, left upper gluteus." The charting did not specify whether the injection was given in the upper outer or upper inner quadrant of the gluteus. An intramuscular injection administered in this area must fall within the upper outer quadrant or serious trauma may result. As a matter of fact, many hospitals recommend or require the use of the ventrogluteal area in children to avoid injection-related problems. This area is used because it is free of major blood vessels and nerves.

The nurse who administered the injection testified that it was in fact given in the upper outer quadrant. According to testimony by this nurse, however, the angle of hypodermic needle insertion was incorrect. She stated that the needle is "always inserted at a 45-degree angle." The needle for an intramuscular injection (of correct length and gauge) must be inserted at a right angle to the skin. If the needle is not inserted at a 90-degree angle to the skin, the material may be injected into the subcutaneous tissue and/or into a nerve or blood vessel.

The plaintiff's case was based on the determination that improper injection technique, caused the serious injury to the patient. The case settled with payment to the child's parents.

## Case 10–5
## *Wrong Medication Dosage*

### Problem and Outcome

A medication error caused a phenobarbital overdose in a pre-term infant. The drug overdose impacted the child's growth and development.

### The Patient

Patient O was born on 9 November by Cesarean section because of prenatal problems. The initial one-minute Apgar score was nine, and he weighed three pounds and two ounces.

### Treatment

Patient O was admitted to the newborn nursery as a pre-term infant and was noted to be small for his gestational age. Soon after birth, the infant developed apneic spells. He was transferred to another hospital and admitted to the high-risk nursery.

The infant was placed on a warmer-servocontrol, and the peripheral umbilical artery line was maintained with an infusion of 10 percent dextrose in water, at 4 milliliters per hour. He was also placed on a transcutaneous oxygen monitor and was observed carefully. Vital signs and general physical condition were unremarkable. The baby was noted to be "somewhat jittery."

On 12 November, Patient O developed generalized multifocal seizures. During an acute seizure episode, he was intubated and placed on a ventilator for approximately two hours. He was started on phenobarbital and Dilantin (phenytoin sodium).

On the evening of 13 November, a medication error resulted in an overdose of phenobarbital. Immediately after this incident, the phenobarbital and Dilantin (phenytoin sodium) were discontinued, and the baby's phenobarbital level was monitored. On the morning of 14 November, the phenobarbital level was 86.4 milligrams per liter (mg/L). This level slowly decreased to 30.4 mg/L by 26 November.

Over time, Patient O's lethargy slowly decreased. He had no episodes of respiratory embarrassment and his vital signs remained stable. No more seizure activity was observed during the hospital stay, and the baby continued to gain weight. On 15 December the baby was discharged.

Questions still remain about the full impact of the phenobarbital overdose on this child. Mental development along with general growth and development has not been within normal limits.

### Departures from the Standard of Care

The departure from the prevailing professional standard of nursing care in this case was the failure to administer the correct dosage of a medication to the patient.

### Discussion

The general nursing care that Patient O received conformed to acceptable standards of nursing practice, but the administration of phenobarbital did not.

Nurse P, was asked by Nurse K to administer the 12:00 A.M. dose of phenobarbital to Patient O, because Nurse K was busy with change-of-shift activities. Nurse P stated that she went to the nursery and "saw a syringe that said 'phenobarbital.' . . . I took it, and since I saw 'phenobarbital,' I gave the medication intravenous push in the line, and as soon as I finished, I told [Nurse K] that I had given the medication." Nurse P further testified that Nurse K asked her which syringe she used. She told her she used the syringe labeled "phenobarbital." This syringe, however, was not labeled with the Patient O's name or dose of medication.

Nurse K stated that she had placed two syringes on top of Patient O's isolette. One syringe, labeled "phenobarbital," contained 130 milligrams per milliliter of phenobarbital; the other, with no label, contained 2 milligrams of phenobarbital. She informed Nurse P that she had used the wrong syringe.

This medication error was absolutely preventable. Nurse P had the responsibility to administer the correct medication to the correct patient, in the correct dosage, by the proper route, at the appropriate time. This is a basic, standard procedure to ensure patient safety. Nurse P did not prepare the medication to be administered and, thereby, failed to administer the correct dose.

The plaintiff's case was based on the determination that, within reasonable nursing probability, the departure from the prevailing professional standard of nursing care contributed to the child's delayed growth and development. This case settled during trial with payment made to a trust account for the child for future care and education.

## Case 10–6

### *Intramuscular Injection: Incorrect Site*

#### Problem and Outcome

A 45-year-old woman sustained a severe sciatic nerve injury secondary to an intramuscular injection. The injection was administered in the wrong site.

#### The Patient

Patient F was a single mother with a ten-year-old-son. She was admitted to the hospital 11 September with the chief complaint of low back pain. The patient had injured her back four years prior to admission. The injury occurred at work when Patient F attempted to lift a box. At the time, Patient F was working as an insurance agent, but she had not worked since the accident. Numerous hospitalizations and surgical procedures had provided little relief from the low back pain.

#### Treatment

A percutaneous discectomy at lumbar vertebrae numbers four and five (L4–5) and a repeat discectomy at lumbar vertebra five and sacral vertebra one (L5–S1) were performed 12 September. In the immediate postoperative period, Patient F was stable from a neurological standpoint, but she did complain of back pain, for which Demerol (meperidine) 50 milligrams was administered intramuscularly.

The next day, 13 September at 1:00 P.M., Patient F was given Demerol (meperidine) 50 milligrams intramuscularly in the "left outer quadrant— gluteal area" for "back pain." Following the injection, Patient F complained immediately of severe left buttock pain radiating down her thigh to the left foot. Weakness of the left leg rapidly developed.

The attending neurosurgeon ordered diagnostic studies, but the studies were negative both with regard to nerve root compression and infection from the surgical procedure. Further evaluation indicated that Patient F sustained an injection neuropathy of the femoral nerve during the Demerol (meperidine) injection on 13 September at 1:00 P.M.

### Departures from the Standard of Care

The departure from the prevailing professional standard of nursing care was the administration of an intramuscular injection in the wrong site.

### Discussion

Testimony by the nurse who administered the injection revealed that the injection was given in the "left outer quadrant of the gluteus area . . . in the meatier somewhat lower outer quadrant because she was skinny." Examination of the gluteal area by the physician was consistent with this testimony, because a needle puncture was evident in the left lower outer quadrant. Intramuscular injections must be given in the upper outer quadrant of the gluteal area. The use of proper landmarks for determining the correct injection site is necessary to avoid nerves and blood vessels.

Patient F was discharged from the hospital 22 September with a complete left-foot drop. At the time, she was unable to walk well and required the services of a physical therapist on a daily basis in her home. In addition, an aide for eight hours per day was necessary for housekeeping chores.

Patient F became quite depressed by the constant burning pain in the left calf posteriorly and laterally, radiating down to the foot. The depression affected the relationship with her ten-year-old son. The child became withdrawn and developed a stress-related bleeding gastric ulcer. At the recommendation of a psychologist and a physician, the child was withdrawn from school and placed on homebound instruction.

The plaintiff's case was based on the determination that the departure from the prevailing professional standard of nursing care caused the sciatic nerve injury. The case settled with payment to the plaintiff.

## Case 10–7
### *Intramuscular Injection: Incorrect Volume*

### Problem and Outcome

The intramuscular administration of an excessive volume of solution resulted in foot drop in a 73-year-old patient.

## The Patient

Patient H, a retired stockbroker, was admitted to the hospital on 6 April with the diagnosis of adenocarcinoma of the right upper lobe of the lung. Past medical history was significant for hypertension, peptic ulcer disease, and supraventricular tachycardia. Nine years prior to admission, Patient H had a left lower lobectomy for carcinoma of the lung.

## Treatment

On 7 April, Patient H was taken to the operating room for an exploratory right thoracotomy and a right upper lung lobectomy. He tolerated the procedure "reasonably well" and was admitted to the surgical intensive care unit. His early postoperative course was satisfactory, but on 8 April Patient H was described as "awake, confused, requiring frequent orientation to place and time . . . complaining of seeing bugs in bed . . . restless."

This altered state persisted, and he received medications for restlessness. The morning of 9 April, Patient H had a respiratory arrest two minutes after a 5 milliliter intramuscular injection of Paral (paraldehyde). He had no change in vital signs and was intubated promptly.

As Patient H's condition improved, he complained of pain in the right leg below the knee radiating to the right foot. Neurologic examination revealed weakness of the right lower extremity which was confined to the muscle groups below the knee. He could not dorsiflex the right foot or extend or plantar flex the toes of the right foot. It was determined that Patient H had an acquired lesion of the high sciatic and inferior gluteal nerve or the low plexus region. It was noted that the lesion occurred between surgery and discharge from the hospital.

## Departures from the Standard of Care

The departure from the prevailing professional standard of nursing care in this case was the intramuscular administration of an excessive volume of solution into one site.

## Discussion

Nerve damage may result from an intramuscular injection as a function of faulty technique, chemical irritation by the medication, and/or pressure exerted by the volume of fluid injected.

The alarmed and struggling individual, or the violent, aggressive, obstreperous, encephalopathic patient who requires sedation is at increased risk for an injection injury to the sciatic nerve. In addition, Paral (paraldehyde), a chemically irritating medication, is a well-known cause of sciatic nerve injury when administered improperly. On 9 April, when Patient H received Paral (paraldehyde), he was described as combative and resisting treatment. It was noted in the medical record that the entire 5 milliliters of this medication was given intramuscularly in one site in the "right gluteal."

The nurse administering the Paral (paraldehyde) documented the medication, the dose, the time, and the route, but not the specific site of the intramuscular injection. For medication administered in the dorsogluteal area, the nurse must specify the buttock as well as the quadrant. Intramuscular injections in the dorsogluteal area not given in the upper outer quadrant may cause injury by penetrating surrounding nerves and blood vessels. Volume in excess of a maximum of 3 milliliters, injected into one site, can also cause tissue damage. Patient H received 5 milliliters of fluid in the one site.

The plaintiff's case was based on the determination that the excessive volume of solution injected into one site along with possible improper site of injection caused the neuropathy. The case settled with payment to the plaintiff.

## Case 10–8
### *Medication Omitted*

#### Problem and Outcome

A 48-year-old diabetic man in a hospital died because insulin was not administered.

#### The Patient

Patient Z, a self-employed shopkeeper and the father of two children, was admitted to the hospital with abdominal pain, nausea, and vomiting. The patient had become diabetic at the age of twelve. The type I diabetes mellitus was controlled by diet and daily insulin injections.

#### Treatment

Patient Z's physician ordered a number of tests to be performed. He also ordered capillary blood glucose-monitoring and urine-testing for

ketone bodies four times a day along with sliding-scale insulin administration. Sixteen hours after admission, Patient Z was found dead in bed.

### Departures from the Standard of Care

Departures from the prevailing professional standard of nursing care
were as follows:

1. Failure to assess the patient systematically
2. Failure to perform capillary blood glucose-monitoring and
   urine-testing for ketone bodies
3. Failure to administer insulin

### Discussion

According to the medical record, the only capillary blood glu-
cose–monitoring and urine-testing for ketone bodies that was performed
was at 9:00 P.M. (six hours after admission). The capillary blood glu-
cose–level was markedly elevated. Accordingly, insulin was to be administered, but it was not given to Patient Z.

At 10:00 P.M. it was noted that the patient's pulse rate was 146, and
the blood pressure was 180/90 mmHg. This was a change when compared
with the admission pulse rate of 72 and blood pressure of 120/68 mmHg.
No further nursing care was provided to Patient Z except for that documented in the medical record as follows:

11:00 P.M.   Patient sleeping soundly.
4:00 A.M.   Patient sleeping.
6:00 A.M.   Patient sleeping well.
7:00 A.M.   Patient found not breathing; no pulse; cardiopulmonary
            resuscitation; pronounced by [Dr. S].

This patient entrusted himself to the care and treatment of the nursing staff and the hospital. Patient Z was basically abandoned. The nursing care was deplorable.

The plaintiff's case was based on the determination that, within reasonable probability, the failure to administer insulin along with inadequate assessment and observation caused the death of this patient. The
case settled with payment to the estate of the plaintiff.

Case 10–9
## *Wrong Medication Time*

### Problem and Outcome

Heparin administration at the wrong time caused a 62-year-old man to develop cardiac tamponade. Decreased cardiac output, caused by the tamponade, ultimately led to cerebral hypoxia. Patient P is now confined to a wheelchair and suffers from severely impaired memory and speech.

### The Patient

Patient P, a prominent retired chief of police, was admitted to the hospital for elective mitral valve repair because of severe mitral insufficiency and regurgitation (class four). He had a known history of mitral valve prolapse secondary to bacterial endocarditis four years prior to this admission. This led to progressive congestive heart failure.

### Treatment

On 28 June, Patient P entered the hospital to undergo an elective repair or replacement of his mitral valve. On 29 June, Patient P underwent open heart surgery with attempted repair of the mitral valve. When the repair failed, a #33 St. Jude mitral valve was implanted.

Postoperatively, Patient P was hemodynamically stable but pacemaker-dependent. Heparin was administered because of the prosthetic heart valve to prevent the formation of blood clots. Complete heart block developed and on 7 July, a permanent pacemaker was implanted. Prior to this surgery, anticoagulation was discontinued to protect him from bleeding during the procedure. The temporary epicardial pacing wires were left in place. Postoperatively, he was transferred to the telemetry unit in "excellent condition."

At 10:45 A.M. on 8 July, a physician, assisted by Nurse C, removed the temporary epicardial pacing wires. Shortly thereafter, Patient P suffered a cardiopulmonary arrest. Resuscitation was successful, but anoxic brain damage occurred. After the cardiopulmonary resuscitation, Patient P was taken back to surgery, and he had evidence of bleeding around the heart and cardiac tamponade.

### Departures from the Standard of Care

Departures from prevailing professional standards of nursing care included the following list (see page 237):

## Case 10–9 Flow Sheet

**Assessment Standard for Patient**                    **Minimum Frequency of Assessment**

| Assessment | Variable | to telemetry unit 7 July 4:00 pm | 4:30 | 5:00 | 5:30 | 6:00 | 6:30 |
|---|---|---|---|---|---|---|---|
| **Respiratory status** | Patency of airway | | | | | | |
| | Respiratory rate | 20 | | | | | |
| | Respiratory character | | | | | | |
| | Respiratory rhythm | | | | | | |
| | Breath sounds | | | | | | |
| **Circulatory status** | Heart rate | 72 | | | | | |
| | Heart rhythm | | | | | | |
| | Heart sounds/quality | | | | | | |
| | Blood pressure | $\frac{140}{70}$ | | | | | |
| | Skin color / temperature | | warm dry color fair | | | | |
| | Peripheral pulses | | | | | | |
| | Capillary refill | | | | | | |
| | Pacemaker: rhythm, capture, firing, sensing | | | | | | |
| **Neurological status** | Level of consciousness | | alert | | | | |
| | Orientation | | oriented x3 | | | | |
| | Behavior | | | | | | |

(entries indicate assessments that were made)

| 7 July 7:00 pm | 7:30 | 8:00 | 8:30 | 9:00 | 9:30 | 10:00 | 10:30 | 11:00 | 11:30 | 8 July 12:00 am | 12:30 |
|---|---|---|---|---|---|---|---|---|---|---|---|
| | | | | | | | | | | | |
| | | 24 | | | | | | | | 22 | |
| | | | | | | | | | | | |
| | | | | | | | | | | | |
| | scattered rales | | | | | | | | | | |
| | | 72 | | | | | | | | 72 | |
| | | | | | | | | | | | |
| | | | | | | | | | | | |
| | | $\frac{134}{70}$ | | | | | | | | $\frac{120}{72}$ | |
| | | | | | | | | | | | |
| | present strong | | | | | | | | | | |
| | | | | | | | | | | | |
| | in capture | in capture | | | | | | | | | |
| | awake alert | | | | | | | | | | awake |
| | oriented x3 | | | | | | | | | | |
| | very apprehensive | restless apprehensive | | | | | | remains restless | | | very restless |

## Case 10–9 Flow Sheet (continued)

**Assessment Standard for Patient**                    **Minimum Frequency of Assessment**

| Assessment | Variable | 8 July 1:00 am | 1:30 | 2:00 | 2:30 | 3:00 | 3:30 |
|---|---|---|---|---|---|---|---|
| **Respiratory status** | Patency of airway | | | | | | |
| | Respiratory rate | | | | | | |
| | Respiratory character | | | | | | |
| | Respiratory rhythm | | | | | | |
| | Breath sounds | | | | | | |
| **Circulatory status** | Heart rate | | | | | | |
| | Heart rhythm | | | | | | |
| | Heart sounds/quality | | | | | | |
| | Blood pressure | | | | | | |
| | Skin color / temperature | | | | | | |
| | Peripheral pulses | | | | | | |
| | Capillary refill | | | | | | |
| | Pacemaker: rhythm, capture, firing, sensing | | | | | | |
| **Neurological status** | Level of consciousness | | | | | | |
| | Orientation | | | | | | |
| | Behavior | | | | | out of bed | |

**(entries indicate assessments that were made)**

| 4:00 | 4:30 | 5:00 | 5:30 | 6:00 | 6:30 | 7:00 | 7:30 | 8:00 | 8:30 | 9:00 | 9:30 |
|------|------|------|------|------|------|------|------|------|------|------|------|
|      |      |      |      |      |      |      |      |      |      |      |      |
|      |      |      |      |      |      |      |      | 18   |      |      |      |
|      |      |      |      |      |      |      | un-labored |  |      |      |      |
|      |      |      |      |      |      |      | regular |   |      |      |      |
|      |      |      |      |      |      |      |      |      |      |      |      |
|      |      |      |      |      |      |      |      | 76   |      |      |      |
|      |      |      |      |      |      |      |      |      |      |      |      |
|      |      |      |      |      |      |      |      |      |      |      |      |
|      |      |      |      |      |      |      |      | $\frac{100}{70}$ |      |      |      |
|      |      |      |      |      |      |      | warm dry fair |  |      |      |      |
|      |      |      |      |      |      |      |      |      |      |      |      |
|      |      |      |      |      |      |      |      |      |      |      |      |
|      |      |      |      |      |      |      |      |      |      |      |      |
|      |      |      |      |      |      |      |      |      |      |      |      |
|      |      |      |      |      |      |      |      |      |      |      |      |
|      |      |      |      |      |      |      |      |      |      |      |      |

## Case 10–9 Flow Sheet (continued)

**Assessment Standard for Patient**          **Minimum Frequency of Assessment**

| Assessment | Variable | 8 July 10:00 am | 10:30 | 10:45 | 10:50 | 11:00 | 11:15 |
|---|---|---|---|---|---|---|---|
| **Respiratory status** | Patency of airway | | | | | | |
| | Respiratory rate | | | | | | |
| | Respiratory character | | | | | | acute distress |
| | Respiratory rhythm | | | | | | |
| | Breath sounds | | | | | | |
| **Circulatory status** | Heart rate | | | | | | |
| | Heart rhythm | | | | | | |
| | Heart sounds/quality | | | | | | |
| | Blood pressure | | | | | | $\frac{180}{80}$ |
| | Skin color / temperature | | | | | | |
| | Peripheral pulses | | | | | | |
| | Capillary refill | | | | | | |
| | Pacemaker: rhythm, capture, firing, sensing | | | | | | pacing at 65 |
| **Neurological status** | Level of consciousness | | | | | | |
| | Orientation | | | | | | |
| | Behavior | | | | | | |

1. Failure to assess the patient systematically after the permanent pacemaker implantation until the cardiopulmonary arrest
2. Failure to clarify and obtain a complete order for heparin administration after the permanent pacemaker implantation
3. Failure to assess hemodynamic status at least every fifteen minutes for one hour after removal of the temporary epicardial pacer wires

## Discussion

After the permanent pacemaker was implanted, Patient P was transferred to the telemetry unit at 4:00 P.M. on 7 July. According to the medical record, systematic nursing assessment was not accomplished. The flow sheet documenting Patient P's nursing care from 4 00 P.M. on 7 July until the cardiopulmonary arrest is on pages 232–36 and 238–39.

Postoperatively, on the evening of 7 July, Dr. D, the cardiovascular surgeon, wrote an order to restart the heparin at 12:00 noon the next day, after the temporary pacemaker wires were removed. Dr. D did not include in his order the dosage or route for administration of the heparin. The nurses on duty that evening signed the order off but did not transcribe the order onto the medication record. The order was not clarified. The following day (8 July), Dr. R, the cardiologist, saw Patient P at approximately 8:00 A.M. and wrote an order to restart the heparin. He wrote the dosage and route of administration but did not indicate the time the medication was to be given. His only indication as to time was that the heparin was to be given "after the wires are removed." The nurses again made no attempt to clarify the order.

On 8 July, at approximately 10:15 A.M., Dr. L removed the temporary epicardial pacer wires. The medication record indicates that Nurse C administered heparin 7,000 units by intravenous push at 10:20 A.M. No nursing observations were made after the removal of the temporary epicardial pacing wires on 8 July until 11:15 A.M., and by 11:18 A.M. it was noted that Patient P was in full cardiopulmonary arrest.

The patient's wife, testified that she was with Patient P after the "wires were removed." She stated that Patient P "became very restless, then dizzy. We called for the nurse, and the light was on for probably twenty minutes. Before she ever came, he had trouble breathing and his color became very bad. I got frightened and ran to call the nurse." According to the medical record, a code was called at 11:18 A.M., and it was noted that pulse and blood pressure were lost for fifty-two minutes.

Testimony by Nurse C revealed that she administered the heparin

## Case 10–9 Flow Sheet (continued)

**Assessment Standard for Patient**          **Minimum Frequency of Assessment**

| Assessment | Variable | to telemetry unit 7 July 4:00 pm | 5:00 | 6:00 | 7:00 | 8:00 | 9:00 | 10:00 |
|---|---|---|---|---|---|---|---|---|
| Thermoregu-latory status | Body temperature | | | | | 98 | | |
| Gastrointes-tinal status | Appearance of abdomen | | | | soft | | | |
| | Bowel sounds | | | | hypo-active | | | |
| Pain status | Qualitative aspects | | | pain | | | | |
| | Quantitative aspects | | | | | | | |
| | Temporal aspects | | | | | | | |
| | Topographic aspects | | | incision | | | | |
| Renal status | Urinary output | | | Foley draining | | | | |
| | Character of urine | | | | dilute | | | |
| Fluid status | Intake-amount/kind | | | | | | | |
| | Intake vs. output | | | | | | | |
| Wound status | Incision: appearance/ drainage | | | pacer incision ok | | | dressing dry | |

according to Dr. R's order because "the last order stands." She further stated that the order was clear and complete, even though the time of heparin administration was not specified.

Dr. D testified that he wanted the heparin given at 12:00 noon because he assumed that the epicardial wires would be removed early in the morning. Dr. L and Dr. R both testified that heparin should not be given until two to four hours after the epicardial wires are removed and the patient

**(entries indicate assessments that were made)**

| | 11:00 | 8 July 12:00 am | 1:00 | 2:00 | 3:00 | 4:00 | 5:00 | 6:00 | 7:00 | 8:00 | 9:00 | 10:00 | 11:00 |
|---|---|---|---|---|---|---|---|---|---|---|---|---|---|
| | | 97.8 | | | | | | | | 97.2 | | | |
| | | | | | | | | | | | | | |
| | | | | | | | | | | | | | |
| | | | | | | | | | | | | | pain |
| | | | | | | | | | | | | | |
| | | | | | | | | | | | | | |
| | | | | | | | | | | | | | |
| | 2000 ml | | | | | | | | 1450 ml | | | | |
| | | | | | | | | | | | | | |
| | 350 ml | | | | | | | | 400 ml | | | | |
| | | | | | | | | | | | | | |
| | | | | | | | | | sternal incision ok | | | | |

is stable. Dr. R further stated that if the nurse was unsure as to the time of the heparin administration, she should have asked him for clarification.

The plaintiff's case was based on the determination that the administration of heparin immediately after the epicardial wires were removed caused bleeding and cardiac tamponade. The resulting decreased cardiac output contributed to the hypoxic encephalopathy suffered by Patient P. The case settled with payment to the plaintiff.

Case 10–10

## *Wrong Intravenous Infusion Solution*

### Problem and Outcome

Administration of the wrong intravenous infusion solution caused the death of a premature infant.

### The Patient

Patient E was born 30 September to a 30-year-old woman at thirty weeks estimated gestational age. The couple had wanted children for a number of years, but the mother had difficulty conceiving. This was her second pregnancy. Her first pregnancy resulted in a miscarriage. Several days after the birth of Patient E, the mother was diagnosed as having systemic lupus erythematosus (SLE). The couple were informed that the SLE may interfere with their future attempts to have children.

### Treatment

Patient E, a 1,300-gram infant, was admitted 30 September to the neonatal intensive care unit in serious but stable condition with the diagnoses of extreme prematurity, intrauterine growth retardation, and respiratory distress syndrome. The newborn intensive care unit protocol was instituted along with intubation and mechanical ventilation. Vital signs remained stable and the infant was responsive, pink, and breathing comfortably.

On 4 October, it was discovered that Patient E was receiving the wrong intravenous infusion fluid. The wrong solution was discontinued and the correct solution was administered. Although the fluid was changed, Patient E's condition deteriorated, and the infant was pronounced dead at 8:50 P.M. on 7 October.

### Departures from the Standard of Care

Based upon review of the medical record of Patient E, serious departures from the prevailing professional standard of nursing care were as follows:

1. Failure to administer the correct intravenous infusion fluid on 4 October
2. Failure to document that the wrong intravenous infusion fluid was administered
3. Failure to inform the physician in a timely manner of a significant change in heart rate, beginning 4 October at 8:00 A.M.

## Discussion

Patient E was receiving continuous intravenous infusion fluids while in the neonatal intensive care unit. On the day of the incident, according to the nurse's notes and medication record, a new plastic bottle of intravenous infusion solution was provided to the patient sometime during the morning of 4 October. The time the solution was started was not charted, and the name of the solution was indicated only by the word "same." The solution ordered by the physician was "dextrose 7.5 percent in water E48 with 0.5 units of heparin per milliliter."

At 8:00 A.M. on 4 October, according to the neonatal intensive care unit flow chart, it was noted that the infant's heart rate had increased to 196 from the previous range of 150–160. The heart rate remained between 196 and 208 throughout the day. The nurse's notes at 4:45 P.M., when Patient E's parents were visiting, stated that the parents "commented on baby being pale." Not until 6:00 P.M. was the physician called and informed of the increased heart rate. The physician was in the hospital at the time and came immediately to the neonatal intensive care unit to examine Patient E. The physician's progress note written at 6:00 P.M. read as follows:

Reported by nursing to be tachycardiac. Intravenous fluid found with 800 milligrams per 500 milliliters of fluid of theophylline. Baby calculated to have received approximately 90 milligrams of theophylline over an eight- to nine-hour period. Immediately corrected fluids to dextrose 10 percent in water E48 with calcium gluconate and heparin.

There was no mention of this incident in the nurse's notes.

On 5 October at 7:00 A.M., the physician's progress note read: "Aminophylline level 95.8 micrograms per milliliter (mcg/ml). Heart rate remains about 200 beats per minute. Parents aware of medication error."

Examination of the intravenous infusion fluid bottle that the physician found at 6:00 P.M. on 4 October revealed the following: (1) The hospital pharmacy placed a label on one side of the bottle with the patient's name on it as well as the name of the correct solution; (2) On the other side of the bottle, the manufacturer's label read "0.16 percent Theophylline and 5 percent Dextrose Inj." The words *Theophylline 800 milligrams* were printed in big red letters.

The pharmacy department had sent the wrong solution to the neonatal intensive care unit. Compounding this error, the nurse failed to read the complete labels on both sides of the bottle before administering the solution to the patient.

The plaintiff's case was based on the determination that this tragic death could have been prevented by (1) the pharmacy double-checking solutions before sending them to the neonatal intensive care unit, or (2) the nurse following the principles and practices of safe medication administration. The case settled with payment to the infant's parents.

# Chapter 11

# Problems Associated with Environmental Safety

Providing a safe environment and protecting the patient from avoidable injury, especially from falls, is an important nursing responsibility. Hospitalized patients are prime candidates for falls. Risk factors in this population may include advanced age, medication reactions that influence equilibrium, unfamiliar surroundings, disorientation at night, a generalized weakened condition, altered mental status, impaired sensory perception, and impaired mobility. Falls generally are avoidable. The development of nursing interventions based upon an assessment for the risk of falling is key to the prevention of falls. Nursing interventions may employ a variety of safety measures such as the use of bedside rails, night lights, restraints, and beds placed in the low position nearer the floor.

Cases 11–1 through 11–5 illustrate varying circumstances in which falls have occurred, involving patients not in restraints. Cases 11–6 through 11–9 analyze instances in which patients have fallen while supposedly in restraints. A common theme in the testimony of nurses involved in these cases is that "somehow" the patient "got out of the restraints." Frequently patients are described as "Houdinis" in their ability to escape from restraints. Such testimony puzzles me because I never observed, in all the years of my clinical experience, a patient's "escape" from a restraint that was appropriate for the situation and also properly applied.

Since this puzzling testimony was the same in every case, especially regarding the Posey vest, I decided to do an experiment. I applied a Posey vest to a very bright, very strong six-foot-four-inch male weighing 200 pounds to ascertain whether he could find a way to free himself. He was unable to escape. This confirmed my belief that, if the appropriate restraint is applied according to the manufacturer's instructions, the restraint will be effective.

When a nurse cares for a patient in restraints, certain systematic nursing assessments must be documented in the medical record. These nursing observations should include at least the following:

1. Patient's behavior precipitating use of restraint

2. Type of restraint used
3. Condition of the skin while restrained and skin care given
4. Frequency of observation of restrained patient (at least every hour)
5. Frequency of removal of restraint (at least every four hours)
6. Date and time of restraint application, and date and time of restraint discontinuance
7. Patient's response to the restraint

Unfortunately, in all of the cases involving "escape" from restraints, the patient was inadequately restrained and not observed systematically.

The falls reported in this chapter caused serious injury to the patient. Each case was settled with payment to the plaintiff.

## Case 11–1
### *Fall: Patient Unattended*

#### Problem and Outcome
A 75-year-old woman fell in the X-ray department. She sustained a compound fracture of the left ankle.

#### The Patient
Patient E, a widow, lived in a large house with a live-in companion and nurse's aide. She was admitted to the hospital for comprehensive evaluation of back pain and mild congestive heart failure. Outpatient diagnostic evaluation was not feasible because of the patient's debilitated condition.

#### Treatment
Patient E's back pain was diagnosed as a degenerative joint disease and was treated with nonsteroidal anti-inflammatory agents. The congestive heart failure was successfully managed by adjusting cardiac medications. Patient E's hospitalization was prolonged, however, because of a fall and a compound fracture of the left ankle. Treatment of the fracture required two surgical procedures.

#### Departures from the Standard of Care
Failure to protect the patient from avoidable injury represented the

departure from the prevailing professional standard of nursing care in this case.

### Discussion

According to the medical record, Patient E was taken to the X-ray department by wheelchair. The nurse caring for Patient E was willing to accompany her into the X-ray room, but the X-ray technician advised that she could not enter. The nurse informed the X-ray technician that Patient E was "very unstable," that she "falls very easily," and "becomes confused at times." The X-ray technician insisted that the nurse leave. At this point, both the nurse and the X-ray technician left the room to discuss the situation. Patient E was left sitting on the X-ray table.

In the meantime, while waiting, Patient E stepped off the X-ray table, fell, and sustained a compound fracture of the left ankle.

The nurse caring for Patient E later testified, "I knew she was going to fall, but what could I do about it? X-ray isn't my department." This nurse had the obligation to remain with the patient and inform a superior of the situation. This fall in the X-ray department could have been prevented.

The plaintiff's case was based on the determination that, within reasonable nursing probability, the departure from the prevailing professional standard of nursing care caused the fall. The case settled with payment to the plaintiff.

### Case 11–2

## *Fall: No Assistance*

### Problem and Outcome

A 59-year-old postoperative cardiac surgery patient repeatedly called for a nurse to assist her to the bathroom. The calls were ignored, and in desperation the patient attempted to go to the bathroom without assistance. This resulted in a fall.

### The Patient

Patient L was admitted to the hospital for a prosthetic mitral valve replacement. She presented with a history of rheumatic heart disease, progressive mitral stenosis, and pulmonary hypertension secondary to rheumatic mitral valvular disease.

Past medical history was significant because Patient L suffered from chronic atrial fibrillation. Associated with this arrhythmia were episodes of cerebral emboli, which left Patient L with a paresis on the left side of the body. In addition, the patient had been a diabetic (type I diabetes mellitus, insulin dependent) for approximately fifteen years.

### Treatment

Patient L was taken to surgery, where the mitral valve was replaced. She tolerated the procedure well and progressed as expected. The atrial fibrillation continued with a moderate ventricular response. On the fourth postoperative day, Patient L had two episodes of paroxysmal atrial tachycardia (PAT) with syncope.

On this day, after attempting repeatedly to call a nurse, Patient L tried to go to the bathroom without assistance. The patient fell and sustained an angulated fracture of the left femoral neck in the subcapital region. Open reduction and internal fixation was accomplished the next day.

Six days after the hip surgery, Patient L complained of vertigo, and conjugate deviation of the eyes to the left was noted. A brain scan demonstrated a lesion consistent with a cerebral infarct. The neurological symptoms improved within forty-eight hours. Patient L continued to progress and was discharged from the hospital one month after admission.

### Departures from the Standard of Care

Departures from prevailing professional standards of nursing care included the following:

1. Failure to provide a safe environment for the patient
2. Failure to protect the patient from harm associated with disease processes
3. Failure to document the incident of the fall properly

### Discussion

Patient L's condition was such that close nursing supervision during ambulation was necessary. Risk factors included the following:

1. Limited mobility prior to hospitalization as a function of cardiac decompensation
2. Residual neurologic deficits from prior cerebral vascular accidents

3. Diabetes mellitus, type I, with episodes of vertigo related to hypoglycemia

4. Physical and psychological exhaustion associated with open heart surgery

5. Potential side effects of medications such as Inderal (propranolol hydrochloride) and Percodan (oxycodone), affecting equilibrium

6. Cardiac arrhythmias with the potential of decreasing end diastolic ventricular volume and decreasing cardiac output, resulting in decreased tissue oxygenation with consequent fatigue, vertigo, etc.

7. Minimal ambulation prior to the fall as documented in the medical record

Patient L was instructed by the nursing staff to "seek assistance at all times" with ambulation. But, the nursing staff did not respond on the fourth postoperative day to Patient L's repeated requests for assistance in going to the bathroom. Patient L got up alone, became "faint," and fell, and this was on the day she had two episodes of PAT with syncope.

In addition, correction of errors in the nurse's notes regarding the fall was not consistent with the acceptable standard of nursing care. The credibility of the medical record in this case was severely jeopardized because numerous sentences were completely obliterated with ink. A single line should have been drawn through the error, with the word "error" written above and the initials of the nurse. The corrected notation then should have followed.

The plaintiff's case was based on the determination that the departures from the prevailing professional standard of nursing care caused the fall. The case settled with payment to the plaintiff.

## Case 11–3
### *Fall: No Documentation*

#### Problem and Outcome

A 56-year-old woman fell while hospitalized. The fall was not charted, and the patient consequently did not receive treatment for injury to the lower extremity. As a result, she suffered a permanent partial disability.

### The Patient

Patient M was admitted to the hospital with the diagnosis of herniated nucleus pulposus of lumbar vertebrae numbers four and five (L4–5), bilateral. Patient M had been in excellent health except for a back injury two years prior to admission. The patient injured her back initially when lifting a grandchild. Patient M took care of her daughter's four children (ages three, four, six, and seven) so that her daughter, who was divorced, could pursue employment.

### Treatment

Surgery for the back injury was effective, and the low back pain improved. Toward the latter part of the hospitalization, Patient M fell in the bathroom and injured her right lower extremity. She was discharged from the hospital but was readmitted later that day with neurovascular embarrassment of the right lower extremity. This required immediate surgical intervention. As a result of the injury, Patient M sustained a peroneal nerve palsy with foot drop and reflex sympathetic dystrophy. Patient M became quite depressed over the injury.

### Departures from the Standard of Care

Departures from prevailing professional standards of nursing care were as follows:

1. Failure to chart the fall
2. Failure to inform the physician of the fall and the injury to the lower extremity
3. Failure to perform an initial comprehensive nursing assessment after the injury
4. Failure to assess systematically the lower extremity

### Discussion

There was no documentation of a fall in the medical record. Patient M testified that she fell in the hospital the day before discharge. Patient M further stated that, "I told the nurses about the fall and that my leg hurt." The nursing progress record does not mention a fall, but states that warm compresses were applied to the right calf commencing the afternoon before discharge. The nursing progress record for that evening read, "right leg elevated on pillow; some redness and swelling noted on right ankle. Ice-pack applied to area."

The factual information regarding the fall should have been charted, and the physician should have been informed of the incident. In addition, the patient should have been examined by a physician, and a comprehensive nursing assessment regarding injuries should have appeared in the record. Continuing nursing assessments of the extremity should have included a description of the following:

1. Pain (quantitative, qualitative, topographic, and temporal aspects)
2. Skin color
3. Temperature of the extremity
4. Edema, presence or absence
5. Ecchymosis, presence or absence
6. Peripheral pulses
7. Ability to flex and extend toes
8. Blanching sign
9. Sensory function
10. Motor function

Systematic assessment of the lower extremity was mandatory because groups of muscles are enclosed within tough fascial compartments. In addition, blood vessels and nerves enter and exit these compartments through small openings. In the lower leg, compartments include the anterior, peroneal, and posterior. In addition to these compartments, each muscle is covered by a fibrous sheath (epimysium). The muscle bellies, in contrast to the skin and subcutaneous tissue, require an abundant supply of well-oxygenated blood or they are rapidly and profoundly affected by the ischemia.

Trauma to a muscle or a group of muscles in the lower extremity may cause bleeding into the soft tissues and/or edema of the soft tissues. This edema and/or bleeding may cause the pressure within a compartment to increase greatly because of the restricting fascial envelope enclosing the muscles. The increasing intramuscular pressure, in turn, causes compression of the small openings through which blood vessels and nerves enter and exit the compartment. A sufficient pressure increase can result in nerve damage and decreased blood supply, producing a progressive irreversible necrosis of the involved muscle tissue. Injury to a muscle may be apparent within four to forty-eight hours after the injury, and a limb with a compromised neurovascular supply may sustain irreversible pathologic changes within approximately one and one-half hours. Assessment enables the nurse to detect these problems early, so that treatment can be instituted before permanent damage occurs.

Patient M sustained an injury of this type, but she was discharged from the hospital on the physician's order written the morning before and prior to the incident. The physician had not been informed of the fall, nor had he examined Patient M on the day of discharge. The patient was reassured by the nursing staff, who told her "You are fine," even though she had severe pain and areas of decreased sensation in the right lower extremity.

The plaintiff's case was based on the determination that, within reasonable nursing probability, the departures from the prevailing professional standard of nursing care caused the peroneal nerve palsy and reflex sympathetic dystrophy. The case settled with payment to the plaintiff.

## Case 11–4

### *Three Falls*

#### Problem and Outcome

Three falls and the development of a sacral decubitus ulcer complicated the hospitalization of a 66-year-old woman.

#### The Patient

Patient L, a patient of Dr. G, suffered from paranoid schizophrenia along with a moderate degree of organic brain deterioration. She was described by her physician as delusional about herself and the people around her. Patient L was very insecure and did not trust anyone. Brought up in the Jewish faith, Patient L turned to Christian Science in her later years as the answer to all her problems. Frequently, her behavior became uncontrollable. When she decompensated to the point of losing reality-orientation and became totally nonfunctional at home, she was admitted to a general hospital.

#### Treatment

Patient L was admitted to the hospital with the diagnosis of psychotic depressive reaction. On this occasion, she had decompensated not only mentally but physiologically as well. Her behavior was delusional with frequent hallucinations. She also was not eating, was very uncooperative with her family, and was totally nonfunctional. Treatment consisted of daily psychotherapy along with tranquilizers and antidepressant agents.

Six days after Patient L's admission, Eskalth (lithium carbonate), in addition to therapeutic milieu, was prescribed. At this time, other antipsychotic and antidepressant medications were discontinued. Patient L improved and became more lucid, rational, and less psychotic. But, two days after commencement of this treatment (8 days postadmission), Patient L became tremulous, agitated, ataxic, and unable to ambulate. She fell three times in the hospital. The third fall resulted in a fracture of the femur and subsequent decubitus ulcers.

### Departures from the Standard of Care

Departures from prevailing professional standards of nursing care were as follows:

1. Failure to provide a safe environment and protect the patient from avoidable injury
2. Failure to follow the physician's orders
3. Failure to maintain the integrity of the skin

### Discussion

Eight days after admission, the nurse's notes describe Patient L as "very tremulous, unsteady in gait, and very weak." The nurse's notes on the ensuing days continue to address increasing confusion, difficulty in ambulation progressing to a totally bedridden state, increasing agitation, disorientation, and increasing tremulousness.

Nine days after admission, Patient L fell but was not injured. At this point, the physician ordered private-duty attendants around the clock for the protection of the patient. It was reported in the nurse's notes, eight days after the first fall, that Patient L "refuses to stay in bed – removed Posey repeatedly, attempted to run from special attendant, fell against chairs, then to floor on left side, striking head on door frame."

Ten days after this second fall, the nurse's notes read, "Patient sitting on floor. When helped to chair, patient complained of right thigh pain. Refused to bear weight. Patient had been in bed and [attendant] left only for lunch break."

The third fall, which resulted in a displaced comminuted intertrochanteric fracture of the right femur with avulsion of the lesser tuberosity, was confirmed by X-ray examination. Investigation of the incident revealed that the private-duty attendant did have permission to go to lunch. The nurse manager testified, "We were short-staffed and there was no one to stay with [Patient L] while her aide was at lunch." This nurse was also aware that the physician did not want Patient L to be unattended at any time.

The nurse manager had the obligation to protect the patient from injury and to execute the physician's order regarding patient safety. Leaving Patient L unattended because of being short-staffed was unacceptable. The  nurse manager had the responsibility to obtain additional staffing so that nursing care could be delivered according to acceptable standards.

Patient L's hospitalization became more complicated after the open reduction and internal fixation of the right femur. During the postoperative period, Patient L developed a sacral decubitus ulcer. A decubitus ulcer, regardless of how debilitated a patient may be, is preventable with proper nursing care. Skin care along with turning and positioning of Patient L was not documented in the nurse's notes. Furthermore, no description of the lesion and its treatment was found in the nurse's notes. Documentation of this lesion was found only in the physician's progress notes.

After two and one-half months, Patient L was transferred to an extended-care facility. Her course of hospitalization had been complicated by inadequate nursing care.

The plaintiff's case was based on the determination that the departures from the prevailing professional standard of nursing care caused injury to Patient L. The case settled with payment to the plaintiff.

## Case 11–5
### *Fall: No Assistance*

#### Problem and Outcome

A fall complicated the hospitalization of an independent 88-year-old woman. The fall resulted in the patient being discharged to an extended-care facility rather than to her home.

#### The Patient

Patient M, a retired schoolteacher, lived alone. A niece assisted her with shopping and "heavy" household chores, thereby enabling Patient M to remain independent. Patient M, despite her age, was energetic and in good health except for "aches and pains" and diminished eyesight associated with aging.

## Treatment

Patient M was admitted to the hospital on 12 October because of rectal bleeding and rectal prolapse. She was alert, oriented to person, place, and time, and most concerned about her condition. Gastrointestinal evaluation, including colonoscopy, revealed diverticulosis coli. The rectal prolapse was treated conservatively, but it persisted. Repair by the Teirch procedure was performed, but Patient M's hospitalization was complicated by a fall.

### Departures from the Standard of Care

Departures from prevailing professional standards of nursing care were as follows:

1. Failure to provide a safe environment
2. Failure to protect the patient from harm associated with advanced age, the added risks of diagnostic tests, and the foreseeable consequences of such a situation
3. Failure to follow the physician's orders

### Discussion

According to the physician's admission orders, Patient M was to be on complete bed rest without bathroom privileges. Gastrointestinal examinations were scheduled, and Patient M was given laxatives and enemas for bowel preparation.

At approximately 11:00 P.M. on 13 October, Patient M put on the call light because she needed to evacuate her bowels. Shortly thereafter, a nurse informed Patient M via the intercom that someone would assist her after the change-of-shift report. Patient M stated that she needed help urgently because she had received various cathartics. There was no reply. Patient M got up and went to the bathroom. She fainted and was found on the bathroom floor at 11:45 P.M. Patient M sustained a laceration to the right supraorbital area and a badly comminuted fracture of the subcapital region of the right humerus.

Bowel preparation increases the risk for accident by falling, particularly if the patient is elderly. Nursing care was not provided to protect Patient M from the consequences of her advanced age, weakened condition, and bowel preparation. The fall prolonged Patient M's hospitalization and caused her to be admitted to an extended-care facility because she could not use her right arm with the short-arm immobilizer.

The plaintiff's case was based on the determination that the departures from the prevailing professional standard of nursing care caused injury to the patient. The case settled with payment to the plaintiff.

## Case 11–6
### *Fall: Posey Vest Tied to Bed*

#### Problem and Outcome

An 82-year-old woman "escaped" from a Posey vest and sustained a fractured wrist. The patient was found on the floor while the Posey vest was found tied to the bed frame.

#### The Patient

A daughter, who cared for Patient M in her own home, noted discoloration of the left great toe which appeared in the other toes over a period of two to three weeks. No previous similar trouble had been noted. Patient M had been in excellent health except for some generalized cerebral deterioration over the past twelve to eighteen months. It was noted that her memory was poor, and that she became easily confused.

#### Treatment

Patient M was admitted to the hospital on 12 August with the diagnosis of gangrene of the left great toe. In addition, she was in a confused mental state.

An arteriogram revealed total occlusion of both internal iliac arteries with stenosis of the left common iliac artery. A femorofemoral arterial bypass and left femoropopliteal arterial bypass was performed on 14 August. Circulation to the left foot markedly improved. Postoperatively, Patient M did well and slowly recuperated. On 24 August, however, Patient M fell and sustained a fractured wrist, which required an open reduction with internal fixation.

#### Departures from the Standard of Care

Departures from prevailing professional standards of nursing care included the following:

1. Failure to apply the restraint properly
2. Failure to observe systematically the restrained patient

### Discussion

A physician's order for the use of a Posey vest restraint (as needed) was written when Patient M was admitted. On 24 August, only two nursing entries were found in the chart between 7:00 A.M. and 3:00 P.M. At noon, it was noted, "liquid stools times three," and at 3:00 P.M. , "patient found on floor with Posey tied securely to bed frame . . . states she was going to bathroom – large amount of stool in bed and on floor." The Posey vest had not been properly applied; the vest was tied too loosely to restrain her in the bed. Patient M was not observed systematically while in the restraint.

The plaintiff's case was based on the determination that the departures from the prevailing professional standard of nursing care caused injury to Patient M. The case settled with payment to the plaintiff.

### Case 11–7

## *Fall: Posey Vest Tied to Patient*

### Problem and Outcome

A 65-year-old male patient "escaped" from a Posey vest and was found on the floor with the Posey vest tied around his body. He sustained a fractured hip.

### The Patient

Patient B was known to his physician because of previous hospitalizations. Past medical history significantly indicated chronic obstructive pulmonary disease, chronic renal failure, mild congestive heart failure, chronic venous stasis, severe peripheral arterial insufficiency, chronic dementia, and chronic depression.

### Treatment

Patient B was taken by his family to the emergency department of a hospital at 9:31 P.M. on 6 October with chief complaints of ataxia of gait, lethargy, increasing confusion, and urinary incontinence. The plan for this hospitalization was to evaluate the patient's condition in light of his chief complaints. While hospitalized, Patient B fell and fractured the right hip, necessitating an open reduction and internal fixation.

### Departures from the Standard of Care

Review of the medical record revealed departures from prevailing professional standards of nursing care that included the following:

1. Failure to observe the patient systematically
2. Failure to provide a safe environment and to protect the patient from avoidable injury

### Discussion

According to the medical record, Patient B's condition was such that restraints were ordered on 7 October to be applied throughout his hospital stay.

The documentation on 7 October by the nursing staff did not reflect systematic nursing observations with regard to the use of restraints. Moreover, in the medical record on 8 October at 3:35 A.M., it was noted that "Patient found sitting on the floor in front of room 3105. States he fell. Lifted into wheelchair and put back to bed. [Dr. R] called and notified. Patient complains of pain in right leg." In addition, it was noted that the Posey vest was "securely tied around him" but "not tied to the bed." The fall resulted in a fracture of the right hip.

This fall could have been prevented by systematic observation of the patient and proper application of the Posey vest.

The plaintiff's case was based on the determination that the departures from the prevailing professional standard of nursing care caused injury to Patient B. The case settled with payment to the plaintiff.

### Case 11–8

## *Fall: Posey Vest Tied to Side Rails*

### Problem and Outcome

A 79-year-old man "escaped" from a Posey vest and fractured his hip. Again, the patient was found on the floor, but the Posey vest, in this case, was found tied to the side rail.

### The Patient

Patient G was admitted to the hospital from an extended-care facility for the treatment of a possible bowel obstruction. Patient G also presented with a history of Alzheimer's disease and was noted to be disoriented to person, place, and time. Because of this, the physician ordered a "Posey vest at all times."

### Treatment

Bowel obstruction was ruled out after the first day, and Patient G was to be discharged the next morning. But Patient G fell during the night. X-rays revealed a fractured hip, and Patient G's hospitalization was prolonged for two weeks.

### Departures from the Standard of Care

Departures from prevailing professional standards of nursing care were as follows:

1. Failure to provide a safe environment and protect the patient from avoidable injury
2. Failure to apply the Posey vest properly

### Discussion

The nurse's note read: "Heard noise and found patient lying on floor with Posey vest on, side rails up." Testimony by the nurse responsible for the care of Patient G revealed that the Posey vest was "tied very securely to the side rails." The Posey vest was applied improperly, because the product is designed to be secured to the bed frame and not the side rails. This fall would have been prevented had the Posey vest been applied properly.

The plaintiff's case was based on the determination that the departures from the prevailing professional standard of nursing care caused injury to the patient. The case settled with payment to the plaintiff.

## Case 11–9

### *Fall: Patient Jumped out the Window*

#### Problem and Outcome

A 27-year-old man sustained multiple injuries in a motor-vehicle accident. Behavioral problems resulted, and the patient jumped out of the hospital window. He was rendered paraplegic.

## The Patient

Patient E was involved in a motor-vehicle accident on 18 August. He sustained multiple injuries which included a closed head injury with a large scalp laceration, a left cerebral contusion with an intraventricular hematoma, and a fractured mandible. Ethanol intoxication (.263 grams per decaliter [gm/DL]) was evident on admission.

## Treatment

Patient E was evaluated and stabilized in the emergency department. The scalp laceration and the fractured mandible were repaired in the operating room on the evening of admission.

According to the physician's progress notes, behavioral problems secondary to the closed head injury resulted in "very slow neurologic improvement." On 11 September, Patient E jumped out of the window of his hospital room. He survived the fall but suffered an acute subdural hematoma and a complex fracture of the thoracic spine. The fracture of the spine rendered him immediately paraplegic. An emergency left frontal craniotomy with removal of an acute subdural hematoma was performed that evening. On 9 October, an open reduction and stabilization of the thoracic spine was performed. Patient E remained paraplegic.

## Departures from the Standard of Care

The departures from prevailing professional standards of nursing care included the following:

1. Failure to provide a safe environment for the patient
2. Failure to restrain the patient properly
3. Failure to inform the physician that the patient's behavior was becoming more uncontrollable on 11 September

## Discussion

In the intensive care unit, the nursing care plan noted, among other things, a "potential for self-harm secondary to head injury, disorientation, agitation, and combativeness." Restraints and sedation were to be used as needed. While in the intensive care unit, Patient E was variously described as disoriented, agitated, combative, screaming, cursing, and having episodes of bizarre behavior. It was noted several times that Patient E was "able to rip off wrist restraints." After "very slow neurologic improvement," Patient E was transferred to a medical-surgical unit on 30 August. The intensive care unit nursing-transfer summary emphasized: "Restrain at all times, as unsteady and continually tries to get out of bed by self. Requires four point restraints and vest restraint." Patient E was still noted as "confused, disoriented, screaming, cursing, combative, and trying to get out of bed."

Between 31 August and 11 September, there were numerous nursing notations referring to Patient E "getting out of restraints," "pulling out Foley," and "pulling out nasogastric tube." On 10 September, it was noted in the medical record by the nurse caring for Patient E, "Suggest private-duty nurse or attendant to family and social service."

At 6:10 A.M. on 11 September, the nurse's note read: "Patient getting worse. Patient got out of vest and wrist restraints and got out of bed." The next note was at 9:00 P.M.: "Patient found on third-floor roof (jumped out of window)." Patient E survived the fall but sustained a complex fracture of thoracic vertebrae nine through twelve (T9–T12), which rendered him paraplegic, and an acute subdural hematoma.

Patient E 's condition was known to the nursing staff, and the potential for self-harm was obvious from the notations in the medical record. In addition, a notation in the medical record on the day before the incident suggested private-duty attendants, but no action was taken. On the day of the incident, Patient E's behavior was described as becoming "worse." Nothing was done about this situation.

Nurses have the obligation to provide a safe environment for the patient. Private-duty attendants or transfer to a facility with personnel competent to manage such behavioral problems should have been discussed with the physician and/or hospital administration.

The plaintiff's case was based on the determination that the departures from the prevailing professional standard of nursing care rendered Patient E paraplegic. The case settled with payment to the plaintiff.

While investigating this tragic case, it was found through police reports that Patient E was the third patient that year to "jump out the window." In March, an 84-year-old man admitted with the diagnosis of encephalopathy "slipped out of restraints." He had been insistent upon seeing his wife, and when his wife arrived at his room, two blankets had been tied together and were hanging out the window. The patient fell three stories and broke both feet.

In June, a 78-year-old man with the diagnosis of urinary-tract infection and kidney problems was noted to be missing at medication-administration time. When the nursing staff looked for the man, the bedridden patient in the room next door reported having heard a loud thump and feeling some type of vibration. A nurse went to the missing patient's room and found the window open. She looked out and saw the patient five storeys below. The patient had been dead for about one and one-half hours before being found.

These three incidents should have been prevented by basic nursing care. These episodes of "escape" from restraints warranted serious investigation by the nursing staff. Restraints that are appropriate to the situation and that are applied properly should, in fact, contain the patient.

# Chapter 12

# Documentation

In the nursing malpractice cases discussed in this book, one important problem recurs – namely, inadequate or inappropriate documentation. The importance of nursing documentation, along with maintaining an accurate and timely medical record, cannot be overemphasized.

Nursing documentation in the medical record is inseparable from the actual nursing care rendered. Documentation is as critical to patient care as the actual nursing care provided. This chapter reviews the purpose of the medical record and the purpose and importance of documentation. It discusses what to document and provides guidelines for documentation.

The basic purpose of a medical record is to document throughout hospitalization (1) the patient's condition, (2) the care received, and (3) the patient's response to that care. This record provides for continuity of care and serves as a basis for planning and evaluating the patient's condition. Other functions of the medical record include the following: (1) documenting communication between members of the health-care team who provide care to a patient, (2) quality-assurance management, (3) risk management, (4) billing and reimbursement, (5) financial planning, (6) preparing health-service statistics, (7) supporting education and clinical research, (8) providing a record that may be used to protect the legal interests of the patient and the hospital or health-care team, and (9) utilization review.

The medical record is a vital element for evaluation of nursing care in the analysis of a potential nursing malpractice case. Problems associated with nursing documentation in the medical record are present not only in the majority of cases discussed in this book but in the majority of medical records that I have reviewed over the years. Because of these problems, a discussion of the importance of documentation along with suggested guidelines follows.

Historically, nursing documentation has come full circle. In the past, detailed charting was expected. Subsequently, the emphasis was on recording entries briefly with some "routine" aspects of care not being charted in detail. Today, with increasingly complex health-care delivery and the involvement of many members of the health-care team in providing care, it is expected that all patient care will be documented.

Nursing care and documentation go hand in hand. Care and documentation cannot be separated or considered as two actions, because they are one act. Documentation of nursing care is as important as providing the actual care. In fact, documentation of care is inseparable from the care itself; the absence of documentation implies absence of care.

Documentation responsibilities and the associated standards are a part of the basic education that every nurse receives. In addition, professional organizations and health-care accrediting agencies provide recommendations, suggestions, and standards for nursing documentation. According to the American Nurses' Association *Standards of Nursing Practice*, documentation regarding the patient's health status must include a systematic and continuous collection of data that is accessible, communicated, and recorded. The Joint Commission on Accreditation of Healthcare Organizations also sets standards for documenting nursing care of hospitalized patients. These standards require that the nursing process (assessment, problem identification, planning, intervention, and evaluation) be documented for each hospitalized patient from admission through discharge.

A hospital policy-and-procedure manual typically provides nursing documentation standards. This is particularly helpful to the nurse because the hospital usually integrates appropriate laws, regulations, and standards into its own policy-and-procedure statements.

These standards have become increasingly important, because nursing care has become more and more complex. The expanded role of the nurse demands greater accountability and responsibility. Similarly, nursing documentation has taken on greater legal significance. Good documentation is a critical element in the nurse's duty to a patient.

The medical record is a witness that cannot be ignored and that never dies. Adequate documentation can prevent malpractice claims from being initiated. In the event of litigation, the strongest defense is provided by clear, concise, accurate, and relevant nurse's notes demonstrating continuous care and treatment. The medical record is a nurse's best friend or worst enemy in a malpractice action. The weight a medical record carries in legal proceedings cannot be overemphasized, because the medical record provides legal proof of the nature and quality of care a patient received.

A nurse's failure to document the care provided to a patient significantly affects the outcome of a malpractice case by weakening or eliminating the hospital's defense. A jury tends to believe a black-and-white copy of a medical record over a person's memory. Courts recognize that in many cases nurses are very busy, and that it might be difficult to document findings and actions. Nonetheless, courts do equate this deficiency in the medical record ("failure to chart") with the nurse's failure to perform a nursing action. The old adage "If it was not charted, it was not done" continues to hold true.

Nursing documentation must be complete, accurate, and timely, and must demonstrate continuous care. It must reflect *everything about* the care provided to the patient. Gaps in documentation suggest that the patient was neglected. The actual elements of nursing care – that is, what is being done and what is seen, felt, and heard – must be recorded.

The *nursing process* is the organizational framework for the elements of nursing practice and it must be reflected in documentation. The nursing process is a problem-solving technique based upon the scientific method. During a patient's hospitalization, the nursing process is applied and is modified as a patient's condition changes. The *nursing care plan* is a written statement of this process.

Patient *assessment* is the initial activity of the nursing process. Here, biopsychosocial data is collected and analyzed. This forms the data base for identification of patient *problems* and *nursing diagnoses*. *Goals* or desired outcomes are formulated in relation to patient problems, and a *plan of action* is devised to address problems. *Implementation* of the plan of action follows, and the plan of action is then continually *evaluated*. Nursing actions are evaluated in relation to the patient problem(s) and desired outcome(s).

The format of the nursing care plan is usually determined by the individual agency. The nurse's responsibility is to ensure that the nursing care plan is specific to patient problems and is modified to reflect the nursing process on a continuing basis as the patient's condition changes. Appendix A provides a representative excerpt from a nursing care plan.

Nursing documentation should reflect the following:

1. Initial nursing assessment and history (see chap. 4)
2. Patient problem(s)
3. Ongoing systematic assessments and observations (see chap. 4 )
4. Nursing interventions

5. Treatments, procedures, diagnostic tests
6. Notation of visits by other members of the health-care team (care rendered by others)
7. Patient response to treatment
8. Pertinent statements made by the patient
9. Comfort and safety measures provided to the patient
10. Patient teaching
11. Nursing discharge summary (patient's condition, teaching, special instructions given for follow-up and/or home care)

Nursing documentation covers all aspects of nursing care, including routine interventions and normal findings as well as the abnormal. If some aspect of nursing care, such as administering a medication, is omitted, the omission must be documented along with the reason for the omission.

The nurse is responsible for complete and accurate documentation in all sections of the medical record concerned with nursing care, such as the medication administration record, intake and output sheet, parenteral-fluids form, flow sheets, graphic record, and preoperative checklist.

All telephone calls regarding patient care must be carefully documented. This is especially important when a call is placed to a physician to clarify an order, report a change in the patient's condition, report laboratory or other diagnostic results, etc. The date, time, and content of the conversation must be documented. If the nurse is unable to contact a patient's physician (that is, if the call is not returned in a timely manner or there is no answer at the physician's phone number), the nursing supervisor should be informed and appropriate help should be obtained. All of this information should be documented.

Telephone and verbal orders should be taken only when the physician cannot attend the patient or cannot in person write the order. Careful documentation (with date, time, and the order-verbatim) is essential. In addition, the order must be read back to the physician for verification. These orders should be countersigned by the physician as soon as possible.

Finally, potentially harmful patient actions must be documented in detail, and actual patient statements should be utilized. Documentation is necessary, for example, if an alert, oriented patient, instructed to be on complete bed rest, is found walking around. The nurse must ascertain the patient's reason for being out of bed and must record it in direct quotes, if possible. Some potentially harmful patient acts that must be documented include the following:

1. Refusal of prescribed treatments
2. Refusal of medications or misuse of prescribed medications
3. Refusal to follow instructions or physician's orders
4. Failure to provide a complete and accurate health history and health-status information
5. Interference with the delivery of health care (that is, any behavior which hinders delivery of care such as tampering with equipment [e.g., intravenous infusion apparatus, traction apparatus] used in the patient's treatment)
6. Use of unauthorized items and substances such as a heating pad, alcoholic beverages, tobacco, and medications
7. Leaving the hospital against medical advice

Any potentially harmful act done to a patient by a visitor or family member must also be documented. This may include, among other things, tampering with dressings and patient-care equipment, preventing or delaying delivery of health care, providing unauthorized substances and items, and assisting the patient with actions contrary to orders and instructions.

A review of some guidelines for effective documentation is in order. These guidelines apply to both of the charting methods commonly used: source-oriented charting (narrative notes organized by discipline); and problem-oriented charting (narrative notes organized around a master problem list). First, knowledge and understanding of hospital policies and procedures concerning documentation is imperative. Periodic review by nurses of these policies and procedures provides for reinforcement of this basic knowledge.

Accurate documentation begins with proper preparation of each page of the medical record with patient name, medical record number, and nursing unit or room number. Recording information promptly and in proper sequence ensures accuracy. Every entry in the medical record must have a complete date and precise time.

Depending on hospital policy, a nurse may choose between time-charting and block-charting. Using time-charting, nursing care is recorded as it occurs, whereas with block-charting, care is recorded at the end of a block of time (frequently a shift). From my experience, time-charting is more accurate when nursing care is recorded shortly after it is administered.

Regardless of the type of charting used, legible handwriting, the use of standard and approved abbreviations, correct grammar and spelling, and a factual, objective, professionally stated entry lends credibility to the record. Vague, general, and subjective entries like "patient taking fluids well" or "patient complains of pain" are meaningless to the reader. Factual and objective observations best communicate information regarding the patient. For example, "The patient drank 600 milliliters of water between 7:00 A.M. and 11:00 A.M." And another example, "Patient reports severe burning pain at incision. The onset was sudden and not associated with activity. Medicated by mouth with Tylenol #3."

The nurse must sign all entries made in the medical record with his/her first initial, full last name, and title. The signature should be placed on the right side of the page to verify that he/she entered all of the information between the previous signature and the current one. The nurse should draw a line through any empty spaces in front of the signature to prevent subsequent additions.

The nurse should document and sign only for the actual nursing care he/she provides, and only *after* the care has been provided. Precharting of nursing care departs from acceptable standards. In addition, it jeopardizes the credibility of a record if, for example, a patient unexpectedly expires and nursing care (such as medication administration) is precharted and thereby falls after the death.

If an error is made in documentation, a single line is drawn through the error and the word "error" is written above the line. This is initialed, and the correction follows. If absolutely necessary, an addition to the medical record or a late entry can be made. This should be done promptly, because the later in time the addendum is made, the less credibility it will have, especially with a jury. This entry should have the correct date and time and must be headed "addendum (or late entry) to the nurse's notes of (date and time)." Any time a nurse alters a medical record, he/she must include the date, time, and reason for the alteration along with his/her signature and title. Finally, the nurse should never obliterate or erase any entry and should never tear out or destroy any pages of the medical record. Errors not properly corrected undermine the credibility of the medical record in court. Entries obliterated with white-out can be X-rayed, and the original entries can be read by the court.

The nurse should not insert corrections and/or information between lines, in margins, or between other entries. If the record appears in court, credibility will be jeopardized because this will seem to be an attempt to reconstruct the record in a more favorable light.

Rewriting nursing notes, particularly after a patient-care incident, should be absolutely avoided. In a number of cases, the discovery process revealed that the nurse involved in an incident decided to rewrite the nursing notes to make them neat and "more complete." Discovery also revealed that on occasion a nurse was told or requested to rewrite the nursing notes under the supervision of the risk manager and/or nursing supervisor.

In the event of any legal action, the nurse should never correct or revise a medical record, even if there is a reason to do so. The nurse should keep private notes if necessary, because altering the medical record at this point creates suspicion regarding the validity of the record.

One final comment is necessary concerning *incident reports* (situation, event, occurrence reports) with regard to patient care and medical record documentation. The incident report is a management tool. It is an important component of the risk-management system because it is the means whereby physicians, nurses, and all employees of a hospital can report unusual occurrences. The incident report serves as a vehicle to gather data for the prevention of actual or potential problems. When an incident report involves a patient, the report itself is not a part of the medical record.

Only a factual, detailed, and objective description of an incident involving a patient should be documented in the medical record. Opinions and speculation are to be avoided. The filing of an incident report should not be documented in the medical record unless it is required in rare circumstances by hospital policy. In the contemporary hospital, incident reporting is encouraged, and the incident report is no longer used by the nursing department as a punitive tool for disciplinary action.

In summary, all nursing care must be documented in the medical record. Nursing care and documentation go hand in hand and are inseparable. The absence of documentation implies absence of care. Nursing documentation must be accurate and timely and must demonstrate continuous care. The nurse should alter records for patient-care purposes only if absolutely necessary. This must be done with the greatest of care to prevent the appearance of misrepresentation. A fraudulent medical record is difficult, if not impossible, to defend.

# Chapter 13

# Summary and Recommendations

Nursing malpractice exists because it is human to make mistakes under stress, and nurses must function in a stressful environment. Contributing to this stressful environment are sicker patients in today's hospitals, heavier work loads, and frequent interruptions and distractions while providing nursing care (such as medication preparation). With the current emphasis on decreasing the costs of health care, nurses are burdened with many non-nursing tasks such as housekeeping chores and clerical work. This adversely affects patient care in that nurses have less time to spend with patients. Staffing levels are often inadequate, and, in addition, nurses are frequently given patient-care assignments for which they may not be qualified. Nurses have an obligation to insist on an adequate level of staffing and to refuse patient-care assignments not within their areas of expertise.

Nursing malpractice can be minimized if the nurse utilizes the nursing process and delivers patient care that conforms to the prevailing professional standard. Fundamental to the nursing process is a complete initial nursing assessment and history, followed by continuous systematic patient assessment. Assessment forms the basis for defining patient problems, setting goals with corresponding objectives, and planning nursing-care actions. Implementation of the plan of action, with attention to providing a safe environment, safe medication administration, prevention of infection, systematic assessment, accurate execution of treatments/procedures, and safe use of equipment and supplies, will protect the patient from harm. Knowledge of hospital policies and procedures will facilitate the formulation of the nursing care plan and will contribute to safe patient care. Ongoing reevaluation and modification of the plan in response to changes in a patient's condition will assure an effective and dynamic process.

Communication throughout the nursing process is crucial for the provision of safe patient care consistent with the prevailing professional standard. Spoken communication among all members of the health-care team, and especially between nurse and physician for clarifying orders, planning patient care, and reporting significant patient observations is vital to the nursing process. Equally important is written communication by the nurse in the form of prompt and accurate entries in the medical record. In addition, interactive discourse between the nurse, nursing administration, and hospital administration should address all aspects of patient care, including instances of inadequate patient care.

Nurses in general are well educated, and they provide competent patient care throughout hospitals in the United States. Yet, nursing malpractice occurs. Utilizing the practices and principles embodied in the nursing process can serve to prevent much nursing malpractice. This would eliminate the mistakes and omissions reflected in the following remarks, typical of those that recur in nursing malpractice testimony:

"You only chart positive things – that is, abnormal findings – not negative things."

"I am not really that familiar with the policy-and-procedure manual because it contains a lot of theoretical stuff."

"I didn't have time to chart everything, and it's really not that important."

"I observed the patient as often as possible, but you know we were really busy [later, admitting to being short-staffed]."

"I was very busy, and it was more important to care for my patients than to chart."

"Oh yes, I looked at the policy-and-procedure manual when I was hired, but you know, you can't remember all that stuff and you don't have time to fool around looking things up."

"I observed the patient a lot, but I must have forgotten to chart."

"I told the head nurse [about inadequate physician care] but she didn't do anything, and I couldn't do anything else. I did my part."

"We do those things [vital signs] all the time and always watch our patients, but we don't chart it."

"It's not good to disturb a doctor at night."

## Nursing Malpractice Data

It is unfortunate that no authoritative national data regarding nursing malpractice is available. The development of data would provide awareness of the incidence and consequences of nursing malpractice on a national basis. Cases of nursing malpractice are generally not addressed as such because the hospital is named as the defendant. It is not common for a nurse to be named individually as a defendant in a malpractice suit, though this practice is increasing. The hospital is usually named as defendant and is held responsible for the actions of all employees, and that includes the nurse. Information can be found, for example, on the number of health-care malpractice cases closed in a particular year, or the percentage of hospital admissions that experience a potentially compensable event, but no data is available specific to nursing.

Attempts to collect nursing malpractice data are being made. In 1987, the American Nurses' Association established "The National Nurses Claims Data Base" to collect information on nursing malpractice claims. Data collection relies on voluntary reporting by the nurse involved in a malpractice claim. The United States government established the National Practitioner Data Bank (NPDB) to collect information on malpractice payments and professional disciplinary actions. This organization was mandated by the Health Care Quality Improvement Act of 1986, and it was implemented in the summer of 1990. Its primary purpose is to identify and discipline physicians and dentists who are incompetent. Moreover, insurance-claim payments involving nursing malpractice must also be reported. It is hoped that accessible information regarding nursing malpractice will be generated by these organizations.

For the time being, one must accept the assumption that nursing malpractice is a serious problem. Certainly a substantial number of lawsuits document the delivery of substandard basic nursing care. This book provides a sample of such cases in a single large urban community. Hospital malpractice cases almost always involve nurses, because the nurse is the only health-care team member in the hospital setting responsible for patient care on a 24-hour basis. The nurse with this responsibility has increased exposure to the risk of malpractice. Nurses as professionals with specialized knowledge and clinical skills hold the lives of patients in their hands. Nursing care that does not conform to the prevailing professional standards of nursing practice may result in patient injury or death. Analysis of the cases in this book provides some insight into the complex, tragic, and far-reaching consequences of nursing malpractice. These cases can be used to define problems and to develop strategies for minimizing nursing malpractice.

For the nurse, malpractice litigation can be physically stressful, emotionally devastating, and financially catastrophic. Awareness of nursing malpractice and the development of strategies aimed at its prevention is a first step toward dealing constructively with this problem.

The recommendations made in this chapter discuss ways of limiting nursing malpractice and are directed specifically to (1) nursing service and

(2) nursing education. Discussion focuses on issues of risk management, inservice education, curriculum, and communication.

## Recommendations: Nursing Service

### Recommendation I: Risk Management

An effective hospital risk-management system will help curtail nursing malpractice. All nurses need to be active participants in hospital risk-management systems. Nurses involved in clinical practice must feel free to identify risks. Nurses should analyze risks and communicate the results to hospital administration. Incidents and potential risks should not be ignored or shrouded in secrecy. Analysis of risks and effective communication will improve patient care.

The nurse is critical to risk management because of the daily contact with patients, family members, and visitors. The nurse is the only member of the health-care team who is with the hospitalized patient 24 hours a day and is thereby in the best position to learn from patients. Patients can provide a wealth of information regarding problems or potential problems. If problems are identified early, corrective action can be taken. If someone is harmed, direct settlement may take place instead of costly legal action. The nurse is in an excellent position to utilize interpersonal skills with the hospitalized patient to facilitate damage control.

A patient who is stressed and angry because of a diagnosis or treatment, for example, may find fault with all the care provided. In this situation, by heeding the patient attentively while at the same time offering a strong dose of reassurance, the nurse will demonstrate his/her genuine concern for the patient in an otherwise depersonalized environment. This may well prevent unfounded legal action that can be time-consuming, costly, and in many instances counter to the patient's best interest.

Hospital inservice education programs for nurses must be designed to enhance risk awareness. Open discussion of actual and potential problems along with a strategy for prevention is needed. All too often nurses report unusual incidents to their supervisor only to have the report "disappear" in the bureaucratic muddle with no apparent action. Feedback is essential if nurses are to feel free to identify risks and become a part of the team responsible for resolving the problem.

Nursing educators and nursing service practitioners must function as partners in risk management. Nursing service administrators must communicate malpractice problems and identify potential problems/risks to educators, with the expectation that this information will be used to improve the curriculum. In geographic areas with a high concentration of hospitals and nursing education programs, it might be worthwhile for nursing service administrators and educators to meet formally at least once a year to discuss those problems. For such a meeting to be effective, of course, the agenda must be carefully planned and structured. It should be agreed that an educator and nursing service representative will work together to formulate such an agenda.

## Recommendation 2: Inservice Education

Nursing service and nursing education must also work together to develop effective patient-care inservice education programs. By developing these programs together, educators can obtain valuable input from nursing service administrators about practical clinical problems and can work to overcome deficiencies in the curriculum. By the same token, nursing service administrators can learn more about the curriculum and the educational programs that prepare those whom they employ as nurses. The communitywide meeting proposed for risk management could also serve as the basis for improving inservice education.

The standard of nursing care delivered within a hospital is the responsibility of the nursing service division. Policies or statements of purpose are the vehicles that define minimum standards of nursing care for the institution. A misconception causes some nurses in clinical practice to regard standards as unreachable ideals with little application to actual clinical practice. Programs of inservice education can dispel this misconception by emphasizing the nurse's responsibility to meet the prevailing professional standards of nursing care for each and every nursing intervention.

Structured programs of inservice education are necessary to assist recent nurse graduates to translate theory into practice. The effective design of these educational programs requires an understanding of the curriculum and products from the various nursing education programs. Inservice education must be responsive to the needs of both the technically prepared nurse (ADN/Diploma) and the professionally prepared nurse (BSN).

For the experienced nurse involved in everyday clinical practice, programs must be developed to reinforce fundamental nursing care principles and their biopsychosocial basis. Strong emphasis must be given to reinforcing those procedural principles most frequently breached in practice, i.e., the common departures from the standard of care. The recurring departures described in the cases in this book need to be translated into inservice education programs to include the following:

1. Nursing assessment, with emphasis on
   a. Nursing history and initial assessment
   b. Formulation and execution of a realistic and individualized nursing care plan
   c. Ongoing systematic nursing assessment
2. Communication, with emphasis on
   a. Medical record documentation
   b. Effective communication of patient condition changes
   c. Effective communication of departures from the standard of care by members of the health-care team
   d. Effective communication of staffing needs
3. Practice elements, with emphasis on
   a. Nursing treatments and procedures
   b. Environmental safety
   c. Principles of medication administration
   d. Principles of infection control
   e. Equipment and product safety
4. Repetition and reinforcement of hospital policies and procedures

In summary, team management in a hospital, with nursing service playing a key role in risk management, is necessary to curtail nursing malpractice. Identification of risks, analysis of risks, communication of and about risks, and the development of preventive strategies is a nursing service obligation.

Inservice education is another vital element in the strategy to curtail nursing malpractice. Communication between nursing service and nursing education will maximize the effectiveness of both the hospital's risk-management system and its inservice education programs.

# Recommendations: Nursing Education

## Recommendation 3: Curriculum

The curriculum of nursing education programs is soundly conceptualized and is planned and revised as needed by dedicated, hard-working faculty members. The National League for Nursing sets standards for accreditation of nursing education programs, as do state boards of nursing. Licensure is controlled, but the issue of one licensure examination for both technical and professional nurses currently needs to be resolved. (It is beyond the scope of these recommendations to address the protracted issue of entry into practice.)

The curriculum in schools of nursing today provides a solid foundation based upon progression from basic to complex nursing principles in an integrated fashion. There is, however, a need to strengthen some areas of the curriculum. Many basic principles, such as those associated with documentation in the medical record, are presented carefully and well in several sessions in the initial phase of the curriculum. But there is little if any systematic reference back to the fundamentals as the curriculum becomes more complex. It is difficult if not impossible for students to assimilate fully these core principles in the initial stages of their education and training. It is therefore most important that, throughout the entire curriculum, these students be exposed to repeated review of these principles and their application.

Based on analysis of nursing malpractice cases, nursing educators must accept the fact that some elements of the curriculum need improvement. Certain fundamentals of nursing care are not being mastered by their students. Review does occur in the curriculum, but it is neither systematic nor frequent. A strategy needs to be developed for regularly and systematically reinforcing basic principles throughout the curriculum. Actual nursing malpractice problems, such as those discussed in this book, can provide a basis for determining which nursing care principles need to be reinforced. Using the repeated departures from the prevailing professional standard of nursing care, the following basic nursing activities can be defined:

1. Nursing history and initial nursing assessment
2. Nursing care planning and implementation
3. Systematic nursing assessment based upon the patient's condition

4. Medical-record documentation and communication of significant observations
5. Communication on behalf of the patient to assure an appropriate level of care by all members of the health-care team.
6. Environmental safety
7. Medication administration
8. Independent and dependent nursing treatments and procedures
9. Infection control
10. Equipment and product safety

Specific nursing care principles within the above categories must be identified and reinforced by all faculty members in both theoretical and clinical courses. Nursing school faculties must reach consensus on the basic principles to be reinforced throughout the curriculum. Each faculty member, when teaching a course, should accept responsibility for implementing review of these fundamental principles of nursing care. The teaching burden is increased only minimally, because one is not teaching new concepts, one is instead reviewing and reinforcing previous learning. Students must master basic nursing principles to the extent that they can apply them automatically in patient care.

## Recommendation 4: Communication

To reduce nursing malpractice, nursing educators should continually consult about the curriculum with nursing service practitioners. All too often, nursing educators plan the curriculum for the graduate nurse with little or no ongoing consultation as to the continuing needs of nursing service. Valuable understanding and input is lost both to educators and to nursing service practitioners.

The ideal would be to have nursing service representatives on the nursing program curriculum committee. This is not cost efficient, however, in a community with multiple nursing education programs and numerous hospitals. As suggested previously, a formal meeting held at least once a year between nursing service and nursing education representatives would also constitute an effective forum for addressing problems of nursing education and practice. Again, for success, the agenda should be well-conceptualized and structured. Representatives of nursing education and nursing service should work together to formulate such an agenda and coordinate the meeting. Particular attention should be directed at avoiding a meeting where only "politically correct and polite" issues are discussed. Educators and service representatives must be frank in identifying problems and in discussing solutions.

In summary, reinforcement of basic nursing care principles throughout the curriculum will enhance mastery of the subject. Communication between education and service is vital. Through communication, nursing service administrators can better understand the continuing educational needs of recent graduates of nursing programs, and nursing educators can better perceive the most common deficiencies in nursing clinical practice.

## Comments on Malpractice Litigation

Nurses who do not provide nursing care according to the prevailing standard should be held accountable for their actions. While it is true that some unjustified lawsuits are filed, nonetheless, as the cases in this book illustrate, poor nursing care that constitutes malpractice does cause serious injury and even death. Legal recourse is justified in such cases. The patient (or guardian, or estate) is entitled to compensation for the injury, past and future medical expenses, loss of income, disruption of life, and stress suffered because of nursing malpractice. For most victims of nursing malpractice, even large financial payments do not make up for what the patient and/or family has suffered.

Nursing service and nursing education administrators must encourage qualified nurses to serve as expert witnesses. Hospitals and schools of nursing are a valuable source of competent expert witnesses, and these agencies should be willing to provide the names of appropriate expert witnesses. By making well-qualified experts available, honest and objective reviews of cases will be made. Unjustified cases can be eliminated, and cases of breach of duty with harm can be settled promptly. The standards of the nursing profession will be upheld by this important process.

A major criticism of malpractice litigation is that plaintiffs' lawyers profit excessively. The contingency fee system, under which the plaintiff's attorney receives a percentage of the settlement or judgment, is in many cases lucrative for the attorney. But the strength of this system is that it assures legal representation for everyone, regardless of his/her financial capabilities. Malpractice litigation is costly. In complex cases, the plaintiff-discovery process alone can cost $50,000 or more. This figure represents only the actual expenses associated with the discovery process and does not include the attorney's time. If the case goes to trial, there may well be another $50,000 or more in expenses incurred by the plaintiff's attorney. How many people can afford this kind of money up front? The plaintiff's attorney makes this money available for the case to assure legal representation. The plaintiff does not have to repay these expenses until the case is concluded.

The money for malpractice settlements or jury awards in most cases comes from the defendant's malpractice insurer. If a defendant does not have malpractice insurance, payment generally comes from the defendant's property and/or future salary.

In the event of a nursing malpractice action arising from hospital-employment duties, malpractice insurance is usually provided by the hospital. However, a nurse, even though a hospital employee, is licensed as a professional and may be sued individually. Such lawsuits are becoming more common. Therefore, the nurse needs an individual nursing malpractice insurance policy to protect personal assets. Nursing malpractice policies for most specialties are available at a reasonable cost. Various policies exist, and they must be carefully compared because of significant differences among them. It is highly recommended that, as professionals, nurses involved in any aspect of clinical practice procure individual malpractice insurance coverage.

Changes in patient care result from malpractice actions. In a number of instances of which I am aware, hospital policies and procedures have been changed and/or mechanisms to ensure implementation of policies and procedures have come about as a result of malpractice actions. In particular, I know that a number of hospitals have changed their systems of nursing documentation to reflect the information and format of the flow sheets used throughout this book. Patient care has thereby been improved. These changes have often been precipitated rapidly in response to a large financial settlement. In these circumstances, the needed changes do not get deferred or lost in protracted committee discussions. They happen.

Serving as an expert witness in nursing malpractice cases has been one of the most rewarding experiences of my career. The work is demanding and challenging, but it can make a difference. To uphold the standards of the nursing profession, thereby improving clinical practice, is an exhilarating responsibility, one that provides tremendous satisfaction.

# Appendixes

The following information, presented at various places in the text, is combined here for convenient cross-reference.

## Appendix A
## The Nursing Process

The nursing process, a problem-solving technique, is the framework for nursing practice and organizes the elements of nursing care. The nursing process as applied to patient care includes:

1. *Assessment*: biopsychosocial data is collected and analyzed
2. *Problem(s)*: the data base, established by assessment, permits identification of patient problems and nursing diagnoses
3. *Goal(s)*: desired outcomes are then formulated in relation to patient problems
4. *Plan and implementation*: a plan of action is devised to address problems and is implemented
5. *Evaluation*: nursing actions are evaluated in relation to the patient problem(s) and desired outcome(s)

The *nursing care plan* is a written statement of this process. The format of a nursing care plan is usually determined by the individual agency. The nurse's responsibility in caring for a patient is to ensure that the nursing care plan reflects the nursing process on a continuing basis as the patient's condition changes. An excerpt from a nursing care plan follows:

| Date | Nursing problem/ diagnosis | Goal(s) | Assessment(s) | Nursing interventions(s) | Evaluation (date, time, & initial) |
|---|---|---|---|---|---|
| 1/19/94 | Postoperative abdominal pain | Relief of pain | 1) General level of comfort<br><br>2) Qualitative, quantitative, topographic, and temporal aspects when pain present | 1) Position change and back rub<br><br>2) Medicated per order | 1) Pain not relieved 1/19/94, 9:00 am J.B.<br>2) Pain relieved 1/19/94, 9:15 am J.B. |

## Appendix B

# Common Departures from the Standard of Nursing Care

Analysis of 60 nursing malpractice cases revealed the following repeated departures from prevailing professional standards of nursing care:

1. Failure to observe or monitor a patient adequately
2. Failure to document and/or communicate a significant change in a patient's condition
3. Failure to execute a complete nursing history
4. Failure to formulate and/or follow the nursing care plan
5. Failure to perform a nursing treatment or procedure properly
6. Failure to provide a safe environment and to protect the patient from avoidable injury
7. Failure to execute a physician's order correctly and/or promptly
8. Failure to administer medications correctly
9. Failure to observe a medication's action
10. Failure to prevent infection
11. Failure to obtain help for a patient not receiving proper care from a physician
12. Failure to report that a patient is not receiving proper care from a physician
13. Failure to use equipment properly
14. Use of known defective equipment
15. Failure to make prompt, accurate entries in a patient's medical record
16. Altering a medical record
17. Failure to follow hospital policy and/or procedure.

## Appendix C
# Initial Nursing Assessment and Nursing History

Upon the patient's admission to the hospital, a nursing assessment with a nursing history should be documented in the medical record. This information is necessary for formulating the nursing care plan and should include such data as the following:

1. Patient's chief complaint (onset of illness, complete description of symptoms and condition)
2. Past medical history
3. Social and family history
4. Behavioral status
5. Respiratory status
6. Circulatory status
7. Neurological status
8. Body temperature status
9. Integumentary status
10. Renal function and fluid status
11. Gastrointestinal status
12. Weight and height
13. Musculoskeletal status
14. Endocrine and metabolic status
15. Sensory and perceptual status
16. Immune status

## Appendix D
## Systematic Nursing Assessment

In a hospital setting, ongoing systematic nursing assessment consists of nursing observations made and recorded over a 24-hour period. The nurse determines the frequency with which these observations are made as well as their specificity based on the patient's condition. These include, among other things, the following:

1. Respiratory status assessment
2. Circulatory status assessment
3. Body temperature status assessment
4. Neurological status assessment
5. Integumentary status assessment
6. Renal status assessment
7. Fluid status assessment
8. Pain status assessment (when applicable)
9. Gastrointestinal status assessment
10. Musculoskeletal status assessment (when applicable)
11. Endocrine and metabolic status assessment (when applicable)
12. Sensory and perceptual status assessment (when applicable)
13. Immune status assessment (when applicable)

## Appendix E
# Independent Nursing Assessments

The nurse has the knowledge base to observe, record, and report, without a physician's order, the following major assessments:

1. Respiratory status assessment
   a. Patency of airway
   b. Respiratory rate
   c. Respiratory rhythm
   d. Respiratory character
   e. Breath sounds
   f. Ease of respiration
   g. Duration of inspiration vs. expiration
   h. General chest expansion
   i. Presence/absence of intercostal retractions
   j. Posture of the patient and facial expression
   k. Presence/absence of fatigue with breathing
   l. Effectiveness and frequency of cough
   m. Sputum amount and character
   n. Percussion of chest (noting intensity, pitch, quality, duration and equality of sound.
   o. Arterial blood gas interpretation
   p. Tidal volume
   q. Minute volume
   r. Vital capacity
2. Circulatory status assessment
   a. Pulse rate
   b. Pulse rhythm
   c. Pulse quality
   d. Blood pressure
   e. Skin color

    f.  Skin temperature

    g.  Central venous pressure and other hemodynamic line measurements

    h.  Circulation in extremities (peripheral pulses, temperature and color of extremity, blanching sign, motor and sensory function)

3. Body temperature status assessment

4. Neurological status assessment

    a.  Response to stimuli

    b.  Orientation

    c.  Level of consciousness

    d.  Response to commands

    e.  Pupillary response (size, equality, and reaction to light)

    f.  Ocular movements (noting if eyes move, if movement is conjugate [together] or disconjugate [separate], and direction of eye movement when head rotated [doll's head maneuver])

    g.  Motor and sensory function (movement and strength in extremities, abnormal sensations)

    h.  Reflexes

    i.  Behavioral changes

    j.  Headache or seizure activity

5. Integumentary and wound status assessment

    a.  Description of trauma

    b.  Character of drainage

    c.  Amount of drainage

    d.  Condition of dressings and/or suture lines

    e.  Condition of skin

6. Renal status assessment

    a.  Urinary output

    b.  Character of urine

7. Fluid status assessment

    a.  Intake (amount, kind, route, rate)

    b.  Intake vs. output

    c.  Estimated or actual fluid loss

8. Pain status assessment

    a.  Qualitative aspects

    b.  Quantitative aspects

    c.  Topographic aspects

    d. Temporal aspects
    e. General level of comfort
9. Gastrointestinal status assessment
    a. Appearance of abdomen
    b. Bowel sounds
    c. Presence/absence of nausea, emesis
10. Musculoskeletal status assessment
    a. Sensory and motor function
    b. Mobility
11. Endocrine and metabolic status assessment
12. Sensory and perceptual status assessment
13. Immune status assessment
14. Psychosocial status assessment

These observations must be systematic and all applicable categories of the patient status assessments outlined above must be present in the medical record throughout each day. The frequency and detail included in a particular patient status assessment is, of course, determined by the patient's primary problem and condition.

## Appendix F

## Nursing Documentation

Every page of the medical record should be labeled to identify the patient by name, with the medical record number and the nursing unit or room number. Every entry in the record must have a complete date and accurate time. Nursing documentation should reflect the following:

1. Initial nursing assessment and history
2. Patient problem(s)
3. Ongoing systematic assessments and observations
4. Nursing interventions
5. Treatments, procedures, diagnostic tests
6. Notation of visits by other members of the health-care team (care rendered by others)
7. Patient response to treatment
8. Pertinent statements made by the patient
9. Comfort and safety measures provided to the patient
10. Patient teaching
11. Nursing discharge summary (patient's condition, teaching, special instructions given for follow-up and/or home care)

# Selected Bibliography

Because nurses are familiar with the monographic, textbook, and periodical literature in the field, this bibliography is for the non-nurse and is limited to textbooks covering fundamental principles and practices of nursing and medical-surgical nursing concepts.

Bass, Linda S., ed. 1991. *Essentials of Cardiovascular Nursing*. Gaithersburg, Md.: Aspen Publishers.

Beare, Patricia G., and Judith L. Myers, eds. 1990. *Principles and Practice of Adult Health Nursing*. St. Louis: C. V. Mosby.

Bellack, Janis P., and Barbara J. Edlund. 1992. *Nursing Assessment and Diagnosis*. 2d ed. Boston: Jones and Bartlett.

Belland, Kathleen H., and Mary A. Wells, eds. 1984. *Clinical Nursing Procedures*. Monterey, Ca.: Wadsworth Health Sciences Division.

Boggs, Rochelle, and Maribeth Wooldridge-King, eds. 1993. *AACN Procedure Manual for Critical Care*. Philadelphia: W. B. Saunders.

Bowers, Arden C., and June M. Thompson. 1992. *Clinical Manual of Health Assessment*. St. Louis: Mosby Year Book.

Burrell, Lenette O., ed. 1992. *Adult Nursing in Hospital and Community Settings*. Norwalk, Ct.: Appleton and Lange.

Christensen, Barbara, and Elaine Kockrow, eds. 1991. *Foundations of Nursing*. St. Louis: Mosby Year Book.

Clark, Julia B. Freeman, *et al.* 1993. *Pharmacologic Basis of Nursing Practice*. 4th ed. St. Louis: C. V. Mosby.

Clayton, Bruce D., and Yvonne N. Stock. 1992. *Basic Pharmacology for Nurses*. 10th ed. St. Louis: Mosby Year Book.

Clochesy, John M., *et al.*, eds. 1993. *Critical Care Nursing*. Philadelphia: W. B. Saunders.

*Code for Nurses with Interpretive Statements*. 1985. Kansas City, Mo.: American Nurses' Association.

Creasia, Joan L., and Barbara Parker, eds. 1991. *Conceptual Foundations of Professional Nursing Practice*. St. Louis: Mosby Year Book.

deWitt, Susan C. 1992. *Keane's Essentials of Medical-Surgical Nursing*. 3d ed. Philadelphia: W. B. Saunders.

Doenges, Marilyn E., and Mary F. Moorhouse. 1993. *Nurse's Pocket Guide: Nursing Diagnoses with Interventions*. Philadelphia: F. A. Davis.

Earnest, Vicki V. 1993. *Clinical Skills in Nursing Practice*. 2d ed. Philadelphia: J. B. Lippincott.

Felver, Linda, and Maxine Patrick. 1991. *Study Guide for Medical-Surgical Nursing: Pathophysiological Concepts.* 2d ed. Philadelphia: J. B. Lippincott.

Ferri, Fred, ed. 1991. *Practical Guide to Care of the Medical Patient.* 2d ed. St. Louis: Mosby Year Book.

Flynn, Janet-Beth M., and Ritva Hackel, eds. 1990. *Technological Foundations in Nursing.* Norwalk, Ct.: Appleton and Lange.

Frost, Elizabeth A. M., ed. 1990. *Post-Anesthesia Care Unit: Current Practices.* St. Louis: C. V. Mosby.

Gahart, Betty L. 1993. *Intravenous Medications: A Handbook for Nurses and Allied Health Professionals.* St. Louis: Mosby Year Book.

Gorzeman, Joy, and Carol Bowdoin. 1990. *Decision-Making in Medical-Surgical Nursing.* Toronto and Philadelphia: B. C. Decker; St. Louis: C.V. Mosby.

Grimes, Jorge, and Elizabeth Burns. 1992. *Health Assessment in Nursing Practice.* 3rd ed. Boston: Jones and Bartlett.

Hartshorn, Jeanette, Marilyn Lamborn, and Mary Lou Noll. 1993. *Introduction to Critical Care Nursing.* Philadelphia: W. B. Saunders.

Hathaway, Rebecca G., ed. 1988. *Nursing Care of the Critically Ill Surgical Patient.* Rockville, Md.: Aspen Publishers.

Holloway, Nancy M., ed. 1993. *Medical-Surgical Care Planning.* 2d ed. Springhouse, Pa.: Springhouse Corporation.

*Hospital Accreditation Program Scoring Guidelines: Nursing Services, Infection Control. Special Care Units.* 1987. Chicago: Joint Commission on Accreditation of Healthcare Organizations.

Hudak, Carolyn M., Barbara M. Gallo, and Julie J. Benze, eds. 1990. *Critical Care Nursing: A Holistic Approach.* 5th ed. Philadelphia: J. B. Lippincott.

Ignatavicius, Donna D., and Marilyn Varner Bayne. 1991. *Medical-Surgical Nursing: A Nursing Process Approach.* Philadelphia: W. B. Saunders.

Iyer, Particia W., *et al.* 1991. *Nursing Process and Nursing Diagnosis.* 2d ed. Philadelphia: W. B. Saunders.

Johanson, Brenda Crispell, *et al.* 1988. *Standards for Critical Care.* St. Louis: C. V. Mosby.

Kee, Joyce L. 1991. *Laboratory and Diagnostic Tests with Nursing Implications.* 3rd ed. Norwalk, Ct.: Appleton and Lange.

Kee, Joyce L., and Evelyn Ruth Hayes. 1993. *Pharmacology: A Nursing Process Approach.* Philadelphia: W. B. Saunders.

Kinney, M., D. Packa, and S. Dunbar, eds. 1993. *AACN's Clinical Reference for Critical Care Nursing.* St. Louis: C. V. Mosby.

Kozier, B., *et al.* 1993. *Techniques in Clinical Nursing.* 4th ed. Redwood City, Ca.: Addison-Wesley.

Kozier, Barbara, Glenora Erb, and Rita Olivieri. 1991. *Fundamentals of Nursing: Concepts, Process, and Practice.* 4th ed. Redwood City, Ca.: Addison-Wesley.

Lewis, Sharon Mantik, and Idolia Cox Collier, eds. 1992. *Medical-Surgical Nursing: Assessment and Management of Clinical Problems.* 3rd ed. St. Louis: Mosby Year Book.

Litwack, Kim. 1991. *Post-Anesthesia Care Nursing.* St. Louis: Mosby Year Book.

Long, Barbara C., Wilma J. Phipps, and Virginia L. Cassmyer, eds. 1993. *Medical-Surgical Nursing: A Nursing Process Approach.* St. Louis: C. V. Mosby.

Luckmann, Joan, and Karen C. Sorensen. 1993. *Luckmann and Sorensen's Medical-Surgical Nursing: A Psychophysiologic Approach.* Philadelphia: W. B. Saunders.

Lyke, Evelyn. 1992. *Assessing for Nursing Diagnosis: A Human Needs Approach.* Philadelphia: J. B. Lippincott.

Mathewson-Kuhn, Merrily. 1991. *Pharmacotherapeutics: A Nursing Process Approach.* 2d ed. Philadelphia: F. A. Davis.

McFarland, Gertrude K., and Elizabeth A. McFarlane, eds. 1993. *Nursing Diagnosis and Intervention: Planning for Patient Care.* St. Louis: Mosby Year Book.

Meeker, Margaret Huth, and Jane C. Rothrock. 1991. *Alexander's Care of the Patient in Surgery.* St. Louis: Mosby Year Book.

Morton, Patricia Gonce, ed. 1993. *Health Assessment in Nursing.* 2d ed. Springhouse, Pa.: Springhouse Corporation.

*Outcome Standards for Nursing Care of the Critically Ill.* 1990. Laguna Niguel, Ca.: American Association of Critical Care Nurses.

Pagana, Kathleen D. 1994. *Diagnostic Testing and Nursing Implications. A Case Study Approach.* Chicago: C.V. Mosby.

Patrick, Maxine L., *et al.* 1991. *Medical-Surgical Nursing: Pathophysiological Concepts.* 2d ed. Philadelphia: J. B. Lippincott.

Patterson, Carol, *et al.* 1986. *Guide to JCAH Nursing Service Standards.* Chicago: Joint Commission on Accreditation of Hospitals.

Perry, Ann G., and Patricia A. Potter, eds. 1990. *Clinical Nursing Skills and Techniques.* 2d ed. St. Louis: C. V. Mosby.

Phipps, Wilma J., *et al.*, eds. 1991. *Medical-Surgical Nursing: Concepts and Clinical Practice.* St. Louis: Mosby Year Book.

Potter, Patricia Ann. 1993. *Fundamentals of Nursing: Concepts, Process, and Practice.* St. Louis: Mosby Year Book.

Potter, Patricia A., and Ann G. Perry. 1991. *Basic Nursing: Theory and Practice.* 2d ed. St. Louis: Mosby Year Book.

Rorden, Judith W., and Elizabeth D. Taft. 1990. *Discharge Planning Guide for Nurses.* Philadelphia: W. B. Saunders.

Rudy, Ellen B., and V. Ruth Gray. 1991. *Handbook of Health Assessment.* Norwalk, Ct.: Appleton and Lange.

Sands, Judith K. 1991. *Clinical Manual of Medical-Surgical Nursing.* St. Louis: Mosby Year Book.

Scherer, Jeanne C. 1991. *Introductory Medical-Surgical Nursing.* 5th ed. Philadelphia: J. B. Lippincott.

Schroeder, Patricia, ed. 1991. *Approaches to Nursing Standards.* Gaithersburg, Md.: Aspen Publishers.

Shannon, Margaret T., *et al.* 1992. *Govoni and Hayes Drugs and Nursing Implications.* 7th ed. Norwalk, Ct.: Appleton and Lange.

Sheehy, Susan, B. 1994. *Manual of Clinical Trauma Care: The First Hour.* St. Louis: C. V. Mosby.

Shekleton, Maureen, and Kim Litwack. 1991. *Critical Care Nursing of the Surgical Patient.* Philadelphia: W. B. Saunders.

Smith, Sandra, and Donna D. Duell. 1992. *Clinical Nursing Skills: Nursing Process Model, Basic to Advanced Skills.* 3rd ed. Norwalk, Ct.: Appleton and Lange.
Snyder, Mariah, ed. 1992. *Independent Nursing Interventions.* 2d ed. Albany, N.Y.: Delmar Publishers.
Sorensen, Karen C. 1986. *Basic Nursing: A Psychophysiologic Approach.* 2d ed. Philadelphia: W. B. Saunders.
*Standards of Cardiovascular Nursing Practice.* 1981. Division on Medical-Surgical Nursing Practice, and Council on Cardiovascular Nursing (American Heart Association). Kansas City, Mo.: American Nurses' Association.
*Standards of Neurological and Neurosurgical Nursing Practice.* 1977. Division on Medical-Surgical Nursing Practice, and American Association of Neurosurgical Nurses. Kansas City, Mo.: American Nurses' Association.
*Standards of Nursing Practice.* 1973. Kansas City, Mo.: American Nurses' Association.
*Standards for Nursing Services in Hospitals, Community Health Agencies, Nursing Homes, Industry, Schools, Ambulatory Services, and Related Health Care Organizations.* 1973. Commission on Nursing Services. Kansas City, Mo.: American Nurses' Association.
*Standards for Organized Nursing Services and Responsibilities of Nurse Administrators Across All Settings.* 1991 Kansas City, Mo.: American Nurses' Association.
*Standards for Professional Nursing Education.* 1984. Kansas City, Mo.: American Nurses' Association.
Sundberg, Mary C. 1989. *Fundamentals of Nursing: Clinical Procedures.* 2d ed. Boston: Jones and Bartlett.
Swearingen, Pamela. 1991. *Addison-Wesley's Photo Atlas of Nursing Procedures.* 2d ed. Redwood City, Ca.: Addison-Wesley.
Swearingen, Pamela, ed. 1990. *Manual of Nursing Therapeutics: Applying Nursing Diagnoses to Medical Disorders.* St. Louis: C. V. Mosby.
Tucker, Susan Martin, *et al.* 1992. *Patient Care Standards: Nursing Process, Diagnosis and Outcome.* 5th ed. St. Louis: Mosby Year Book.
Ulrich, Susan, Suzanne Canale, and Sharon Wendell. 1990. *Nursing Care Planning Guides: A Nursing Diagnosis Approach.* Philadelphia: W. B. Saunders.
Wasorick, Bonnie. 1990. *Standards of Nursing Care: A Model for Clinical Practice.* Philadelphia: J. B. Lippincott.
Wingate, Sue, ed. 1991. *Cardiac Nursing: A Clinical Management and Patient Care Resource.* Gaithersburg, Md.: Aspen Publishers.

# Index

The increasing number of nursing malpractice cases is cause for serious concern and has clear implications for clinical practice and nursing education. Nursing malpractice not only causes injury or even death to patients, but it is also contributing to the rising cost of health care because the consumer ultimately pays for the cost of malpractice. This book analyzes nursing malpractice and suggests ways to reduce its occurrence. No other systematic analysis of nursing malpractice currently exists in either the nursing or the legal literature.

Janet Beckmann brings to her book an authoritative awareness of the legal implications of nursing malpractice. She has a broad background in nursing education and clinical practice and draws on more than fifteen years of experience serving as an expert witness in nursing malpractice cases. She presents a wealth of complex information in straightforward, accessible prose and makes clear the integral role of the nurse as a member of the hospital health-care team. She also provides practical advice for the nurse expert witness.

Beckmann presents sixty case studies in which she analyzes common departures from the standard of nursing care. In this context, she offers principles for the improvement of patient care. Case studies are grouped into problem areas associated with nursing assessment, communication between nurse and physician, physicians' departures from the standard of care, nosocomial infection, equipment and products, nursing interventions and treatments, administration of medications, environmental safety, and documentation. Useful charts are provided and appendixes afford easy cross reference. In her conclusion, Beckmann provides general recommendations aimed at curtailing nursing malpractice; she focuses on issues of risk management, inservice education, curriculum, and communication.

This book is intended for all persons concerned with quality patient care—nursing students, nurses in clinical practice, nursing educators, nursing service administrators, hospital administrators, physicians, attorneys, the insurance industry, and risk managers.

*Janet Pitts Beckmann* is a consultant and is an affiliate professor in the School of Nursing, University of Washington.